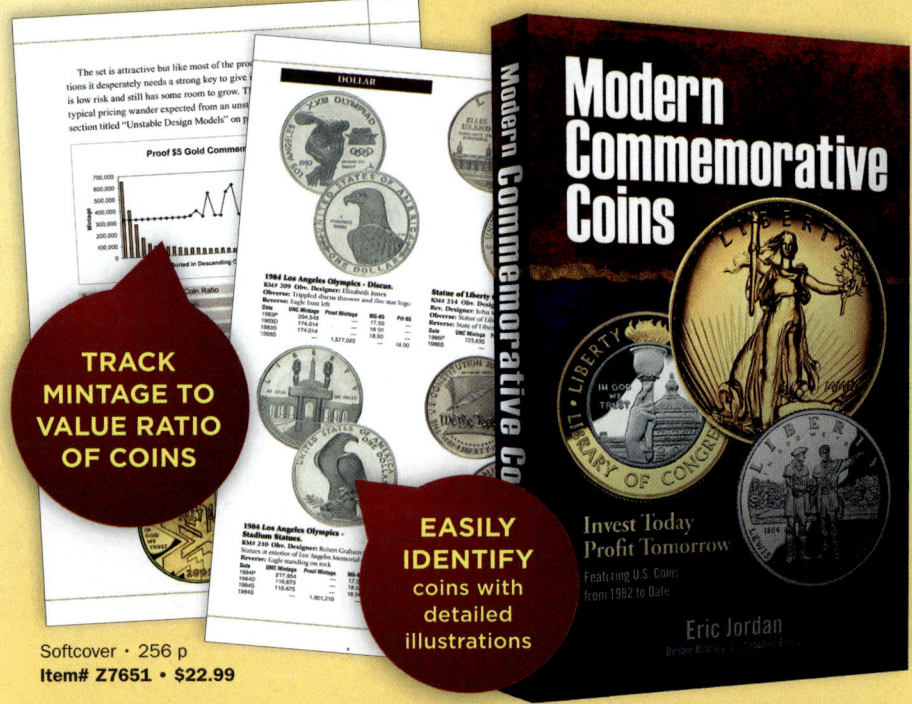

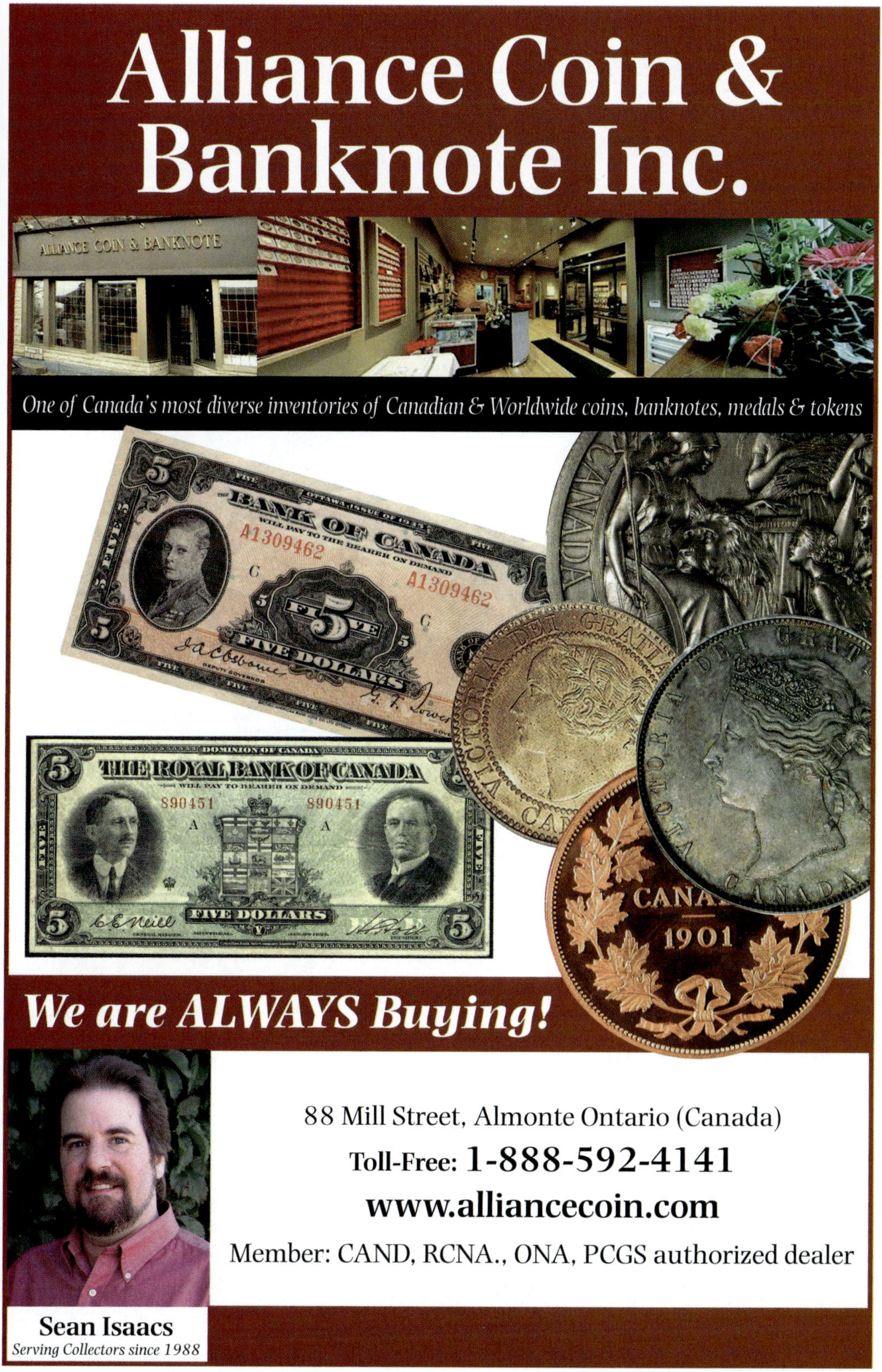
Alliance Coin & Banknote Inc.
ALLIANCE COIN & BANKNOTE
One of Canada's most diverse inventories of Canadian & Worldwide coins, banknotes, medals & tokens
We are ALWAYS Buying!
88 Mill Street, Almonte Ontario (Canada)
Toll-Free: 1-888-592-4141
www.alliancecoin.com
Member: CAND, RCNA., ONA, PCGS authorized dealer
Sean Isaacs
Serving Collectors since 1988

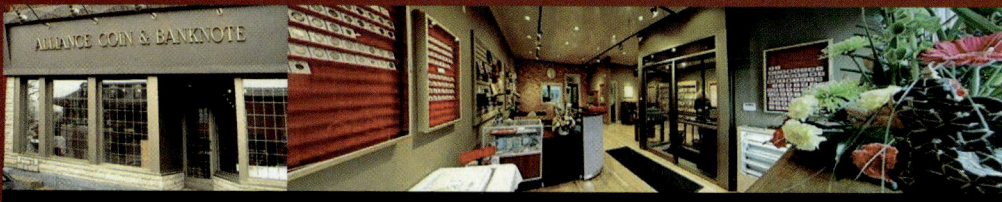

CANADIAN
COIN DIGEST

George S. Cuhaj, Editor
Thomas Michael, Market Analyst

Published by

Krause Publications, a division of F+W Media, Inc.
700 East State Street • Iola, WI 54990-0001
715-445-2214 • 888-457-2873
www.krausebooks.com

To order books or other products call toll-free 1-800-258-0929
or visit us online at www.shopnumismaster.com

ISBN-13: 978-1-4402-2985-5
ISBN-10: 1-4402-2985-6

Cover Design by Jana Tappa
Designed by Sandi Carpenter
Edited by George Cuhaj

Printed in the United States of America

Table of Contents

Letter From the Editor

Welcome to this second edition of Krause Publications' *Canadian Coin Digest*!

For 40 years Krause Publications has brought to serious coin collectors the *Standard Catalog of® World Coins*, now we present, a special catalog for the collector of Canadian issues. These include the early provincial issues of Newfoundland, Nova Scotia and Prince Edward Island.

The listings are in the Standard Catalog format, which collectors have come to recognize. The listings are presented in denomination and date order, and then include weight, fineness and size; descriptive information and designer names follow.

Then what most collectors are really interested in - the date, mintmark and variety mintage and price information! The headings are the commonly used commercial grading terms, with both descriptive and numerical equivalents so collectors can be confidant on accurate determination on the items they are interested in buying or selling. Enjoy this book, and remember you can always check for new listings on-line at www.numismaster.com and look for additional books at www.shopnumismaster.com.

George S. Cuhaj, Editor
Thomas Michael, Market Analyst

Introduction

The starting point for the national coinage of Canada is popularly fixed at 1858. In that year a large cent was first produced for use in Upper and Lower Canada (Ontario and Quebec). These pieces were intended to supplant local copper coinage, which in turn had been attempts to give various regions a medium of exchange.

What was circulating in Canada at the time was a hodgepodge of world issues. The large cent predates a unified national government by nine years, but it is considered the beginning of national issues nevertheless.

There are many similarities between the United States and Canada and their respective monetary systems. Both continent-sized nations thought in terms of taming the frontier, new settlements, and growth. Both came to use the dollar as the unit of account because of the pervasiveness of the Spanish milled dollar in trade. For each, the dollar divides into 100 cents.

However, Canada had a far longer colonial history. Many of its residents resisted the tide that carried the United States to independence and worked to preserve their loyalties to the British crown. As a result, Canada was firmly a part of the British Empire. So even today with its constitution (the British North America Act transferred from Westminster to Ottawa in 1982), parliamentary democracy, and a national consciousness perhaps best symbolized by the maple leaf, Canada retains a loyalty to the crown in the person of Queen Elizabeth II of the United Kingdom. Canada is a member of the British Commonwealth of Nations.

The effect of this on coins is obvious. Current issues carry the queen's effigy. How Canada got its coins in the past was also influenced. The fledgling U.S. government set about creating its own mint as one of its earliest goals, despite that better-quality pieces could be purchased abroad at lower cost. Canada found

that ties to mints located in England were logical and comfortable.

The Royal Canadian Mint was not established until 1908, when it was called the Ottawa branch of the British Royal Mint, and it was not given its present name until 1931. Canadian coins, therefore, have a unique mixture of qualities. They are tantalizingly familiar to U.S. citizens yet distinctly different.

The coinage of a monarchy brings its own logic to the organization of a collection. Type collecting is delineated by the monarch. United Canada has had six. The first was Queen Victoria, whose image appeared on those large cents of 1858. Her reign began in 1837 and lasted until 1901.

She was followed by Edward VII, 1901-1910; George V, 1910-1936; Edward VIII, 1936; George VI, 1936-1952; and Queen Elizabeth II, 1952-present. All but Edward VIII had coins struck for circulation in Canada. The collectible monarchs, therefore, number five, but the longer reigns inspired changes of portraits over time to show the aging process at work. Legends also changed. When George VI ceased being emperor of India, Canada's coin legends were modified to recognize the change.

Like U.S. coins, sizes and alloys were altered to meet new demands placed on the coinage. However, the separateness of each nation might best be summed up this way: Though the United States abolished its large cent in 1857, Canada's was just getting under way in 1858. The United States put an end to the silver dollar in 1935, the very year Canada finally got its series going.

And Canada, the nickel-mining giant, used a small-sized silver five-cent coin until 1921, almost 50 years after the half dime was abolished in the United States. But whereas the Civil War was the major cause of the emergence of modern U.S. coinage as specified by the Coinage Act of 1873, World War I influenced the alterations that made Canada's coins what they are today.

It might be assumed that change in the monarch also signaled a change in the reverse designs of the various denominations. A

check of the Canadian price guide section shows this is not necessarily the case. Current designs paired with Queen Elizabeth II basically date back to the beginning of her father's reign. The familiar maple-leaf cent, beaver five-cent piece, schooner 10-cent, caribou 25-cent, and coat-of-arms 50-cent have been running for nearly 75 years. Significant changes were made to the 50-cent coin in 1959, but the reverse design remains the coat of arms.

So where does that leave type collectors? It puts them in a situation similar to categorizing the various eagles on U.S. coins. They can be universalists and accept the broadest definitions of type, or they can narrow the bands to whatever degree suits them best.

By checking the price-guide section, date and mintmark collectors will quickly note that their method of organization more or less turns into collecting by date. Historically there have been three mints in Canada – Hull, Quebec; Ottawa, Ontario; and Winnipeg, Manitoba but they don't use mintmarks. Historically, few mintmarks were employed.

Ottawa used a "C" on gold sovereigns of 1908-1919 and on some exported colonial issues. The private Heaton Mint in Birmingham, England, used an "H" on coins it supplied to Canada from 1871 to 1907.

But the coins supplied to Canada by the British Royal Mint and later by its Ottawa branch did not carry any identifying mark. Collectors who confine their activities to the more recent issues need never think about a mintmark.

It would be easy to slant a presentation on Canadian issues to stress similarities or differences to U.S. issues. One should remember that the monetary structures of each evolved independently, but each was always having an impact on the other.

Common events, such as World War II, had a similar impact. For example, the Canadian five-cent coin changed in much the same way as the U.S. nickel. In Canada, nickel was removed and replaced first by a tombac (brass) alloy and then by

chromium-plated steel. Peace brought with it a return to the prewar composition.

To see an example of differences between the United States and Canada, take the Canadian approach to the worldwide trend of removing silver from coinage. Canada made its move in 1968, three years after the United States. Instead of choosing a copper-nickel alloy as a substitute for silver, Canada looked to its own vast natural resources and employed pure nickel.

Canada also seems more comfortable with its coinage than the United States. Whereas the United States often feared confusion and counterfeiting from making the least little changes in its coins, Canada has long embraced coinage to communicate national events, celebrations and culture. Its silver-dollar series actually began as a celebration of George V's 25th Anniversary on the throne.

Succeeding years saw additional commemorative $1 designs interspersed with the regular Voyageur design. When the centennial of national confederation was observed in 1967, all of the circulating denominations were altered for one year. The United States only reluctantly tried out the idea on three of its denominations for the nation's Bicentennial.

Ultimately, Canada began an annual commemorative dollar series in 1971. Im most years silver was struck for collectors and copper-nickel for circulation. It issued multi-year commemorative programs for the 1976 Montreal Olympic Games and again in 1988 for the Calgary Olympic Games and 2010 for the Vancouver games. Bullion coins were created to market its gold, silver and platinum output. A commemorative series of gold $100 coins was also undertaken. Canada, too, issues special proof, prooflike and specimen sets, similar to the United States.

When collecting Canada, another thing to remember is the importance varieties play in the nation's various series. Certainly, a type collector has no need to dwell on this information, but the date and mintmark collector may puzzle over the many extra identifying abbreviations in the price guide

for certain coins. These varieties should not be confused with the U.S. variety-and-error category.

Here the varieties are not mistakes; they are deliberately created and issued variations of the standard design. We see Voyageur dollars on which the number of water lines changes. Other dollars count the number of beads.

These differences are minor. Though they were deliberately done to meet varying mint needs, they were not intended to be set apart in the public mind. The hobby, however, likes to look at things under a microscope.

Some varieties were indeed intended to be deliberately and noticeably different. An example of this occurs with 1947-dated issues. A maple leaf was placed on the 1947-dated cent through 50-cent issues. This indicated the coin was struck after George VI lost his title of emperor of India, as proclaimed in the Latin legend, but that the design had not yet been altered to reflect this. All of these varieties are considered integral parts of the Canadian series, and they are listed as such.

Do not construe any of this to mean there is no collecting of varieties and errors of the type common in the United States. There is. Collecting Royal Canadian Mint mistakes is just as active, just as interesting, and just as rewarding. After all, mint errors are universal. The methods of manufacture are the same. So the mistakes can be classified in the same manner.

Canada's numismatic listings also include items from various provinces issued before they were part of the confederation. The largest portion of this section is devoted to Newfoundland, because it retained a separate status far longer than the other provinces – until 1949, in fact.

A bit of advice to collectors: Collect what interests you. Collect what you can afford. Create sets of uniform grade coins.

Ten Marks that Have Made Their Mark on Canadian Coins

BY MARK FOX

Since its creation in 1792, the Philadelphia Mint has been aided by a total of eight branch mints in the enormous workload of supplying America's domestic, colonial, and non-circulating coinages, as well as providing minted money for other countries. All had, or eventually developed, their own special mintmark to identify their respective coins. Even the Mother Mint ultimately began marking all of her coins on a regular basis in 1980, with the exception of the cent.

Although only a fraction of American mints continue to strike coins today, most veteran collectors know every mints' numismatic symbol by heart—perhaps with the exception of Manila, which was the only U.S. mint erected outside the continental U.S. In contrast, the Royal Canadian Mint (RCM) in Ottawa has had only two branches: one in Winnipeg, Manitoba, and another in Hull, in southwestern Québec, although it is no longer in operation. In addition, the Canadian government had contracted three mints outside Canada to strike coinage: the Royal Mint in London, the Heaton Mint in Birmingham, and U.S. Mint at Philadelphia. Except for one of the contracted mints, none of the Canadian coin makers, including the RCM itself, regularly used a true mintmark.

What has been just outlined is one of the important distinctions between U.S. and Canadian numismatics that may come as a disappointment to many mintmark enthusiasts. But it really shouldn't. Canadian coins are not without interesting and collectible coin marks, which bring us to the focus of this article. Soon to follow is a specially selected list of 10 marks found on Canadian coins, beginning with the earliest. Some are

mintmarks, but the majority are not, which will hopefully illustrate a more fascinating feature of Canadian coinage that US coins simply lack.

This list isn't meant to be complete. Some readers may be quick to point out that the author neglected to mention the various Canadian privy marks that have appeared in recent years. Nevertheless, it was felt that the marks were less interesting historically and were solely a commemorative coin and bullion phenomena as opposed to the sort of coins more collectors would be familiar with and collect.

1. HEATON/BIRMINGHAM "H" MINTMARK

Before the Ottawa Mint opened its doors in 1908, Canadian coinage was an entirely English affair, carried out mostly by the Royal Mint in London. They didn't use a mintmark, but a private mint located in Birmingham contracted to mint Canadian coins did.

These coins bore an "H" mintmark, placed under the wreaths on the silver coins and usually below the dates on the cents. This letter stood for the Heaton Mint, owned by Ralph Heaton & Sons. It was headed by Ralph Heaton II (1794–1862), and later by his son, Heaton III (1827–1891). Richard Doty in *The Soho Mint and the Industrialization of Money* (1998) regarded this mint as a "stepchild" of Matthew Boulton's famed Soho Mint, since most of the minting equipment, including the steam powered coin presses, were bought by the Heatons when the grandson of Boulton closed the Soho operation and auctioned off the equipment in 1850.

The purchased machinery went to work again in a new minting facility only a few hundred yards away from their old home. However, there is solid evidence that the Heatons' coining ambitions predate the building of this mint. In *A Numismatic History of the Birmingham Mint* by James O. Sweeney (1981), the author found among the Heaton archives of

Photos courtesy of Heritage Auctions (HA.com)

An extraordinary example of a 1902-H large H Canadian ten cents struck by the Birmingham (Heaton's) Mint. According to Heritage Auctions, this MS-67 PCGS graded specimen is the "finest existing." Even so, it sold for only $1,495 in their 2010 January Signature World Coin Auction. An interesting aspect of this coin is that it bears the outdated St Edward's Crown instead of the Imperial State Crown, which was finally introduced the following year.

cardboard impressions of dies, a reverse for an 1846 Rutherford Brothers halfpenny token. Unlike earlier tokens minted for these merchants in St. John's, Newfoundland, this type in question bore an "RH" mintmark above the date, which Sweeney confidently attributed to Ralph Heaton. Presumably the actual minting was contracted to someone else with the proper minting equipment.

Once the Heaton Mint was up and running other Canadian token issues followed in addition to a busy flow of newly minted money to other parts of the world, especially France. From 1858 to 1859, the Heatons provided the bronze planchets to the Royal Mint that would become Canada's first decimal cent coins. These were minted for the Province of Canada. A few years after the Canadian Confederation of 1867, the Heaton Mint started producing colonial coinages for a couple of the remaining British colonies in North America: Newfoundland

Photos courtesy of Heritage Auctions (HA.com)

An 1890-H Canadian half dollar, one of only two known in mint state. Its provenance can be traced back to the famous Heaton Archive Collection which was slowly dispersed between 1975 and 1984. Graded MS-64 by PCGS, it is little wonder Heritage was able to raise a winning bid of $149,500 for this rarity in the 2010 January Signature World Coin Auction.

and Prince Edward Island. For the latter, an issue of large cents struck in 1871 would be the Island's only decimal coinage before joining the Dominion of Canada two years later. The reverse displayed a large oak tree sheltering three maple saplings. Sweeny writes that "this is generally taken to suggest the benevolent protection of the Provincial Government over the three counties of Prince Edward Island." For some unknown reason, these coins contain no mintmark. So many were minted (2,000,000) that the stockpile wasn't depleted until almost a decade later.

1871, the second year Canadian dominion coinage was issued, would also be the beginning of a long series of instances when the Royal Mint would be too busy to satisfy the coinage needs of Canada. As elsewhere, particularly in Britain itself, the Royal Mint would call on Heaton to help fill in. The 1871 Heaton coinages are significant in that they were the first silver

coins minted by the firm. In commenting on the beginning of production, Sweeney notes that "one thousand 50 Cent pieces were struck on 18 December 1871 under close supervision by Royal Mint personnel." In total, only 45,000 pieces would be minted, along with 748,000 25-cent pieces, and 1,870,000 10-cent coins. The following year silver 5-cent pieces were added to Heatons' roster of minted coins and the half dollar dropped a year later by both mints until the 1880s.

After a few more years of brisk minting came the Birmingham coiner's first order for large cents in 1876. This was the first year of issue for dominion cents, and since the Royal Mint was having a tough enough time keeping Britain supplied with bronze change, Heaton became the sole minter of this denomination up to the early 1880s.

In 1882 and 1883, the entire production of Canadian coinage was in the hands of the Heaton mint. It was also during this time that they ended up partly sabotaging their own business by furnishing the Royal Mint with new coin presses and other machinery. Afterwards, the "Deputy Master of the Royal Mint made it clearly known to the High Commissioner for Canada in London that hereafter Canada's requirements would be handled by the Royal Mint." But eventually they would need help again in 1890. By this time, the Heaton Mint no longer went by that name. Ralph Heaton III turned his father's mint into a limited liability company in 1889, two years before his death. The mint was now officially called "The Mint, Birmingham, Limited," which has probably been a source of some confusion to collectors. It was the same mint facility, but it was now publicly owned. One of the stipulations of the agreement was that Ralph Heaton IV, would become general manager.

What came out of the coin shipments in 1890 was one of the greatest Heaton rarities in Canadian numismatics: the 1890 50-cent piece, with only 20,000 coins to its name. In the article "Rarities Pose Intriguing Questions," by Michael W. Hurley in the June 1984 issue of the *Canadian Numismatic Journal*, Hurley

writes, "Prior to the 1930s very few people collected coins. All coins, common as well as rare, circulated for decades. Many were lost, mutilated, or they simply wore out. For some reason the toll seems to have been especially heavy on the 1890-H half dollar. Obtaining an 1890H half in any grade is a formidable task today." Only two mint state examples are currently known. Both are from the Heaton Archive Collection. They and numerous other Heaton-minted coins, many Canadian, were slowly auctioned off between 1975 and 1984. One of the 1890-H Heaton Archive half dollars, graded MS-64 by PCGS, sold for $149,500 during Heritage's 2010 January Signature World Coin Auction.

Several more contracts for Canadian (and Newfoundland) coinage were secured all the way up to 1907, when a last order of Canadian cents was filled. Mintages of Canadian coins aren't always reliable in determining rarity, but of the 800,000 examples produced, the value of a 1907-H cent is actually about what one would expect. The coin catalogs from $12 in VG-8 to $550 in MS-63 according to the 2011 *Standard Catalog of World Coins*.

After 1907, the Ottawa Mint was opened and the formative years of Canadian coinage would immediately come to a close with the disappearance of the British minters.

2. OTTAWA 'C' MINTMARK

When the Ottawa branch of the Royal Mint began production in 1908, there was no need to add mintmarks to its products. Well, not quite. In response to the desire of Yukon mine owners wishing to convert their newly found gold into coinage, the new mint was eager from the very beginning to produce gold sovereigns. This very popular gold coin was one of the outward, numismatic signs that the British Empire was indeed an empire. Aside from those minted in the mother country, the 19th and/or early 20th centuries witnessed gold sovereigns,

Photos courtesy of Robert Kokotailo of Calgary Coin

A 1911-C sovereign struck at Ottawa, Canada. Because it was more profitable for Yukon gold miners to convert their gold into coinage at the San Francisco Mint, that is where most of the metal traveled. As a result, the 1911 mintage record for the entire series was only 256,946 pieces. Note the "C" mintmark.

bearing Benedetto Pistrucci's iconic depiction of St. George slaying the dragon, produced at British colonial and dominion mints in Australia (Melbourne, Sydney, and Perth), India (Bombay), Canada (Ottawa), and South Africa (Pretoria). Keeping track of the quality and origin of the gold was important, and so you can be sure each mint used a mintmark. For Canada it was a simple "C", placed inconspicuously like all the others above the date in the plain under St. George's horse.

It is said that gold from the Larder Lake and Peace River districts and the Yukon Territory were used to strike the 636 gold sovereigns minted at Ottawa in 1908. Although these would have to be considered a trial run, production of Canadian sovereigns was never very high. The most populous year was 1911 when 256,946 were produced. The second lowest was 1913 with a measly 3,715 pieces, which also sounds like a drop in the bucket. But it is not the rarest date. That honor goes to the 6,111 pieces minted in 1916. A collector of moderate means will likely have to mortgage his house to own one of those. At Heritage's 2010 April CICF Signature World Coin Auction, an MS-63 1916-C Sovereign, slabbed by NGC, realized

$29,900. With the price of gold around $1,200 at the time of this writing, collectors can expect to pay around $350-400 for the commonest dates in EF.

No sovereigns were issued in either 1912 or 1915. The last were minted in 1919, which begs the question of why so little when one tallies up all 10 years and finds that only 627,834 coins were minted. This figure has been compared to the 1918-I sovereign minted in Bombay. This mint was in service from Aug. 15, 1918, to April 22 the following year, but had managed to strike 1,295,000 sovereigns.

The answer to this perplexing question is, surprisingly enough, the San Francisco Mint. In his article, "Yukon gold becomes Canadian sovereigns, American dollars," in the January 1975 issue of the *Numismatic Scrapbook Magazine*, Edwin E. Wiegand quotes from an unidentified source that "the main factor responsible was that 'the bullion charge imposed at the United States Mint, San Francisco, in the purchase of gold bullion is 1/8 of one per cent less on the gross value of the bullion than at the Vancouver assay office.'" As a result, Canadian gold flowed in great quantities to the same destination as did the gold the forty-niners mined.

In addition to Canadian sovereigns, the "C" mintmark also appeared on coinages struck for Newfoundland and Jamaica from 1917-1919. These foreign contracts were likely the start of something bigger for Ottawa, but when the Royal Mint became interested in expanding its own business, it sought to put its subsidiary mints in their place. Frances C. Rowe, et al., in *The Currency and Medals of Newfoundland* (1983) relates to us what happened:

> "Late in 1922 a letter was drafted advising the Deputy Master of the Ottawa Branch Mint that in future all coinages for colonies not having their own branch mints should be executed by the Royal Mint, London, whenever this would be possible without seriously interfering with British coinage needs. Such coinages

as had been undertaken by the Ottawa mint for Newfoundland and Jamaica were not to be repeated without sanction from the Royal Mint, and any such proposals from the governments concerned were to be referred to the usual British authorities. To these instructions the Canadian mint authorities rather meekly acquiesced."

But with the outbreak of World War II, the supremacy of the Royal Mint faltered. The risk involved in shipping coinage across the Atlantic convinced the Royal Mint that it would be wiser if Ottawa were to supply Newfoundland with coinage for the duration of the war. Again, the 'C' mintmark was used. Coinage began in 1940 and was restricted to cents, and silver 5- and 10-cent pieces. Production ended in 1947, two years before the country elected to become a part of Canada.

3. J.O.P. DOLLARS

Unlike the other marks discussed in this article that are on the die, the J.O.P. dollar mark is not the work of a mint but a counterstamp added privately. It is listed here because many collectors consider J.O.P. dollars to be an "official" part of a Canadian silver dollar collection.

But this wasn't always so. Collectors, at first, didn't have a clue why some 1935 and later Voyageur dollars were punched with the initials "J.O.P" above the date on the reverse. Many thought the coins were mutilated with little or no value over face. In *Canadian Silver Dollars* by Starr Gilmore (1961), the author reported that one dealer even went to the trouble of filling in the punch mark on one coin with silver.

However, thanks to the pioneering research of Larry Gingras, the mystery of the J.O.P. countermark has been mostly solved, although many additional questions still linger. It is a story not worth repeating here in detail, especially when we have Gingras' excellent article to read. "The J.O.P. Silver Dollar"

Photo courtesy of the Paul Bass collection

A 1936 J.O.P. silver dollar. The letters in the oval punch mark above the date at first puzzled collectors, most of whom regarded as damage to the coin. Thanks to the research of the late Larry Gingras, the initials 'J.O.P.' stood for Joseph Olivia Patenaude and told a fascinating story.

originally appeared in the October 1959 issue of the *Canadian Numismatic Journal,* and as a testament to its importance, has been reprinted twice, the latest being in the June 1995 issue.

Briefly, the J.O.P. dollars were the creation of one Joseph Oliva Patenaude, a well-respected jeweler and optometrist in Nelson, British Columbia. Near the end of the First World War, he and several other citizens of Nelson provided financial backing for Mr. (Andrew) French who claimed to have invented a new and cheaper way to refine silver ore. However, the patent for this discovery was challenged in court during the 1920s and eventually won by the "opposing mining interests." The whole affair left Patenaude and his associates nearly penniless.

In 1930 he sold his jewelry business and focused solely on optometry. Even then his interest in promoting silver mining wasn't tarnished. With the aid of influential connections, he persistently pushed for the introduction of a Canadian silver

Photo courtesy of the Paul Bass collection.

A close-up of the J.O.P. countermark on the coin in CoinMark6–7. The doubled lettering possibly suggests that the punch was applied twice. Notice the last initial lacks a period.

dollar. He believed such a coin would greatly benefit the mining region in which he lived. Just how much of an impact he had is not certain, but the Royal Canadian Mint did begin silver dollar production in 1935.

To his deepest joy at achieving this, he is said to have ordered 1,000 of the new coins, counterstamped them with his initials, and gave them out in change at his store. This practice of stamping silver dollars apparently continued for many years— up to 1949 according to Gingras, the year before Patenaude retired from the optometry business. J. O. Patenaude died on May 9, 1956, at the age of 85.

Patenaude was held in the highest regard by the citizenry of Nelson. When Gingras inquired why such an upright man would illegally deface the country's coinage, he was assured by those who knew Patenaude that he would never have done so if he knew it was a crime.

Collectors' should be equally grateful to the recent *Canadian Numismatic Journal* contributions by Chris Boyer ("The J.O.P Dollar," May 2009) and Roger Grove ("J.O.P – The Joseph Oliva Patenaude Story," January/February 2010), which have shed even more light on Patenaude's numismatic activities. Grove

concluded that the main reason for Patenaude countermarking silver dollars was not so much to express his joy over getting the coins minted by the government, as it was to advertise his optometry business. The same researcher learned from George Coletti, a former coin collector who knew Patenaude well, that the former jeweler "only stamped 1935 and 1936 coins for regular distribution. Any other years of coins stamped by Patenaude were done as one-offs for special requests by friends and citizens in Nelson." Even so, Starr Gilmore had reported that, for some reason, many J.O.P. dollars were of the 1947 blunt seven variety.

During the time of Gingras' article, collectors were aware of two types of J.O.P. countermarks. The first, and probably most common, shows the initials in a recessed oval, with periods after the first two letters. The second stamp appears as three incuse initials without periods. According to what Coletti had told Grove, the Type 2 punch was in fact the first one the optometrist had used, "which eventually became lost." Patenaude is said to have created and used the Type 1 punch sparingly in his later years.

Currently there are two other varieties of J.O.P. countermarks known: "Oval, Large Initials [Type 3]" and "Rectangle, Initials [Type 4]." Charlton regards the authenticity of both with some skepticism as they are not recorded in the older literature, but thanks to the findings of Chris Boyer, he was able to vindicate the Type 3 dollars when he learned that Edward Doane had purchased one directly from Patenaude's housekeeper.

Unfortunately there is a darker side to these coins. Robert Kokotailo of Calgary Coin has informed the author that in the 1970s and 1980s one of the punches came into the possession of a Vancouver coin dealer who used it to stamp his own "J.O.P. dollars." Some were countermarked with dates later than 1950 and even after Patenaude's death. While the latter coins certainly cannot be originals, some collectors may have been a bit hasty to regard all J.O.P. dollars dated in the early 1950s (which have come to light since Gingras and Gilmore's works)

with grave doubt. Grove believes Patenaude had continued to stamp silver dollars, on special request, even after his retirement. Coletti explained that Patenaude was having trouble marking the coins in his later years due to poor eyesight and loss of dexterity. This may explain why a few countermarked coins are a sharp departure from the high quality collectors often see and expect. Of course, such pieces could also indicate the work of a poor imitator with a genuine punch.

In spite of all this, J.O.P. dollars continue to be in heavy demand. In AU condition, a collector can expect to pay anywhere from $300 to $1,000 for one of the common dates.

4. 1936 DOT COINAGE

The world was shocked when King Edward VIII abdicated the British throne on Dec. 10, 1936, in order to marry the twice-divorced American socialite Wallis Warfield. Especially unprepared were the Royal Mint in London and its branches across the British Empire. Edward's father, King George V, had died on Jan. 20, but following numismatic tradition, coinage bearing the image of the deceased monarch would continue to be minted for the remainder of the year. Some trials and portrait-less colonial coins of the new king had already been minted when radios on the night of Dec. 11 broadcasted his abdication speech with the famous line, "I have found it impossible to carry the heavy burden of responsibility and to discharge my duties as king as I would wish to do without the help and support of the woman I love." To the dismay of the mints, the Edwardian dies had to be scrapped and new ones made for Edward's younger brother, Prince Albert, who reluctantly ascended the throne as George VI.

This quick succession of British monarchs was particularly troubling for the Royal Canadian Mint. Although they withdrew their role as a branch of the Royal Mint in London in 1931, to become an agency of the Canadian government, they

Photos courtesy of Heritage Auctions (HA.com)

The reader is looking at the finest of three confirmed 1936 dot cents, once owned by John Jay Pittman. This piece was certified Specimen 66 Red by PCGS and is known as the Belzberg or Pittman-Belzberg Specimen. It reaped $402,500 at Heritage's 2010 January Signature World Coin Auction.

would lack a reducing lathe for some years and so still relied on the Royal Mint for master dies to create the working dies. However, the need for 1, 10- and 25-cent coins in early 1937 couldn't wait for the George VI matrices. In later years it would be common practice for the Mint to strike coins dated one year into the next (they often did this to use up leftover dies). But no such thing could be done in the present case for this matter involved a transition of monarchs. And yet, the RCM was compelled to keep on minting coins of George V right into 1937. Somehow they must mark the coins without changing the date. What they settled on was a tiny dot. It was engraved below the date on the cent, and under the wreaths on the 10- and 25-cent denominations.

There is still much mystery surrounding the 1936 dot coins. Supposedly 678,823 cents, 191,237 10-cents, and 153,322 25-cent coins were minted. According to the research of Dean T. Silver on his blog "Three dots three Kings 1936," there are no such

records in the annual mint reports. The earliest source he was able to locate was in the 1958 Charlton coin guide. Where Charlton received his information from is uncertain, but in the 1970 article, "Canada's Dot Coinage of 1936-37," in the December issue of the *Canadian Numismatic Journal*, G. R. L. Potter makes a surprising revelation, which is worth repeating:

> "I believe I was, in a numismatic sense, the second person to learn that 'dot' quarters existed, my knowledge coming from Mr. James Hector, who had found several in circulation. It was not until Mr. Maurice Lafortune joined our small group, which later became the Ottawa Coin Club, and still later became the Canadian Numismatic Association's founding body, that we learned that cents and ten-cent pieces had also been marked in this way. Mr. Lafortune worked in the Mint, and his study of the files brought us the information that the issue was of an emergency character, that some 678,823 cents, 191,237 ten-cent pieces, and 153,322 quarters had been struck, and that all had been promptly placed in circulation."

Regardless of Potter's remarks, it is baffling in that only three dot cents and five dot 10-cent coins are currently known, all specimen coins save for one of the cents. This apparent circulation strike was claimed by its late owner, the famous collector John J. Pittman, to have been found in a pyx box used in a Trial of the Pyx. In this formal procedure, new coins are selected at random from the Mint and tested for weight and purity the following year. Again, according to the findings of Dean Silver in several 1930s RCM reports, the three Assay Commissioners appear to have assayed only silver and gold coins. The author has found this view to be strongly supported by other official documents, but has also happened upon some remarks from the late meteorological instrument researcher William E. K. Middleton (1902-1998), a Pyx

Commissioner "on one occasion," who indicated that "a certain number of each denomination" were assayed. His attendance appears to have been at the 1950 Pyx trial. Of course, Middleton could still have been referring to only silver coins.

Whatever the case may be, all appearances suggest that no 1936 dot cent or dot 10-cent pieces were officially released into circulation. However, there is evidence to suggest that these two denominations were indeed struck in quantity for that expectation, but were presumably withheld and melted, probably when the new master dies for George VI became available. The Mint may have had misgivings about issuing the coins, and yet, the 25-cent coins obviously did circulate in some quantity to the continued puzzlement of numismatists. They are scarce, but worn examples can be obtained by most collectors of moderate means. The *2011 Standard Catalog of World Coins* catalogs them at $26 in VG-8 to $1,800 in MS-63. The designs of the coins often appear weaker than regular 1936 25-cent pieces, leading one to believe that the dot was applied only after the die or dies had been used to strike a considerable number of dot-less coins.

Coins of the two smaller denominations, on the other hand, are strictly reserved for the wealthiest of collectors, and cause sensation whenever they appear at auction. John J. Pittman had actually owned all three dot cents and two of the dot 10-cents. He reputedly obtained all these pieces, except the pyx cent, directly from a former Mint employee (Maurice LaFortune!) and the widow of another, during the early 1950s. It was only after Pittman's death in 1996 that the coins crossed the auction block and circulate among other highbrow collections. One of the other 1936 dot 10-cent pieces is actually a recent discovery. The Dominion Collection Specimen, as it is called, surfaced in 2000 when an elderly former mint employee sold it to a private collector. The two remaining dot ten cent coins are in the possession of the National Currency Collection.

The most recent dot cent appearance was in Heritage's 2010 January Signature World Coin Auction. This piece, often referred to as the Belzberg Specimen after the owners who won it in Part Three of the John Jay Pittman Collection (August 1999), is heralded as the finest of the three Pittman coins. It was graded Specimen 66 Red and sold for a whopping $402,500. Also present in the same auction was a 1936 dot ten cent piece in Specimen 68. 1936 10-cent dot coins traditionally garner less attention from collectors than the one cent pieces, but when the hammer fell, the Heritage coin realized a new record of $184,000.

Naturally, the towering price tags collectors are willing to pay for the 1936 dot rarities has led to numerous instances of fakery. One common method is to drill a tiny hole where the dot should be and fill it with a very fine length of wire, just enough to leave a little extra to form the dot. The dots on the genuine cent pieces are very tiny, tinier than the dots on either the 10- or 25-cent pieces. Often, the wire method has a tendency to leave behind an unusually large dot. Another, perhaps cruder technique, is to scrape metal from the fields and form the dot that way. The main problem here is that the dot appears in a depression.

One interesting piece of news in recent years is the possible discovery of a fourth 1936 dot cent, but with a perplexingly large dot. In the article, "Spotting the Dot" in the November 2004 issue of *The Numismatist*, author Gregory Ingram writes that the coin was reportedly found in change by an employee of a Calgary arcade owner in 1969. After an initial, promising examination at the University of Calgary's Nickle Arts Museum, the coin lay in hibernation until late 1999 when it was brought to the attention of Ingram. He subjected the coin to meticulous testing and consulted a number of experts. Ingram's verdict is that the coin was the real deal. However, the coin has never appeared at auction to the knowledge of this writer, and there has been no news of it for a number of years.

The dot after the date on this 1937 Canadian 5-cent piece apparently had no purpose other than to balance the numerals.

5. 1937 DOT FIVE CENTS

Off hand, one would think the dot on this first year type is connected in some way to the famous 1936 dot coinages. But, as the first edition of *Coins of Canada* (1971) by James Haxby and Robert Willey makes clear, the dot right after the date was created "to balance the design," probably in response to the long-tailed seven. The beaver design chosen for the 5-cent piece was previously considered for the 10-cent denomination, and in a proposed drawing for the latter, a dot after the date also appears, although in this case, both were positioned above the beaver. After 1937, the dot disappears on the five cent piece. The 1947 dot variety is another story which will be discussed later on.

6. 1947 MAPLE LEAF COINAGE

As with the 1936 dot coins, most Canadian coin collectors are probably familiar with this story. In 1947, India was granted independence from Britain, and Pakistan was formed, both

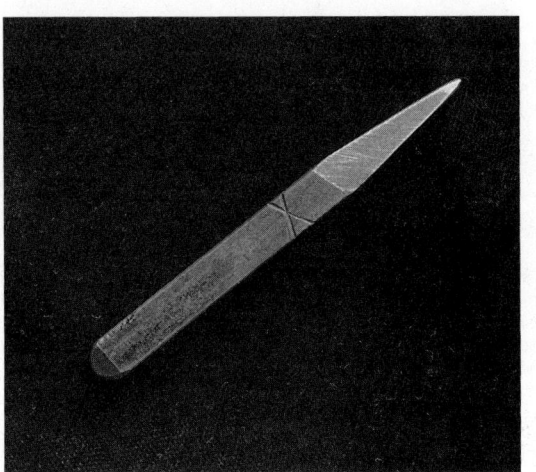

Photos courtesy of the National Currency Collection, Bank of Canada

The obverse legends on Canadian coins had to be modified in 1948 to reflect the fact that King George VI was no longer the emperor of India. However, the necessary obverse master die wouldn't arrive from the Royal Mint in London until late in the year. So as not to halt coin production, the Royal Canadian Mint devised this maple leaf punch, created by Master Engraver Thomas Shingles. It was used to mark 1947-dated coins to show that they were in fact minted in 1948.

countries existing as British dominions for a few years before becoming republics. Normally none of this would cause the Dominion and British colonial mints stress, but one must realize that India was valued by the British Empire almost as much as Algeria was by the French.

Since 1877, the reigning British monarch was also the empress or emperor of India, a fact that the British weren't shy to publicize. On Canadian coins during the reign of George VI, his royal titles first appear in Latin as "GEORGIVS VI D:G: REX ET IND:IMP:" or "George the VI, by the grace of God, King, and Emperor of India." But no more. And the mandatory need to delete the last title once again spelled trouble for the Royal Canadian Mint. In *Striking Impressions*, James Haxby wrote, "Even if there had been advance warning, the Mint was too hard-pressed to do anything more than to meet current

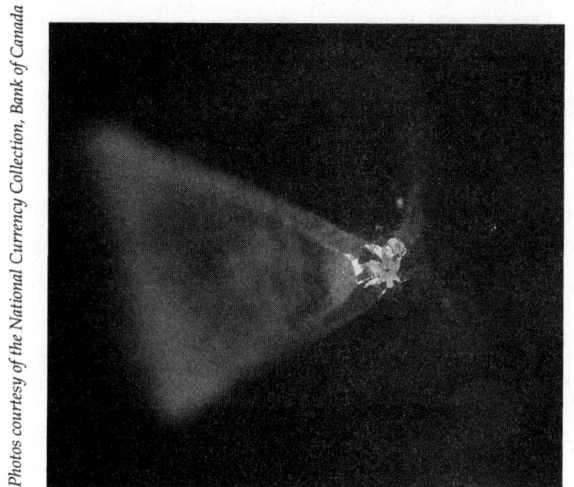

Photos courtesy of the National Currency Collection, Bank of Canada

Seen here is the tiny maple leaf design on the very tip of the 1947 maple leaf punch.

demands. Those demands also meant that there would be no question of simply waiting through several months of the new year until the matrices [hubs] and punches [dies] arrived. Coins were too urgently needed."

For the Canadian minters, solving the problem of an outmoded obverse legend probably felt like déjà vu. They couldn't simply pretend nothing had happened and begin production of 1948-dated coins. No, like the dilemma the RCM faced in 1937, they must continue minting 1947-dated coins into the new year, but somehow mark them. No dots this time though. Instead, it was decided that the dies from cent to dollar were to be marked with a tiny maple leaf after the date. These issues are immensely popular among collectors today and, for the most part, are more easily obtainable than the regular 1947 dated coins without a maple leaf.

The one main exception is the 50-cent maple leaf. More often than not, maple leaf coins were minted in greater numbers than those without the mark, but in this case, only 38,433 half dollars were minted of the former variety as opposed to 424,885 pieces

of the latter type. The prices reflect this to some extent, but really depend upon another consideration. It so happens that 50-cent coins minted in 1947 were struck with two different styles of the numeral seven in the date. This occurred on a couple of other denominations as well, but the variations of the two numbers are different in each case. On the 50-cent piece, the first variety of seven is referred to as a straight seven. One can easily identify it by how the numeral's tail curves to the left. The second variety is known as the curved seven. Coins of this type show the tail curve sharply to the right. Both style sevens can be found with or without a maple leaf huddling close by. For the leafless coins, the *2011 Standard Catalog of World Coins* values the two sevens almost evenly in the low grades, but begins to noticeably favor the curved seven in MS-60 at $100 versus $65 for its straight counterpart. For the maple leaf coins, there is no comparison between the two style sevens. The straight seven is listed at $160 in MS-60, while the curved variety will stop a collector cold at $3,900. It is one of the most sought after Canadian half dollar varieties.

When the new obverse tools did finally arrive in late 1948, the RCM scrambled to put them to work. Considering how little time the minting staff had to produce 1948-dated coins, their efforts were noteworthy, but were not enough to prevent from creating some popular rarities, the king being the 1948 silver dollar. Only 18,780 pieces were minted, but what few collectors there were at the time noticed the dollar's paltry numbers and eagerly saved them. According to the Krause catalog again, this classic rarity catalogs for $1,000 in EF-40 and $1,900 in MS-63.

In about 1969, James Haxby made arrangements to interview the late Thomas Shingles (1903–1984). At this time, the famous engraver was retired from the Royal Canadian Mint and living at his home in Victoria, British Columbia. One of Haxby's questions for Shingles was if he had any souvenirs from his long career at the RCM. The previous Master Engraver looked in his toolbox and retrieved a black, nail-like object. To Haxby's astonishment, it was the 1947 maple leaf

The reverse of a 1947 maple leaf 5-cent piece.

The reverse of a 1947 dot 5-cent piece.

Photos courtesy of Robert Kokotailo of Calgary Coin.

punch! Shingles remarked something along the lines of, "We didn't have one of these lying around so I had to make one." Haxby asked if Shingles would donate the punch to the National Currency Collection, to which Shingles willingly consented, although thinking little of the significance of his past work. The punch still resides in the Collection to this day.

From what Shingles had indicated to Haxby, it seemed clear that the engraver created only one punch. However, according to the research of Calgary coin dealer Robert Kokotailo, "There has to have been more than one punch, because on the dimes one sees two different sizes of maple

The reverse of a 1947 dot 5-cent piece.

Photos courtesy of Robert Kokotailo of Calgary Coin.

A side by side blow-up of the marks on a 1947 dot, and a 1947 maple leaf 5-cents. Notice that the location of the dot is far too low and close to the date to have served as a marker to know where to punch the maple leaf into the die.

leaves. One is enough larger than the other as to be very noticeable." For the inquisitive researcher, here is an area of inquiry worth pursuing further!

7. 1947 DOT COINAGE

The existence of dots after the dates on a few 1947 5- and 25-cent pieces has been a source of much debate among numismatists. What were the meaning of these marks? Some believe that they have none, and are the result of chips in the chromium plated dies. Others, as Robert Kokotailo relates, believe the dots helped mark the spot where the maple leaf would be punched, and that one die was accidentally used without the maple leaf. Of course, there are a couple of serious problems with this theory. As Kokotailo explained, tiny dots appear in other places on both 1947 dot denominations, strongly suggesting that they were not intentionally made. What's more, on the five cent type, "if you punch the ML [maple leaf] over the dot it would have to be much closer to the

Photos courtesy of Robert Kokotailo of Calgary Coin.

A 2000-W Loon dollar, struck by the Winnipeg Mint. Although Winnipeg has been striking all of Canada's circulating coinage without a mintmark for many years, it also has on occasion struck a few proof-like coins with a 'W' in front or below the bust of the Queen.

"7." That dot is just in the wrong place to be a marker for the ML." If this weren't enough, Haxby had even asked Shingles about the 1947 dots during his interview. Haxby said the engraver, who was responsible for creating the maple leaf marked coins "disclaimed any significance to the dots."

Despite this, collectors today are still willing to pay high premiums for the two dot coins. In the *2011 Standard Catalog of World Coins* one finds the 5-cent varieties going from $12.00 in Good to a healthy $300 in MS-63. For the dot 25-cent pieces, examples run from $30 to $500 in the same grades.

8. WINNIPEG 'W' MINTMARK

Gordon Hunter's greatest accomplishment as Master of the Mint from 1970-1975 is said to have been his efforts to construct a new minting facility in Winnipeg. Not only did this former chartered accountant bring this weighty project to a successful conclusion on time, but also under budget. The first coin was struck on March 8, 1975. By the end of April, this super modern

Photos courtesy of Robert Kokotailo of Calgary Coin.

A 2003 "WP" 25-cent piece. This one year type was only minted for proof-like sets, which included the cent through $2. The letters 'WP' are actually a compound mark: the "W" stands for the Winnipeg Mint, and the "P" indicates that the coin was struck on a nickel-plated steel planchet.

branch of the Royal Canadian Mint had struck 46 million 1, 10-, and 25-cent coins. Even so, the official opening ceremony wasn't until April 30 the following year. Gradually, the Winnipeg plant took total charge of striking Canada's circulation coinage while Ottawa concentrated on producing the country's collector and bullion coins.

Most collectors in the U.S., and perhaps even some in Canada, are probably unaware that any of this ever happened, and for one very good reason—Winnipeg didn't use a mintmark. This frustrating mint policy reminds one of the U.S. coinage situation between 1973 and 1986 at West Point, when this other 'W' minting facility (though not designated an official mint until 1988) struck coins for circulation and refused to mark them. In this case though, it was a deliberate and successful attempt to discourage coin collectors from collecting West Point minted coins.

Fortunately for collectors, there was a small policy shift at the RCM during the late 1990s. Hobbyists first got a whiff of it in

1997, when, as the editor of *Canadian Coin News*, Bret Evans, explained to this writer, "The [proof-like] sets were not as nice. Specifically lacking the wire edge of the Ottawa coins. That summer the then Master of the RCM confirmed to me in an interview that production had been started in Winnipeg because there was not enough capacity in Ottawa at the time, but had since moved back to Ottawa. I was informed that the plan had been to shift production back and forth as needed." The Winnipeg sets could also be identified by the fact that "when the set is laid down in its film holder, reverse facing up, the [one dollar] loon is to the left of the $2 in Winnipeg made sets and to the right of the $2 in Ottawa made sets."

Because of the difference in quality, the RCM decided to mark the Winnipeg proof-like (PL) sets with a "W" mintmark to the lower right of the Queen's bust, beginning in 1998. Each contained a near proof quality example of each denomination, cent through $2 Polar Bear. Unfortunately, the exact number of the mintmarked coins struck is not known as the production figures for both the Winnipeg and Ottawa PL sets were lumped together. Just as the RCM had planned, production of the former coins proved to be erratic. They weren't produced again until 2000, and then for only one more time, in 2003. Since then, Ottawa has presumably been capable of handling orders for PL sets by itself, although after 2006 this is harder to be certain of, for reasons that will be explained under the last coin mark we will discuss. Sadly, circulation coinage, which has been under the complete care of Winnipeg for many years, has been content to remain nameless to this day.

For being minted for a period that seems like only three blinks of an eye, most Winnipeg mintmarked coins, regardless of year, are worth only a few dollars more than an average circulation strike from Ottawa in mint state. Even more surprising, but ironically typical, is the fact that these coins seem to be worth about the same or even less when they are all sealed together in a PL set. And to cap off this underdog feeling, Ottawa sets often go for the higher dollar. One final

Photos courtesy of Heritage Auctions (HA.com)

A 2000 "P" Canadian 10-cent piece, graded MS-68 by PCGS. This nearly perfect example is one of an estimated 200 minted for testing purposes by the vending industry. It sold for $3,737.50 in Heritage's 2010 April CICF Signature World Coin Auction. Although 4,899,000 5-cent pieces were officially issued for circulation in 2000, regular production of most of the other "P" plated coins wouldn't begin until 2001.

insult: although the 1997 Winnipeg coins without mintmark are identifiable, they are still not recognized in most price guides.

9. PLATED 'P' MARK

Soon after the first test coins were distributed to the vending companies with the understanding that they would be returned later, several pieces began appearing on the numismatic marketplace where they were sold for substantial prices (over $100) to collectors. In stark contrast to what the U.S. Mint had been known to do in these sorts of situations, the RCM responded in a more creative way. So as not to jeopardize the testing, they sold about 20,000 sets of the 1999 "P" coins directly to collectors in packaging similar to the proof-like sets, thereby making these issues not as insanely expensive as they could have been.

It isn't too hard to understand why nickel was chosen to replace Canadian silver coins, beginning in 1968. It had excellent coinage properties, was considerably cheaper to mint coins from than silver, and was a locally abundant metal in Canada. In fact, Wayne L. Jacobs in his *Canadian Numismatic Journal* article, "Nickel and Nickles," published in 1999 in two parts, noted that Canada was home to "nearly 90 percent of the world's known nickel reserves." But, at the turn of the last century, one of its main attractive qualities was evaporating. Ironically, nickel was no longer seen as a very affordable coinage metal. In 1968, a pound was worth a little less than $1. By early 1999, the metal was trading at around $2.50 for the same amount, which doesn't seem much of a difference, but nickel prices were anything but steady. In May 2007, nickel peaked at $25.51 a pound ($1.59 an ounce) and averages around $8–9 a pound nowadays; so the Mint was apparently looking ahead when they struck a few coins in 1999 and 2000, minted not of pure nickel, but from what is referred to as multi-ply plated steel.

Electroplated over the steel core was a thin layer of nickel, covered by copper, and then nickel again. This composition was used to produce 10-, 25-, & 50-cent coins, and also the 5-cent (which had been minted in copper-nickel since 1982) and lowly small cent (struck from copper-plated zinc since 1997). For the new steel cents, the last nickel layer wasn't applied so as to retain the appearance of copper. All five coins were given to the vending industry for testing purposes and can be distinguished by a letter 'P' below the Queen's portrait. Collectors sometimes confuse this with a mintmark, which it is not. Most likely it stands for "plated." Bret Evans of *Canadian Coin News* remarked to this writer that "in the past the RCM had used test tokens, but in this case decided to use coins. Nobody ever explained exactly why, and I talked to the VP of Production about this in 2000."

At the urging of the vending companies, the Mint took the new plated coins a step further and began issuing them for

circulation, beginning with 4,899,000 5-cent pieces in late 2000 which were needed ahead of schedule to satisfy a shortage of this denomination. These command a modest premium among collectors in uncirculated grade and make for some interesting finds in pocket change or bank rolls. On the other hand, only a handful of the other 2000 "P" denominations are known, since no test coin sets were issued this year nor any other plated coins intentionally issued for circulation. To many collectors, they represent some of the greatest rarities in modern Canadian coins. As one example, the 2000 "P" 50-cent piece can easily reap thousands in mint state.

Evans explained that the move to circulate the new plated coins was so that the vending companies could easily tell whether a coin rejected by their machines was an old nickel or new plated steel coin. Production of the latter type began in earnest in 2001 for all coin denominations below the Loon dollar, with the exception of the cent. Some coins in the old compositions, most notably a small issue of nickel 25-cent pieces, also made a showing, but by the following year the Mint was confident enough to forego minting in the old metals completely. One exception was again the cent piece which was simultaneously produced in both plated metals and which, oddly enough, continues to be done so even today. However, the "P" mark didn't disappear with the disappearance of pure nickel coinage. The countrywide experiment appears to have been still technically in motion, and, in any event, the RCM probably felt committed to identifying the new plated coins. This is obvious from the fact that even specimen and proof coins were so labeled, including the 2003 Winnipeg mintmarked proof-like sets. Ironically, the two marks are positioned so close to one another below the Queen's bust that it looks as if a new mint with the initials "WP" minted them.

In 2006, after over five years in production, the 'P' marked coins finally gave way to a more stylish mark which we will now discuss.

Photos by Mark Fox

In 2006, the Royal Canadian Mint began marking all of its coins with a maple leaf set inside a circle, below the bust of Queen Elizabeth II. This "mintmark" of the RCM is really a corporate logo. Coins with this mark are commonly described in writing with an 'M,''ML,' or 'L' after the date. Seen here is a slightly circulated 2006-ML 25-cent piece.

10. RCM LOGO COINAGE

On July 21, 2010 at the 2006 Canadian Numismatic Association convention in Niagara Falls, Ontario, the RCM unveiled a curious new mark that would from now on grace all Canadian coins below the bust of Queen Elizabeth II. The RCM described it as encompassing "the three elements of the Mint's corporate name: M for Mint, a maple leaf for Canadian and a crown for royal and crown corporation. It features the Mint design within a circle and consists of a symbol depicting a stylized maple leaf emerging from the letter M. The eastern and western points are upturned and reduced in width to suggest a crown." The RCM continued to wax even more poetic. "A majestic M unifies the design, symbolizing the word 'Mint' and its French counterpart, 'Monnaie.' With their conic shape, position and spacing, the two components of the design evoke the action of two dies striking a coin."

Bret Evans, the editor of *Canadian Coin News*, refers to the new mark in a more whimsical way, as the "Circle M." "I like it," he explains. "Because it lets me refer to the Mint as the guys at the Circle M ranch, as a pun on branding." This mint icon is actually the corporate logo of the RCM, and is often referred to in the literature as just that, a logo. Although not completely verified by the author, this led Robert Kokotailo to make an interesting conclusion. "Technically, the Royal Canadian Mint is a private corporation, although wholly owned by the Canadian government, and since the logo is the logo of that private corporation, Canada has the distinction of being what I believe is the only country that allows a private company to advertise their logo on it's coins."

Despite all this stuff about logos, the RCM considers their new maple leaf to be an official mintmark, representing not a single mint, but as described above, the whole corporation. This actually comes as a blow to collectors, because it silently replaces the 'W' mintmark, should Winnipeg produce more proof-like sets in the future. Once again, collectors will have to rely on less obvious means to distinguish the different sets, assuming, of course, the other variations will still exist. Worse yet, the new collective "mintmark" effectively bars the possibility of future Canadian branch mints from marking coins with their own mintmark. Simplicity in the minting process is not always a good thing.

On a more agreeable note, the debut of the RCM maple leaf also spelled the end of the "P" plated mark, which was frankly about time. The last circulating coins dated 2006 with this mark (and without any mark) were actually minted in August and September 2005 while the first logo pieces were ejected from the presses in March and April the following year. This leaves what seems to be a long gap when supposedly no Canadian coinage for commerce was being minted.

The result of the changeover was a bonanza for variety collectors. There weren't just two main varieties of 2006 coins placed into circulation, but actually four, if one is referring to

Photo courtesy of Dan Gosling

Seen here at the 2006 Canadian Numismatic Association convention in Niagara Falls, Ontario, is Ian Bennett, the current Master of the Royal Canadian Mint, showing the new "mintmark" that will appear on all Canadian coins.

the one cent. Collectors can hope to find examples with the "P" mark (copper-plated steel), without the "P" (copper-plated zinc), and coins struck in both compositions with the RCM logo. Only 233,000 pieces of the first variety were supposedly minted. It is considered a fairly scarce coin, even though it is only currently valued around $3 in MS-63. Reportedly, this is due in part to a large number of excess proof-like coins that were released into circulation. Rolls of them are often seen on eBay. The "P" and no "P" varieties also exist in the opposite compositions one would expect to find, which were probably created through error. Both are quite rare. The 2006 no "P" steel cent, for instance, catalogs for $400 CAD (~$390 USD) in MS-63, according to a recent copy of the *Canadian Coin News* value guide, *Trends*. It can be easily identified with a magnet.

As mentioned before, Canadian cents are still produced with both steel and zinc cores, although after 2006 they solely appear with the RCM maple leaf, forcing collectors to keep a magnet handy to tell the two apart. One avid collector also accomplishes this by tasting them, which is hardly recommended.

For the 5-cent piece, there is also a surprising third variety to keep collectors rummaging through their change. Beginning in July 2006, collectors started reporting 2006 5-cent pieces with no RCM maple leaf or mark at all, as on the copper-nickel coins last struck in 2001. Unverified reports claim the Mint used an old stockpile of copper-nickel planchets that had been in storage before 2002 "to fill an unexpected need for 5-cent coins by a large financial institution." They were thought at first to be rare, but have proven to be fairly common.

As we have seen, the switch to the new RCM maple leaf mark was responsible for creating a flurry of different coin varieties, a few that are even regarded as rare. But the mintmark to end all mintmarks has had its effect. Will it be a permanent, unyielding fixture on Canadian coinage? Will tomorrow always look like today? While we don't know the answers to these questions, one thing is a near certainty: as long as the RCM stands, Canadian coinage will not stand still!

CANADA

CENT

KM#1 4.5400 g. Bronze   **Obv:** Laureate head left **Obv. Legend:** VICTORIA DEI GRATIA REGINA. CANADA **Rev:** Denomination and date within beaded circle, chain of leaves surrounds **Rev. Legend:** ONE CENT **Edge:** plain

Date	Mintage	VG-8	F-12	VF-20	XF-40	MS-60	MS-63	Proof
1858	421,000	75.00	100.00	125	200	500	2,000	—
1859 Narrow 9	9,579,000	2.25	3.00	5.00	7.00	45.00	250	—
1859/8 Wide 9	Inc. above	30.00	45.00	60.00	125	350	1,800	—
1859 Double punched narrow 9 type I	Inc. above	200	250	350	550	1,300	5,000	—
1859 Double punched narrow 9 type II	Inc. above	55.00	75.00	125	175	550	3,000	—

KM#7 5.6700 g. Bronze 25.5 mm.   **Obv:** Crowned head left within beaded circle **Obv. Legend:** VICTORIA DEI GRATIA REGINA. CANADA **Obv. Designer:** Leonard C. Wyon **Rev:** Denomination and date within beaded circle, chain of leaves surrounds **Edge:** Plain

Date	Mintage	VG-8	F-12	VF-20	XF-40	MS-60	MS-63	Proof
1876H	4,000,000	3.00	4.00	6.00	9.00	45.00	250	—
1881H	2,000,000	4.00	5.00	11.00	18.00	75.00	300	—
1882H	4,000,000	3.00	3.50	4.00	7.50	40.00	250	—
1884	2,500,000	3.00	4.00	6.50	11.00	60.00	300	—
1886	1,500,000	4.00	7.00	13.00	20.00	95.00	450	—
1887	1,500,000	3.50	5.00	8.00	14.00	70.00	225	—
1888	4,000,000	3.00	4.00	5.00	7.50	40.00	175	—
1890H	1,000,000	8.00	12.00	19.00	30.00	125	450	—
1891 Large date	1,452,000	8.00	11.00	17.00	35.00	150	450	—
1891 S.D.L.L.	Inc. above	65.00	125	200	300	1,000	4,000	—
1891 S.D.S.L.	Inc. above	60.00	95.00	125	200	450	1,750	—
1892	1,200,000	5.50	8.00	12.00	15.00	60.00	225	—
1893	2,000,000	3.00	4.00	5.00	9.50	45.00	200	—
1894	1,000,000	11.00	15.00	20.00	40.00	125	300	—

Date	Mintage	VG-8	F-12	VF-20	XF-40	MS-60	MS-63	Proof
1895	1,200,000	5.00	9.50	13.00	16.00	60.00	225	—
1896	2,000,000	3.00	5.00	6.50	7.50	40.00	150	—
1897	1,500,000	3.00	5.00	6.50	9.00	45.00	200	—
1898H	1,000,000	9.00	13.00	17.00	35.00	100.00	300	—
1899	2,400,000	3.00	3.50	5.00	7.00	45.00	150	—
1900	1,000,000	9.00	13.50	20.00	30.00	125	500	—
1900H	2,600,000	3.00	3.50	5.00	7.50	30.00	95.00	—
1901	4,100,000	3.00	4.00	6.00	11.00	45.00	100.00	—

KM# 8 5.6700 g. Bronze 25.5 mm.   **Obv:** Kings bust right within beaded circle
Obv. Designer: G. W. DeSaulles **Rev:** Denomination above date within circle, chain
of leaves surrounds **Edge:** Plain

Date	Mintage	VG-8	F-12	VF-20	XF-40	MS-60	MS-63	Proof
1902	3,000,000	2.25	3.00	4.00	8.00	27.00	75.00	—
1903	4,000,000	2.25	3.00	4.00	8.00	30.00	90.00	—
1904	2,500,000	2.50	4.00	6.00	10.00	45.00	100.00	—
1905	2,000,000	4.00	6.00	9.00	13.00	55.00	150	—
1906	4,100,000	2.25	3.00	4.00	8.00	40.00	175	—
1907	2,400,000	2.50	3.00	5.00	10.00	40.00	175	—
1907H	800,000	13.00	21.00	30.00	55.00	175	600	—
1908	2,401,506	3.00	4.00	6.00	10.00	40.00	125	500
1909	3,973,339	2.00	3.00	4.00	7.00	30.00	100.00	—
1910	5,146,487	1.50	2.00	3.00	6.00	30.00	85.00	—

KM# 15 5.6700 g. Bronze 25.5 mm.   **Obv:** King's bust left **Obv. Designer:** E. B.
MacKennal **Rev:** Denomination above date within beaded circle, chain of leaves
surrounds **Edge:** Plain

Date	Mintage	VG-8	F-12	VF-20	XF-40	MS-60	MS-63	Proof
1911	4,663,486	0.80	1.50	2.25	3.50	25.00	70.00	800

KM# 21 5.6700 g. Bronze 25.5 mm. **Obv:** King's bust left **Obv. Designer:** E. B. MacKennal **Rev:** Denomination above date within beaded circle, chain of leaves surrounds **Edge:** Plain

Date	Mintage	VG-8	F-12	VF-20	XF-40	MS-60	MS-63	Proof
1912	5,107,642	0.90	1.75	2.50	4.00	30.00	75.00	—
1913	5,735,405	0.90	1.75	2.50	5.00	27.50	95.00	—
1914	3,405,958	1.25	1.75	3.00	5.00	40.00	100.00	—
1915	4,932,134	0.90	1.50	2.50	5.00	35.00	95.00	—
1916	11,022,367	0.60	0.80	1.50	3.00	19.00	60.00	—
1917	11,899,254	0.60	0.80	1.00	2.50	16.00	55.00	—
1918	12,970,798	0.60	0.80	1.00	2.50	14.00	55.00	—
1919	11,279,634	0.60	0.80	1.00	2.50	14.00	55.00	—
1920	6,762,247	0.70	0.90	1.25	2.50	22.00	85.00	—

Dot below date

KM# 28 3.2400 g. Bronze 19.10 mm. **Obv:** King's bust left **Obv. Designer:** E. B. MacKennal **Rev:** Denomination above date, leaves flank **Rev. Designer:** Fred Lewis **Edge:** Plain

Date	Mintage	VG-8	F-12	VF-20	XF-40	MS-60	MS-63
1920	15,483,923	0.20	0.45	0.95	1.75	15.00	50.00
1921	7,601,627	0.45	0.75	1.75	5.00	35.00	250
1922	1,243,635	13.00	16.00	25.00	45.00	200	1,200
1923	1,019,002	29.00	35.00	40.00	60.00	300	2,000
1924	1,593,195	6.00	7.00	12.00	20.00	125	850
1925	1,000,622	22.00	25.00	30.00	50.00	200	1,200
1926	2,143,372	3.50	4.50	7.00	16.00	95.00	650
1927	3,553,928	1.25	1.75	3.50	8.00	40.00	225
1928	9,144,860	0.15	0.30	0.65	1.50	20.00	90.00
1929	12,159,840	0.15	0.30	0.65	1.50	20.00	80.00
1930	2,538,613	2.00	2.50	4.50	9.00	50.00	225
1931	3,842,776	0.65	1.00	2.50	6.00	40.00	200
1932	21,316,190	0.15	0.20	0.50	1.50	16.00	60.00
1933	12,079,310	0.15	0.30	0.50	1.50	16.00	55.00
1934	7,042,358	0.20	0.30	0.75	1.50	16.00	60.00
1935	7,526,400	0.20	0.30	0.75	1.50	16.00	50.00
1936	8,768,769	0.15	0.30	0.75	1.50	14.00	45.00

Date	Mintage	VG-8	F-12	VF-20	XF-40	MS-60	MS-63
1936 dot below date; Rare	678,823	—	—	—	—	—	250,000

Note: *Only one possible business strike is known to exist. No other examples (or possible business strikes) have ever surfaced.*

Date	Mintage	VG-8	F-12	VF-20	XF-40	MS-60	MS-63
1936 dot below date, specimen, 3 known	—	—	—	—	—	—	—

Note: *At the David Akers auction of the John Jay Pittman collection (Part 1, 10-97), a gem specimen realized $121,000. At the David Akers auction of the John Jay Pittman collection (Part 3, 10-99), a near choice specimen realized $115,000.*

Maple leaf

KM# 32 3.2400 g. Bronze 19.10 mm.   **Obv:** Head left **Obv. Designer:** T. H. Paget **Rev:** Maple leaf divides date and denomination **Rev. Designer:** George E. Kruger-Gray **Edge:** Plain

Date	Mintage	VG-8	F-12	VF-20	XF-40	MS-60	MS-63	Proof
1937	10,040,231	0.35	0.45	0.70	0.95	2.50	12.00	—
1938	18,365,608	0.15	0.20	0.30	0.75	2.50	13.00	—
1939	21,600,319	0.10	0.20	0.30	0.70	2.00	8.00	—
1940	85,740,532	0.10	0.15	0.25	0.50	2.50	8.00	—
1941	56,336,011	0.10	0.15	0.25	0.50	8.00	50.00	—
1942	76,113,708	0.10	0.15	0.25	0.50	7.00	50.00	—
1943	89,111,969	0.10	0.15	0.25	0.45	3.50	22.00	—
1944	44,131,216	0.10	0.15	0.30	0.60	11.00	70.00	—
1945	77,268,591	0.10	0.15	0.20	0.35	2.50	22.00	—
1946	56,662,071	0.10	0.15	0.20	0.35	2.50	12.00	—
1947	31,093,901	0.10	0.15	0.20	0.35	2.50	9.00	—
1947 maple leaf	47,855,448	0.10	0.15	0.20	0.35	2.50	9.00	—

KM# 41 3.2400 g. Bronze 19.10 mm.   **Obv:** Modified legend **Obv. Designer:** T. H. Paget **Rev. Designer:** George E. Kruger-Gray **Edge:** Plain

Date	Mintage	VG-8	F-12	VF-20	XF-40	MS-60	MS-63	Proof
1948	25,767,779	—	0.15	0.25	0.70	4.00	27.00	—
1949	33,128,933	—	0.10	0.15	0.35	2.50	9.00	—
1950	60,444,992	—	0.10	0.15	0.25	1.75	9.00	—
1951	80,430,379	—	0.10	0.15	0.20	1.75	14.00	—
1952	67,631,736	—	0.10	0.15	0.20	1.25	9.00	—

  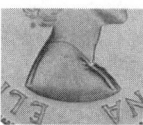 

No strap   With strap

KM# 49 3.2400 g. Bronze 19.10 mm.   **Obv:** Laureate bust right **Obv. Designer:** Mary Gillick **Rev:** Maple leaf divides date and denomination **Rev. Designer:** George E. Kruger-Gray

Date	Mintage	VG-8	F-12	VF-20	XF-40	MS-60	MS-63	Proof
1953	67,806,016	0.10	0.10	0.10	0.25	0.80	2.50	—

Note: *Without strap*

Date	Mintage	VG-8	F-12	VF-20	XF-40	MS-60	MS-63	Proof
1953	Inc. above	0.50	1.00	1.50	2.50	12.00	60.00	—
Note: With strap								
1954	22,181,760	0.10	0.10	0.10	0.40	1.75	6.00	—
Note: With strap								
1954 Prooflike only	Inc. above	—	—	—	—	550	800	—
Note: Without strap								
1955	56,403,193	—	0.10	0.10	0.15	0.45	3.00	—
Note: With strap								
1955	Inc. above	100.00	150	175	250	600	2,000	—
Note: Without strap								
1956	78,658,535	—	—	—	0.15	0.30	2.00	—
1957	100,601,792	—	—	—	0.10	0.10	1.00	—
1958	59,385,679	—	—	—	0.10	0.10	1.00	—
1959	83,615,343	—	—	—	0.10	0.10	0.60	—
1960	75,772,775	—	—	—	0.10	0.10	0.60	—
1961	139,598,404	—	—	—	—	0.10	0.60	—
1962	227,244,069	—	—	—	—	0.10	0.40	—
1963	279,076,334	—	—	—	—	0.10	0.40	—
1964	484,655,322	—	—	—	—	0.10	0.40	—

KM# 59.1 3.2400 g. Bronze 19.10 mm.   **Obv:** Queens bust right **Obv. Designer:** Arnold Machin **Rev:** Maple leaf divides date and denomination **Rev. Designer:** George E. Kruger-Gray **Edge:** Plain

Date	Mintage	VG-8	F-12	VF-20	XF-40	MS-60	MS-63	Proof
1965	304,441,082	—	0.15	0.20	0.40	1.00	5.00	—
Note: Small beads, pointed 5								
1965	Inc. above	—	—	—	—	0.10	0.40	—
Note: Small beads, blunt 5								
1965	Inc. above	1.75	3.00	4.50	7.50	18.00	45.00	—
Note: Large beads, pointed 5								
1965	Inc. above	—	—	—	0.10	0.10	0.40	—
Note: Large beads, blunt 5								
1966	184,151,087	—	—	—	—	0.10	0.40	—
1968	329,695,772	—	—	—	—	0.10	0.40	—
1969	335,240,929	—	—	—	—	0.10	0.40	—
1970	311,145,010	—	—	—	—	0.10	0.40	—
1971	298,228,936	—	—	—	—	0.10	0.40	—
1972	451,304,591	—	—	—	—	0.10	0.40	—
1973	457,059,852	—	—	—	—	0.10	0.40	—
1974	692,058,489	—	—	—	—	0.10	0.40	—
1975	642,318,000	—	—	—	—	0.10	0.40	—
1976	701,122,890	—	—	—	—	0.10	0.40	—
1977	453,762,670	—	—	—	—	0.10	0.40	—

KM# 65 3.2400 g. Bronze 19.10 mm.   **Subject:** Confederation Centennial **Obv:** Queen's bust right **Obv. Designer:** Arnold Machin **Rev:** Dove with wings spread, denomination above, two dates below **Rev. Designer:** Alex Coville

Date	Mintage	VG-8	F-12	VF-20	XF-40	MS-60	MS-63	Proof
1867-1967	345,140,645	—	—	—	—	0.10	0.40	1.00

KM# 59.2 3.2400 g. Bronze 19.10 mm.   **Obv:** Queen's bust right **Obv. Designer:** Arnold Machin **Rev:** Maple leaves **Rev. Designer:** George E. Kruger-Gray **Edge:** Plain **Note:** Thin planchet.

Date	Mintage	VG-8	F-12	VF-20	XF-40	MS-60	MS-63	Proof
1978	911,170,647	—	—	—	—	0.10	0.30	—
1979	754,394,064	—	—	—	—	0.10	0.30	—

KM# 127 2.8000 g. Bronze 19.10 mm.   **Obv:** Queen's bust right **Obv. Designer:** Arnold Machin **Rev. Designer:** George E. Kruger-Gray **Edge:** Plain **Note:** Reduced weight.

Date	Mintage	VG-8	F-12	VF-20	XF-40	MS-60	MS-63	Proof
1980	912,052,318	—	—	—	—	0.10	0.30	—
1981	1,209,468,500	—	—	—	—	0.10	0.30	—
1981 Proof	199,000	—	—	—	—	—	—	1.50

KM# 132 2.5000 g. Bronze 19.10 mm.   **Obv:** Queen's bust right **Obv. Designer:** Arnold Machin **Rev:** Maple leaf divides date and denomination **Rev. Designer:** George E. Kruger-Gray **Edge:** Plain **Note:** Reduced weight.

Date	Mintage	VG-8	F-12	VF-20	XF-40	MS-60	MS-63	Proof
1982	911,001,000	—	—	—	—	0.10	0.30	—
1982 Proof	180,908	—	—	—	—	—	—	1.50
1983	975,510,000	—	—	—	—	0.10	0.30	—
1983 Proof	168,000	—	—	—	—	—	—	1.50
1984	838,225,000	—	—	—	—	0.10	0.30	—
1984 Proof	161,602	—	—	—	—	—	—	1.50
1985	771,772,500	0.95	1.75	2.50	3.50	10.00	19.00	—
Note: Pointed 5								
1985	Inc. above	—	—	—	—	0.10	0.30	—
Note: Blunt 5								

Date	Mintage	VG-8	F-12	VF-20	XF-40	MS-60	MS-63	Proof
1985 Proof	157,037	—	—	—	—	—	—	1.50
Note: Blunt 5								
1986	740,335,000	—	—	—	—	0.10	0.30	—
1986 Proof	175,745	—	—	—	—	—	—	1.50
1987	774,549,000	—	—	—	—	0.10	0.30	—
1987 Proof	179,004	—	—	—	—	—	—	1.50
1988	482,676,752	—	—	—	—	0.10	0.30	—
1988 Proof	175,259	—	—	—	—	—	—	1.50
1989	1,077,347,200	—	—	—	—	0.10	0.30	—
1989 Proof	170,928	—	—	—	—	—	—	1.50

KM# 181 2.5000 g. Bronze 19.10 mm. **Obv:** Crowned Queen's head right **Obv. Designer:** Dora dePedery-Hunt **Rev:** Maple leaf divides date and denomination **Rev. Designer:** George E. Kruger-Gray **Edge:** Plain

Date	Mintage	MS-63	Proof
1990	218,035,000	0.30	—
1990 Proof	140,649	—	2.50
1991	831,001,000	0.30	—
1991 Proof	131,888	—	3.50
1993	752,034,000	0.30	—
1993 Proof	145,065	—	2.00
1994	639,516,000	0.30	—
1994 Proof	146,424	—	2.50
1995	624,983,000	0.30	—
1995 Proof	—	—	2.50
1996	445,746,000	0.30	—
1996 Proof	—	—	2.50

KM# 204 Bronze 19.10 mm. **Subject:** Confederation 125 **Obv:** Crowned Queen's head right **Obv. Designer:** Dora dePedery-Hunt **Rev:** Maple leaf divides date and denomination **Rev. Designer:** George E. Kruger-Gray

Date	Mintage	MS-63	Proof
1992 Proof	147,061	—	2.50
1992	673,512,000	0.30	—

KM# 289 2.2500 g. Copper Plated Steel 19.05 mm. **Obv:** Crowned head right **Obv. Designer:** Dora dePédery-Hunt **Rev:** Maple twig design **Rev. Designer:** George E. Kruger-Gray **Edge:** Round and plain

Date	Mintage	MS-63	Proof
1997	549,868,000	0.30	—
1997 Proof	—	—	2.75
1998	999,578,000	0.30	—
1998 Proof	—	—	3.00
1998W	—	1.75	—
1999P	—	6.00	—
1999	1,089,625,000	0.30	—
1999W	—	—	—
1999 Proof	—	—	4.00
2000	771,908,206	0.30	—
2000 Proof	—	—	4.00
2000W	—	1.75	—
2001	919,358,000	0.30	—
2001P Proof	—	—	5.00
2003	92,219,775	0.30	—
2003P Proof	—	—	5.00
2003P	235,936,799	1.50	—

KM# 289a Bronze 19.10 mm.

Date	Mintage	MS-63	Proof
1998	—	0.75	—

Note: In Specimen sets only

KM# 309 5.6700 g. 0.9250 Copper Plated Silver 0.1686 oz. **Subject:** 90th Anniversary Royal Canadian Mint - 1908-1998 **Obv. Designer:** Dora dePedery-Hunt **Rev. Designer:** G. W. DeSaulles

Date	Mintage	MS-63	Proof
1908-1998	25,000	16.00	—
Note: Antique finish			
1908-1998 Proof	—	—	—

KM# 332 5.6700 g. 0.9250 Silver 0.1686 oz. ASW **Subject:** 90th Anniversary Royal Canadian Mint - 1908-1998 **Obv:** Crowned Queen's head right, with "Canada" added to head **Obv. Designer:** Dora dePedery-Hunt **Rev:** Denomination above dates withn beaded circle, chain of leaves surrounds **Rev. Designer:** G. W. DeSaulles

Date	Mintage	MS-63	P/L	Proof
1908-1998 Proof	25,000	—	—	16.00

Note: Mirror finish

KM#445 2.2500 g. Copper Plated Steel 19.1 mm. **Subject:** Elizabeth II Golden Jubilee **Obv:** Crowned head right, Jubilee commemorative dates 1952-2002 **Obv. Designer:** Dora dePédery-Hunt **Rev:** Denomination above maple leaves **Rev. Designer:** George E. Kruger-Gray **Edge:** Plain

Date	Mintage	MS-63	Proof
1952-2002	716,366,000	0.75	—
1952-2002P	114,212,000	1.00	—
1952-2002P Proof	32,642	—	5.00

KM# 445a 0.9250 Silver **Subject:** Elizabeth II Golden Jubilee **Obv:** Crowned head right, Jubilee commemorative dates 1952-2002 **Obv. Designer:** Dora dePédery-Hunt **Rev:** Denomination above maple leaves **Rev. Designer:** George E. Kruger-Gray

Date	Mintage	MS-63	Proof
1952-2002	21,537	—	3.00

KM# 490 2.2500 g. Copper Plated Zinc 19.05 mm. **Obv:** New effigy of Queen Elizabeth II right **Obv. Designer:** Susanna Blunt **Rev:** Two maple leaves **Edge:** Plain

Date	Mintage	MS-63	Proof
2003	56,877,144	0.25	—
2004	653,317,000	0.25	—
2004 Proof	—	—	2.50
2005	759,658,000	0.25	—
2005 Proof	—	—	2.50
2006	886,275,000	0.25	—
2006 Proof	—	—	2.50

KM# 490a 2.2500 g. Copper Plated Steel 19.05 mm. **Obv:** Bust right **Obv. Designer:** Susanna Blunt **Rev:** Two maple leaves **Rev. Designer:** G. E. Kruger-Gray

Date	Mintage	MS-63	Proof
2003P	591,257,000	0.25	—
2003 WP	Inc. above	0.25	—
2004P	134,906,000	0.25	—
2005P	30,525,000	0.25	—
2006P	137,733,000	0.25	—
2006(ml)	Inc. above	0.25	—
2007(ml)	938,270,000	0.25	—
2007(ml) Proof	—	—	2.50
2008(ml)	787,625,000	0.25	—
2008(ml) Proof	—	—	2.50
2009(ml)	455,680,000	0.25	—
2009(ml) Proof	—	—	2.50
2010(ml)	—	0.25	—
2010(ml) Proof	—	—	2.50
2011(ml)	—	0.25	—
2011(ml) Proof	—	—	2.50
2012(ml)	—	0.25	—
2012(ml) Proof	—	—	2.50

KM# 468 2.5000 g. Copper **Subject:** 50th Anniversary of the Coronation of Elizabeth II **Obv:** 1953 Effigy of the Queen, Jubilee commemorative dates 1953-2003 **Obv. Designer:** Mary Gillick

Date	Mintage	MS-63	Proof
1953-2003 Proof	—	—	2.50

KM# 490b 2.2500 g. Copper Plated Zinc **Obv:** Head right **Rev:** Maple leaf, selectively gold plated **Note:** Bound into Annual Report.

Date	Mintage	MS-63	Proof
2003 Proof	7,746	—	35.00

KM# 1023 Copper 19.1 mm.   **Obv:** George V bust left **Rev:** Value within wreath, dual dates below

Date	Mintage	MS-63	Proof
1935-2010 Proof	—	—	10.00

KM# 1153 Copper 19.1 mm.

Date	Mintage	MS-63	P/L	Proof
1911-2011 Proof	—	—	—	10.00

3 CENTS

KM# 410 3.1100 g. 0.9250 Silver 0.0925 oz. ASW Gilt 21.3 mm. **Subject:** 1st Canadian Postage Stamp **Obv:** Crowned head right **Obv. Designer:** Dora dePédery-Hunt **Rev:** Partial stamp design **Rev. Designer:** Sandford Fleming **Edge:** Plain

Date	Mintage	MS-63	Proof
2001 Proof	59,573	—	12.50

5 CENTS

       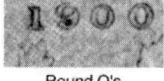

Oval O's   Round O's

KM# 2 1.1620 g. 0.9250 Silver 0.0346 oz. ASW   **Obv:** Head left **Obv. Legend:** VICTORIA DEI GRATIA REGINA. CANADA **Rev:** Denomination and date within wreath, crown above

Date	Mintage	VG-8	F-12	VF-20	XF-40	MS-60	MS-63
1858 Small date	1,500,000	19.00	30.00	45.00	80.00	250	550
1858 Large date over small date	Inc. above	150	225	350	550	1,500	3,500
1870	2,800,000	15.00	24.00	40.00	75.00	250	850
Note: Flat rim							
1870	Inc. above	15.00	24.00	40.00	75.00	250	600
Note: Wire rim							
1871	1,400,000	15.00	24.00	40.00	75.00	300	800
1872H	2,000,000	13.00	20.00	35.00	80.00	350	1,250
1874H Plain 4	800,000	22.00	45.00	90.00	150	450	1,000
1874H Crosslet 4	Inc. above	18.00	40.00	75.00	150	500	1,100
1875H Large date	1,000,000	300	500	800	1,400	5,000	15,000
1875H Small date	Inc. above	150	225	500	700	2,100	6,000
1880H	3,000,000	6.00	12.00	27.00	65.00	300	800
1881H	1,500,000	9.00	15.00	30.00	70.00	300	800
1882H	1,000,000	12.00	18.00	28.00	80.00	300	800
1883H	600,000	23.00	40.00	85.00	200	900	3,000
1884	200,000	125	200	350	750	3,500	9,000
1885 Small 5	1,000,000	16.00	24.00	50.00	125	750	2,900
1885 Large 5	Inc. above	15.00	27.00	55.00	150	850	3,000
1885 Large 5 over small 5	Inc. above	65.00	125	200	500	4,000	—

Date	Mintage	VG-8	F-12	VF-20	XF-40	MS-60	MS-63
1886 Small 6	1,700,000	9.00	15.00	30.00	60.00	400	1,300
1886 Large 6	Inc. above	11.00	18.00	40.00	70.00	425	1,500
1887	500,000	30.00	60.00	75.00	175	500	1,000
1888	1,000,000	6.00	9.00	18.00	50.00	175	450
1889	1,200,000	24.00	40.00	90.00	175	600	1,600
1890H	1,000,000	6.00	12.00	22.00	50.00	200	450
1891	1,800,000	6.00	9.00	15.00	30.00	150	400
1892	860,000	6.00	10.00	20.00	50.00	250	700
1893	1,700,000	6.00	9.00	14.00	30.00	175	500
1894	500,000	19.00	30.00	75.00	125	450	1,400
1896	1,500,000	6.00	9.00	14.00	35.00	175	450
1897	1,319,283	4.50	6.50	20.00	45.00	150	450
1898	580,717	12.00	20.00	40.00	90.00	350	950
1899	3,000,000	4.50	6.50	12.00	25.00	125	350
1900 Oval 0's	1,800,000	4.50	6.50	12.00	25.00	125	400
1900 Round 0's	Inc. above	21.00	40.00	60.00	150	450	1,000
1901	2,000,000	6.00	8.00	16.00	35.00	175	500

KM# 9 3.3200 g. 0.9250 Silver 0.0987 oz. ASW 20.1 mm.   **Obv. Designer:** G. W. DeSaulles **Rev. Designer:** Leonard C. Wyon

Date	Mintage	VG-8	F-12	VF-20	XF-40	MS-60	MS-63	Proof
1902	2,120,000	2.00	3.00	5.00	9.00	45.00	70.00	—
1902	2,200,000	2.00	4.00	7.00	14.00	45.00	80.00	—
Note: Large broad H								
1902	Inc. above	10.00	17.00	30.00	50.00	125	225	—
Note: Small narrow H								

KM# 13 1.1500 g. 0.9250 Silver 0.0342 oz. ASW 15.5 mm.   **Obv:** King's bust right **Rev:** Denomination and date within wreath, crown at top

Date	Mintage	VG-8	F-12	VF-20	XF-40	MS-60	MS-63	Proof
1903 22 leaves	1,000,000	5.00	9.00	22.50	45.00	200	450	—
1903H 21 leaves	2,640,000	2.25	4.00	9.00	20.00	125	400	—
1904	2,400,000	3.00	5.00	9.00	30.00	225	650	—
1905	2,600,000	2.25	4.00	10.00	20.00	125	300	—
1906	3,100,000	2.00	3.00	7.00	17.00	125	250	—
1907	5,200,000	2.00	3.00	5.00	13.00	70.00	175	—
1908	1,220,524	7.00	13.00	30.00	50.00	125	225	—
1909 Round leaves	1,983,725	4.00	8.00	13.00	40.00	250	700	—
1909 Pointed leaves	Inc. above	16.00	24.00	55.00	125	700	1,700	—
1910 Pointed leaves	3,850,325	2.00	3.00	6.00	12.00	65.00	125	—
1910 Round leaves	Inc. above	18.00	24.00	45.00	125	550	1,700	—

KM# 16 1.1620 g. 0.9250 Silver 0.0346 oz. ASW   **Obv:** King's bust left **Obv. Designer:** E. B. MacKennal **Rev:** Denomination and date within wreath, crown above **Rev. Designer:** Leonard C. Wyon

Date	Mintage	VG-8	F-12	VF-20	XF-40	MS-60	MS-63	Proof
1911	3,692,350	2.50	4.00	7.00	12.00	80.00	125	—

KM# 22 1.1300 g. 0.9250 Silver 0.0336 oz. ASW 15.5 mm.   **Obv:** King's bust left **Obv. Designer:** E. B. MacKennal **Rev:** Denomination and date within wreath, crown above **Rev. Designer:** Leonard C. Wyon

Date	Mintage	VG-8	F-12	VF-20	XF-40	MS-60	MS-63	Proof
1912	5,863,170	2.50	3.00	6.00	10.00	70.00	200	—
1913	5,488,048	2.50	3.00	5.00	8.00	35.00	70.00	—
1914	4,202,179	2.50	3.00	6.00	10.00	65.00	200	—
1915	1,172,258	14.00	20.00	35.00	65.00	350	800	—
1916	2,481,675	4.00	7.00	12.00	28.00	125	300	—
1917	5,521,373	2.25	3.00	4.00	9.00	40.00	100.00	—
1918	6,052,298	2.25	3.00	4.00	8.00	40.00	85.00	—
1919	7,835,400	2.25	3.00	4.00	8.00	40.00	85.00	—

KM# 22a 1.1664 g. 0.8000 Silver 0.0300 oz. ASW 15.48 mm.   **Obv. Designer:** E. B. MacKennal **Rev. Designer:** Leonard C. Wyon

Date	Mintage	VG-8	F-12	VF-20	XF-40	MS-60	MS-63	Proof
1920	10,649,851	1.75	2.50	3.00	6.50	28.00	65.00	—
1921	2,582,495	4,000	5,000	6,500	9,000	16,000	28,000	—

Note: *Approximately 460 known; balance remelted. Stack's A.G. Carter Jr. Sale (12-89) choice BU, finest known, realized $57,200*

Near 6   Far 6

KM# 29 4.6000 g. Nickel 21.2 mm.   **Obv:** King's bust left **Obv. Designer:** E. B. MacKennal **Rev:** Maple leaves divide denomination and date **Rev. Designer:** W. H. J. Blakemore

Date	Mintage	VG-8	F-12	VF-20	XF-40	MS-60	MS-63	Proof
1922	4,794,119	0.30	0.95	1.75	7.00	60.00	125	—

Date	Mintage	VG-8	F-12	VF-20	XF-40	MS-60	MS-63	Proof
1923	2,502,279	0.40	1.25	5.50	16.00	150	400	—
1924	3,105,839	0.30	1.00	4.00	10.00	100.00	300	—
1925	201,921	65.00	80.00	150	300	1,600	5,000	—
1926 Near 6	938,162	3.00	7.00	16.00	75.00	450	1,600	—
1926 Far 6	Inc. above	150	175	300	600	2,000	6,000	—
1927	5,285,627	0.30	0.65	3.00	14.50	75.00	200	—
1928	4,577,712	0.30	0.65	3.00	14.50	65.00	125	—
1929	5,611,911	0.30	0.65	3.00	14.50	80.00	200	—
1930	3,704,673	0.30	1.25	3.00	15.00	125	250	—
1931	5,100,830	0.30	1.25	3.50	18.00	175	650	—
1932	3,198,566	0.30	1.00	3.50	16.00	150	500	—
1933	2,597,867	0.40	1.50	6.00	18.00	200	800	—
1934	3,827,304	0.30	1.00	3.00	16.00	150	500	—
1935	3,900,000	0.30	1.00	3.00	11.00	125	350	—
1936	4,400,450	0.30	0.65	1.75	9.00	60.00	150	—

KM# 33 4.5000 g. Nickel 21.2 mm.   **Obv:** Head left **Obv. Designer:** T. H. Paget **Rev:** Beaver on rock divides denomination and date **Rev. Designer:** George E. Kruger-Gray

Date	Mintage	VG-8	F-12	VF-20	XF-40	MS-60	MS-63	Proof
1937 Dot	4,593,263	0.20	0.30	1.25	2.50	12.00	24.00	—
1938	3,898,974	0.30	0.90	2.00	7.00	80.00	175	—
1939	5,661,123	0.20	0.35	1.25	3.00	55.00	90.00	—
1940	13,920,197	0.20	0.30	0.75	2.25	20.00	55.00	—
1941	8,681,785	0.20	0.30	0.75	2.25	28.00	70.00	—
1942 Round	6,847,544	0.20	0.30	0.75	1.75	20.00	50.00	—

KM# 39 Tombac Brass 21.2 mm.   **Obv:** Head left **Obv. Designer:** T. H. Paget **Rev:** Beaver on rock divides denomination and date **Rev. Designer:** George E. Kruger-Gray **Shape:** 12-sided

Date	Mintage	VG-8	F-12	VF-20	XF-40	MS-60	MS-63	Proof
1942	3,396,234	0.40	0.65	1.25	1.75	4.00	16.00	—

KM# 40 Tombac Brass 21.2 mm.   **Subject:** Victory **Obv:** Head left **Obv. Designer:** T. H. Paget **Rev:** Torch on "V" divides date **Rev. Designer:** Thomas Shingles

Date	Mintage	VG-8	F-12	VF-20	XF-40	MS-60	MS-63	Proof
1943	24,760,256	0.20	0.30	0.40	0.80	3.50	12.00	—
1944	8,000	—	—	—	—	—	—	—

Note: 1 known

KM# 40a 4.4000 g. Chrome Plated Steel 21.2 mm.   **Obv:** Head left **Rev:** Torch on "V" divides date

Date	Mintage	VG-8	F-12	VF-20	XF-40	MS-60	MS-63	Proof
1944	11,532,784	0.10	0.20	0.45	0.90	2.50	6.50	—
1945	18,893,216	0.10	0.20	0.40	0.80	2.50	6.50	—

  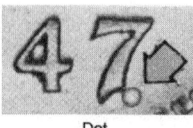 

Dot   Maple leaf

KM# 39a 4.5000 g. Nickel 21.2 mm.   **Obv:** Head left **Obv. Designer:** T. H. Paget **Rev:** Beaver on rock divides denomination and date **Rev. Designer:** George E. Kruger-Gray

Date	Mintage	VG-8	F-12	VF-20	XF-40	MS-60	MS-63	Proof
1946	6,952,684	0.10	0.25	0.50	2.00	16.00	40.00	—
1947	7,603,724	0.20	0.25	0.50	1.25	12.00	28.00	—
1947 Dot	Inc. above	18.00	22.00	35.00	75.00	200	400	—
1947 Maple leaf	9,595,124	0.20	0.25	0.45	1.25	12.00	25.00	—

KM# 42 4.5400 g. Nickel 21.2 mm.   **Obv:** Head left, modified legend **Obv. Designer:** T. H. Paget **Rev:** Beaver on rock divides date and denomination **Rev. Designer:** George E. Kruger-Gray

Date	Mintage	VG-8	F-12	VF-20	XF-40	MS-60	MS-63	Proof
1948	1,810,789	0.40	0.50	1.00	3.00	20.00	40.00	—
1949	13,037,090	0.15	0.25	0.45	0.75	7.00	16.00	—
1950	11,970,521	0.15	0.25	0.45	0.75	7.00	16.00	—

KM# 42a Chromium And Nickel Plated Steel 21.2 mm.   **Obv:** Head left **Obv. Designer:** T. H. Paget **Rev:** Beaver on rock divides date and denomination **Rev. Designer:** George E. Kruger-Gray

Date	Mintage	VG-8	F-12	VF-20	XF-40	MS-60	MS-63	Proof
1951	4,313,410	0.10	0.20	0.45	0.80	3.50	11.00	—
Note: Low relief; Second "A" in GRATIA points between denticles								
1951	Inc. above	400	550	750	1,200	2,400	3,500	—
Note: High relief; Second "A" in GRATIA points to a denticle								
1952	10,891,148	0.10	0.20	0.45	0.80	3.50	8.00	—

KM# 48 4.5500 g. Nickel 21.2 mm.   **Subject:** Nickel Bicentennial **Obv:** Head left **Obv. Designer:** T. H. Paget **Rev:** Buildings with center tower divide dates and denomination **Rev. Designer:** Stephen Trenka **Shape:** 12-sided

Date	Mintage	VG-8	F-12	VF-20	XF-40	MS-60	MS-63	Proof
1951	9,028,507	0.15	0.25	0.30	0.45	1.75	8.00	—

KM# 50 Chromium And Nickel Plated Steel 21.2 mm.   **Obv:** Laureate queen's bust, right **Obv. Designer:** Mary Gillick **Rev:** Beaver on rock divides date and denomination **Rev. Designer:** George E. Kruger-Gray **Shape:** 12-sided

Date	Mintage	VG-8	F-12	VF-20	XF-40	MS-60	MS-63	Proof
1953	Inc. above	300	450	700	900	1,300	3,500	—
Note: Without strap, near leaf								
1953	Inc. above	175	250	350	550	1,600	3,500	—
Note: With strap, far leaf								
1953	16,635,552	0.10	0.20	0.40	0.90	3.00	7.00	—
Note: Without strap								
1953	Inc. above	0.10	0.20	0.40	0.90	5.00	8.00	—
Note: With strap								
1954	6,998,662	0.10	0.25	0.50	1.00	6.00	12.00	—

KM# 50a 4.5900 g. Nickel 21.2 mm.   **Obv:** Laureate queen's bust right **Obv. Designer:** Mary Gillick **Rev:** Beaver on rock divides date and denomination **Rev. Designer:** George E. Kruger-Gray

Date	Mintage	VG-8	F-12	VF-20	XF-40	MS-60	MS-63	Proof
1955	5,355,028	0.15	0.20	0.40	0.75	3.50	6.50	—

Date	Mintage	VG-8	F-12	VF-20	XF-40	MS-60	MS-63	Proof
1956	9,399,854	—	0.15	0.30	0.45	2.50	5.00	—
1957	7,387,703	—	—	0.25	0.30	1.25	3.50	—
1958	7,607,521	—	—	0.25	0.30	1.25	3.50	—
1959	11,552,523	—	—	—	0.20	0.45	1.75	—
1960	37,157,433	—	—	—	0.20	0.45	1.75	—
1961	47,889,051	—	—	—	—	0.40	1.25	—
1962	46,307,305	—	—	—	—	0.40	1.25	—

KM#57 Nickel 21.2 mm.   **Obv:** Laureate queen's bust right **Obv. Designer:** Mary Gillick **Rev:** Beaver on rock divides date and denomination **Rev. Designer:** George E. Kruger-Gray **Shape:** Round

Date	Mintage	VG-8	F-12	VF-20	XF-40	MS-60	MS-63	Proof
1963	43,970,320	—	—	—	—	0.30	0.80	—
1964	78,075,068	—	—	—	—	0.30	0.80	—
1964	—	18.00	20.00	21.00	24.00	40.00	125	—

Note: Extra water line

KM#60.1 4.5400 g. Nickel 21.2 mm. **Obv:** Queen's bust right **Obv. Designer:** Arnold Machin **Rev:** Beaver on rock divides date and denomination **Rev. Designer:** George E. Kruger-Gray

Date	Mintage	MS-63	Proof
1965	84,876,018	0.80	—
1966	27,976,648	0.80	—
1968	101,930,379	0.80	—
1969	27,830,229	0.80	—
1970	5,726,010	1.75	—
1971	27,312,609	0.80	—
1972	62,417,387	0.80	—
1973	53,507,435	0.80	—
1974	94,704,645	0.80	—
1975	138,882,000	0.80	—
1976	55,140,213	0.80	—
1977	89,120,791	0.80	—
1978	137,079,273	0.80	—

KM# 66 Nickel 21.2 mm.   **Subject:** Confederation Centennial **Obv:** Queen's bust right **Obv. Designer:** Arnold Machin **Rev:** Snowshoe rabbit bounding left divides dates and denomination **Rev. Designer:** Alex Coville

Date	Mintage	MS-63	Proof
1867-1967	36,876,574	0.80	1.00

KM# 60.2 Nickel 21.2 mm.   **Obv:** Queen's bust right **Obv. Designer:** Arnold Machin **Rev:** Beaver on rock divides date and denomination **Rev. Designer:** George E. Kruger-Gray

Date	Mintage	MS-63	Proof
1979	186,295,825	0.30	—
1980	134,878,000	0.30	—
1981	99,107,900	0.30	—
1981 Proof	199,000	—	1.50

KM# 60.2a 4.6000 g. Copper-Nickel 21.2 mm.   **Obv:** Queen's bust right **Obv. Designer:** Arnold Machin **Rev:** Beaver on rock divides date and denomination **Rev. Designer:** George E. Kruger-Gray

Date	Mintage	MS-63	Proof
1982	64,924,400	0.30	—
1982 Proof	180,908	—	1.50
1983	72,596,000	0.30	—
1983 Proof	168,000	—	1.50

Date	Mintage	MS-63	Proof
1984	84,088,000	0.30	—
1984 Proof	161,602	—	1.50
1985	126,618,000	0.30	—
1985 Proof	157,037	—	1.50
1986	156,104,000	0.30	—
1986 Proof	175,745	—	1.50
1987	106,299,000	0.30	—
1987 Proof	179,004	—	1.50
1988	75,025,000	0.30	—
1988 Proof	175,259	—	1.50
1989	141,570,538	0.30	—
1989 Proof	170,928	—	1.50

KM# 182 4.6000 g. Copper-Nickel 19.55 mm. **Obv:** Crowned head right **Obv. Designer:** Dora dePedery-Hunt **Rev:** Beaver on rock divides dates and denomination **Rev. Designer:** George E. Kruger-Gray **Edge:** Plain

Date	Mintage	MS-63	Proof
1990	42,537,000	0.30	—
1990 Proof	140,649	—	2.50
1991	10,931,000	0.55	—
1991 Proof	131,888	—	7.00
1993	86,877,000	0.30	—
1993 Proof	143,065	—	2.50
1994	99,352,000	0.30	—
1994 Proof	146,424	—	3.00
1995	78,528,000	0.30	—
1995 Proof	50,000	—	2.50
1996 Far 6	36,686,000	2.25	—
1996 Near 6	Inc. above	2.25	—
1996 Proof	—	—	6.00
1997	27,354,000	0.30	—
1997 Proof	—	—	5.00
1998	156,873,000	0.30	—
1998W	—	1.50	—
1998 Proof	—	—	5.00
1999	124,861,000	0.30	—
1999W	—	—	—
1999 Proof	—	—	5.00
2000	108,514,000	0.30	—
2000W	—	1.50	—
2000 Proof	—	—	5.00
2001	30,035,000	12.50	—
2001P Proof	—	—	10.00
2003	—	0.30	—

KM# 205 4.6000 g. Copper-Nickel 21.2 mm.   **Subject:** Confederation 125 **Obv:** Crowned head right **Obv. Designer:** Dora dePedery-Hunt **Rev:** Beaver on rock divides date and denomination **Rev. Designer:** George E. Kruger-Gray

Date	Mintage	MS-63	Proof
1992	53,732,000	0.30	—
1992 Proof	147,061	—	4.00

KM# 182b 3.9000 g. Nickel Plated Steel 21.2 mm.   **Obv:** Crowned head right **Obv. Designer:** Dora dePedery-Hunt **Rev:** Beaver on rock divides date and denomination **Rev. Designer:** George E. Kruger-Gray **Edge:** Plain

Date	Mintage	MS-63	Proof
1999 P	Est. 20,000	15.00	—
2000 P	Est. 2,300,000	3.50	—
2001 P	136,650,000	0.35	—
2003 P	32,986,921	0.35	—

KM# 182a 5.3500 g. 0.9250 Silver 0.1591 oz. ASW 21.2 mm.   **Obv:** Crowned head right **Obv. Designer:** Dora dePedery-Hunt **Rev:** Beaver on rock divides date and denomination **Rev. Designer:** George E. Kruger-Gray

Date	Mintage	MS-63	Proof
1996 Proof	—	—	5.00
1997 Proof	—	—	5.00
1998 Proof	—	—	5.00
1998O Proof	—	—	5.00
1999 Proof	—	—	5.00
2000 Proof	—	—	5.00
2001 Proof	—	—	5.00
2003 Proof	—	—	5.00

KM# 310 1.1670 g. 0.9250 Silver 0.0347 oz. ASW **Subject:** 90th Anniversary Royal Canadian Mint **Obv:** Crowned head right **Obv. Designer:** Dora dePedery-Hunt **Rev:** Denomination and date within wreath, crown above **Rev. Designer:** W. H. J. Blackmore

Date	Mintage	MS-63	Proof
1908-1998	25,000	12.00	—
1908-1998 Proof	25,000	—	12.00

KM# 400 0.9250 Silver 21.2 mm. **Subject:** First French-Canadian Regiment **Obv:** Crowned head right **Obv. Designer:** Dora dePedery-Hunt **Rev:** Regimental drums, sash and baton, denomination above, date at right **Rev. Designer:** R. C. M. Staff **Edge:** Plain

Date	Mintage	MS-63	Proof
2000 Proof	—	—	9.00

KM# 413 5.3500 g. 0.9250 Silver 0.1591 oz. ASW 21.2 mm. **Subject:** Royal Military College **Obv:** Crowned head right **Rev:** Marching cadets and arch **Rev. Designer:** Gerald T. Locklin **Edge:** Plain

Date	Mintage	MS-63	Proof
2001 Proof	25,834	—	7.00

KM# 446 3.9500 g. Nickel Plated Steel 21.2 mm. **Subject:** Elizabeth II Golden Jubilee **Obv:** Crowned head right, Jubilee commemorative dates 1952-2002 **Obv. Designer:** Dora dePedery-Hunt **Rev. Designer:** George E. Kruger-Gray **Note:** Magnetic.

Date	Mintage	MS-63	Proof
1952-2002P	135,960,000	0.45	—
1952-2002P Proof	32,642	—	10.00

KM# 446a 5.3500 g. 0.9250 Silver 0.1591 oz. ASW 21.2 mm. **Subject:** Elizabeth II Golden Jubilee **Obv:** Queen, Jubilee commemorative dates 1952-2002

Date	Mintage	MS-63	Proof
1952-2002 Proof	21,573	—	11.50

KM# 453 5.3500 g. 0.9250 Silver 0.1591 oz. ASW 21.2 mm. **Subject:** Vimy Ridge - WWI **Obv:** Crowned head right **Rev:** Vimy Ridge Memorial, allegorical figure and dates 1917-2002 **Rev. Designer:** S. A. Allward

Date	Mintage	MS-63	Proof
2002 Proof	22,646	—	11.50

KM# 491 3.9500 g. Nickel Plated Steel 21.2 mm. **Obv:** Bare head right **Obv. Designer:** Susanna Blunt **Rev:** Beaver divides date and denomination **Rev. Designer:** George E. Kruger-Gray **Note:** Magnetic.

Date	Mintage	MS-63	Proof
2003P	61,392,180	0.45	—
2004P	132,097,000	0.45	—
2004P Proof	—	—	2.50
2005P	89,664,000	0.45	—
2005P Proof	—	—	2.50
2006P	139,308,000	0.50	—
2006P Proof	—	—	2.50
2006(ml)	184,874,000	0.45	—
2006(ml) Proof	—	—	2.50
2007(ml)	221,472,000	0.45	—
2007(ml) Proof	—	—	2.50
2008(ml)	278,530,000	0.45	—
2008(ml) Proof	—	—	2.50
2009(ml)	266,488,000	0.45	—
2009(ml) Proof	—	—	2.50
2010(ml)	—	0.45	—
2010(ml) Proof	—	—	2.50
2011(ml)	—	0.45	—
2011(ml) Proof	—	—	2.50
2012(ml)	—	0.45	—
2012(ml) Proof	—	—	2.50

KM# 469 5.3500 g. 0.9250 Silver 0.1591 oz. ASW 21.2 mm. **Subject:** 50th Anniversary of the Coronation of Elizabeth II **Obv:** Crowned head right, Jubilee commemorative dates 1953-2003 **Obv. Designer:** Mary Gillick

Date	Mintage	MS-63	Proof
1953-2003 Proof	21,573	—	11.50

KM# 491a 5.3500 g. 0.9250 Silver 0.1591 oz. ASW 21.1 mm. **Obv:** Crowned head right **Obv. Designer:** Susanna Blunt **Rev:** Beaver divides date and denomination **Edge:** Plain

Date	Mintage	MS-63	Proof
2004 Proof	—	—	3.50

KM# 506 5.3500 g. 0.9250 Silver 0.1591 oz. ASW 21.3 mm. **Obv:** Bare head right **Rev:** "Victory" design of the KM-40 reverse **Edge:** Plain **Shape:** 12-sided

Date	Mintage	MS-63	Proof
1944-2004 Proof	20,019	—	15.00

KM# 627 3.9500 g. Nickel Plated Steel 21.2 mm. **Subject:** 60th Anniversary, Victory in Europe 1945-2005 **Obv:** Head right **Rev:** Large V **Edge:** Plain

Date	Mintage	MS-63	Proof
2005P	59,269,192	4.50	—

KM# 758 5.3000 g. 0.9250 Silver 0.1576 oz. ASW **Obv:** George VI head left **Rev:** Torch and large V

Date	Mintage	MS-63	Proof
2005 Proof	42,792	—	35.00

KM# 758a 5.3000 g. 0.9250 Silver 0.1576 oz. ASW selectively gold plated **Obv:** George VI head left **Rev:** Torch and large V **Note:** Bound into Annual Report.

Date	Mintage	MS-63	Proof
2005 Proof	6,065	—	40.00

KM# 491b 4.6000 g. Copper-Nickel **Obv:** Bust right **Rev:** Beaver

Date	Mintage	MS-63	Proof
2006	43,008,000	5.00	—

KM# 1024 Nickel 21.2 mm. **Obv:** George V bust left **Rev:** Denomination and 1935-2010 anniversary dates, two maple leaves below

Date	Mintage	MS-63	Proof
1935-2010 Proof	—	—	15.00

KM# 1154 Nickel 21.2 mm.

Date	Mintage	MS-63	P/L	Proof
1911-2011 Proof	—	—	—	15.00

10 CENTS

KM# 3 2.3240 g. 0.9250 Silver 0.0691 oz. ASW 18.03 mm. **Obv:** Head left **Obv. Legend:** VICTORIA DEI GRATIA REGINA. CANADA **Rev:** Denomination and date within wreath, crown above **Edge:** Reeded

Date	Mintage	VG-8	F-12	VF-20	XF-40	MS-60	MS-63	Proof
1858/5		900	1,400	2,100	4,000	12,000	—	—
1858	1,250,000	20.00	35.00	65.00	125	350	850	—

Date	Mintage	VG-8	F-12	VF-20	XF-40	MS-60	MS-63	Proof
1870 Narrow 0	1,600,000	18.00	40.00	75.00	125	400	1,300	—
1870 Wide 0	Inc. above	35.00	65.00	125	225	600	2,100	—
1871	800,000	29.00	50.00	125	200	600	2,500	—
1871H	1,870,000	35.00	60.00	125	225	600	2,100	—
1872H	1,000,000	150	225	400	600	1,750	4,000	—
1874H	600,000	14.00	24.00	50.00	125	350	1,100	—
1875H	1,000,000	400	800	1,200	2,000	7,000	16,000	—
1880H	1,500,000	18.00	30.00	65.00	125	350	1,200	—
1881H	950,000	21.00	35.00	70.00	150	400	1,300	—
1882H	1,000,000	21.00	35.00	70.00	150	450	1,500	—
1883H	300,000	65.00	125	250	500	1,300	3,000	—
1884	150,000	300	500	950	1,700	6,000	20,000	—
1885	400,000	65.00	125	250	500	1,700	7,000	—
1886 Small 6	800,000	30.00	65.00	125	300	1,500	4,000	—
1886 Large 6	Inc. above	40.00	80.00	150	350	1,500	4,000	—
1887	350,000	65.00	125	225	450	1,700	4,000	—
1888	500,000	16.00	27.00	55.00	125	350	1,100	—
1889	600,000	750	1,200	2,000	4,000	13,000	35,000	—
1890H	450,000	21.00	45.00	90.00	200	500	1,100	—
1891 21 leaves	800,000	21.00	45.00	90.00	200	500	1,300	—
1891 22 leaves	Inc. above	21.00	45.00	90.00	200	500	1,200	—
1892/1	520,000	250	400	700	1,400	4,000	—	—
1892	Inc. above	20.00	35.00	75.00	150	450	1,200	—
1893 Flat-top 3	500,000	45.00	80.00	150	300	1,000	2,300	—
1893 Round-top 3	Inc. above	850	1,400	2,700	5,000	13,000	35,000	—
1894	500,000	45.00	80.00	150	250	750	1,800	—
1896	650,000	14.00	24.00	45.00	90.00	300	750	—
1898	720,000	14.00	24.00	45.00	90.00	300	750	—
1899 Small 9's	1,200,000	12.00	22.00	40.00	75.00	225	600	—
1899 Large 9's	Inc. above	24.00	45.00	85.00	150	500	1,200	—
1900	1,100,000	8.50	18.00	40.00	85.00	225	650	—
1901	1,200,000	12.00	24.00	50.00	100.00	250	850	—

KM# 10 2.3240 g. 0.9250 Silver 0.0691 oz. ASW 18.03 mm. **Obv:** Crowned bust right **Obv. Designer:** G. W. DeSaulles **Rev:** Denomination and date within wreath, crown above **Rev. Designer:** Leonard C. Wyon **Edge:** Reeded

Date	Mintage	VG-8	F-12	VF-20	XF-40	MS-60	MS-63	Proof
1902	720,000	9.00	18.00	35.00	100.00	450	1,200	—
1902H	1,100,000	4.00	9.00	20.00	45.00	150	350	—
1903	500,000	15.00	35.00	90.00	300	1,200	2,300	—
1903H	1,320,000	8.00	18.00	35.00	90.00	350	800	—
1904	1,000,000	12.00	27.50	50.00	150	400	1,000	—
1905	1,000,000	7.00	27.50	60.00	150	600	1,400	—
1906	1,700,000	7.00	13.00	35.00	80.00	350	900	—
1907	2,620,000	5.00	12.00	25.00	45.00	300	600	—
1908	776,666	9.00	27.50	60.00	150	300	600	—

Date	Mintage	VG-8	F-12	VF-20	XF-40	MS-60	MS-63	Proof
1909	1,697,200	7.00	20.00	45.00	125	500	1,200	—
Note: *"Victorian" leaves, similar to 1902-08 coins*								
1909	Inc. above	11.00	30.00	60.00	150	750	1,800	—
Note: *Broad leaves, similar to 1910-12 coins*								
1910	4,468,331	4.00	9.00	20.00	40.00	150	400	—

KM# 17 2.3240 g. 0.9250 Silver 0.0691 oz. ASW 23.5 mm.   **Obv:** Crowned bust left **Obv. Designer:** E. B. MacKennal **Rev:** Denomination and date within wreath, crown above **Rev. Designer:** Leonard C. Wyon **Edge:** Reeded

Date	Mintage	VG-8	F-12	VF-20	XF-40	MS-60	MS-63	Proof
1911	2,737,584	5.00	12.00	20.00	45.00	150	300	—

  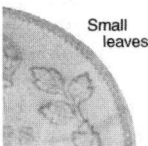
Small leaves

Large leaves

KM# 23 2.3240 g. 0.9250 Silver 0.0691 oz. ASW 17.8 mm.   **Obv:** Crowned bust left **Obv. Designer:** E. B. MacKennal **Rev:** Denomination and date within wreath, crown above **Rev. Designer:** Leonard C. Wyon **Edge:** Reeded

Date	Mintage	VG-8	F-12	VF-20	XF-40	MS-60	MS-63	Proof
1912	3,235,557	BV	5.00	11.00	35.00	250	650	—
1913	3,613,937	BV	3.00	9.00	30.00	200	500	—
Note: *Small leaves*								
1913	Inc. above	125	225	450	1,350	8,500	27,500	—
Note: *Large leaves*								
1914	2,549,811	BV	4.00	9.00	30.00	175	500	—
1915	688,057	7.00	16.00	40.00	125	500	950	—
1916	4,218,114	BV	3.00	6.00	25.00	100.00	225	—
1917	5,011,988	BV	3.00	4.00	12.00	75.00	125	—
1918	5,133,602	BV	3.00	4.00	10.00	65.00	100.00	—
1919	7,877,722	BV	3.00	4.00	10.00	65.00	100.00	—

KM# 23a 2.3320 g. 0.8000 Silver 0.0600 oz. ASW 17.9 mm.   **Obv:** Crowned bust left **Obv. Designer:** E. B. MacKennal **Rev:** Denomination and date within wreath, crown above **Edge:** Reeded

Date	Mintage	VG-8	F-12	VF-20	XF-40	MS-60	MS-63	Proof
1920	6,305,345	BV	2.50	3.50	12.00	75.00	125	—
1921	2,469,562	BV	2.50	6.00	20.00	90.00	225	—
1928	2,458,602	BV	2.50	4.00	12.00	80.00	150	—
1929	3,253,888	BV	2.50	3.50	12.00	75.00	125	—

Date	Mintage	VG-8	F-12	VF-20	XF-40	MS-60	MS-63	Proof
1930	1,831,043	BV	3.00	4.50	14.00	80.00	175	—
1931	2,067,421	BV	2.50	4.00	12.00	70.00	125	—
1932	1,154,317	BV	3.00	9.00	23.00	125	250	—
1933	672,368	2.50	5.00	12.00	35.00	200	400	—
1934	409,067	4.00	7.00	22.00	60.00	350	650	—
1935	384,056	4.00	7.00	19.00	60.00	350	600	—
1936	2,460,871	BV	2.50	3.00	9.00	60.00	100.00	—
1936	—	—	—	—	—	—	150,000	—

Note: *Dot on reverse. Specimen, 4 known; David Akers sale of John Jay Pittman collection, Part 1, 10-97, a gem specimen realized $120,000*

  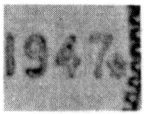

Maple leaf

KM# 34 2.3328 g. 0.8000 Silver 0.0600 oz. ASW 18.03 mm.   **Obv:** Head left **Obv. Designer:** T. H. Paget **Rev:** Bluenose sailing left, date at right, denomination below **Rev. Designer:** Emanuel Hahn **Edge:** Reeded

Date	Mintage	VG-8	F-12	VF-20	XF-40	MS-60	MS-63	Proof
1937	2,500,095	—	BV	2.50	4.00	16.00	24.00	—
1938	4,197,323	—	BV	4.00	7.00	60.00	100.00	—
1939	5,501,748	—	BV	3.00	6.00	50.00	90.00	—
1940	16,526,470	—	—	BV	4.00	20.00	40.00	—
1941	8,716,386	—	BV	3.00	7.00	50.00	100.00	—
1942	10,214,011	—	—	BV	5.00	40.00	60.00	—
1943	21,143,229	—	—	BV	4.00	20.00	35.00	—
1944	9,383,582	—	—	BV	5.00	28.00	45.00	—
1945	10,979,570	—	—	BV	4.00	20.00	35.00	—
1946	6,300,066	—	—	BV	5.00	30.00	45.00	—
1947	4,431,926	—	BV	3.00	7.00	40.00	60.00	—
1947	9,638,793	—	—	BV	4.00	15.00	20.00	—

Note: *Maple leaf*

KM# 43 2.3328 g. 0.8000 Silver 0.0600 oz. ASW 18.03 mm.   **Obv:** Head left, modified legend **Obv. Designer:** T. H. Paget **Rev:** Bluenose sailing left, date at right, denomination below **Rev. Designer:** Emanuel Hahn

Date	Mintage	VG-8	F-12	VF-20	XF-40	MS-60	MS-63	Proof
1948	422,741	BV	3.50	7.50	13.00	60.00	80.00	—
1949	11,336,172	—	—	BV	2.50	12.00	18.00	—
1950	17,823,075	—	—	BV	2.50	10.00	15.00	—
1951	15,079,265	—	—	BV	2.50	7.00	12.00	—
1951	—	—	6.00	8.00	12.00	40.00	65.00	—

Note: *Doubled die*

Date	Mintage	VG-8	F-12	VF-20	XF-40	MS-60	MS-63	Proof
1952	10,474,455	—	—	BV	2.50	6.00	10.00	—

KM# 51 2.3100 g. 0.8000 Silver 0.0594 oz. ASW 18 mm.   **Obv:** Laureate bust right **Obv. Designer:** Mary Gllick **Rev:** Bluenose sailing left, date at right, denomination below **Rev. Designer:** Emanuel Hahn

Date	Mintage	VG-8	F-12	VF-20	XF-40	MS-60	MS-63	Proof
1953	17,706,395	—	—	—	BV	6.00	12.00	—
Note: Without straps								
1953	Inc. above	—	—	—	BV	4.00	8.00	—
Note: With straps								
1954	4,493,150	—	—	—	BV	12.00	20.00	—
1955	12,237,294	—	—	—	BV	4.50	8.00	—
1956	Inc. above	—	3.50	4.00	7.00	15.00	24.00	—
Note: Dot below date								
1956	16,732,844	—	—	—	BV	3.00	6.00	—
1957	16,110,229	—	—	—	BV	3.50	4.00	—
1958	10,621,236	—	—	—	BV	3.50	4.00	—
1959	19,691,433	—	—	—	BV	3.00	4.00	—
1960	45,446,835	—	—	—	BV	3.00	4.00	—
1961	26,850,859	—	—	—	BV	3.00	4.00	—
1962	41,864,335	—	—	—	—	BV	2.50	—
1963	41,916,208	—	—	—	—	BV	2.50	—
1964	49,518,549	—	—	—	—	BV	2.50	—

KM# 61 2.3328 g. 0.8000 Silver 0.0600 oz. ASW 18.03 mm.   **Obv:** Young bust right **Obv. Designer:** Arnold Machin **Rev:** Bluenose sailing left, date at right, denomination below

Date	Mintage	VG-8	F-12	VF-20	XF-40	MS-60	MS-63	Proof
1965	56,965,392	—	—	—	—	BV	2.50	—
1966	34,567,898	—	—	—	—	BV	2.50	—

KM# 67 2.3328 g. 0.8000 Silver 0.0600 oz. ASW 18.03 mm. **Subject:** Confederation Centennial **Obv:** Bust right **Rev:** Atlantic mackerel left, denomination above, dates below **Rev. Designer:** Alex Colville

Date	Mintage	VG-8	F-12	VF-20	XF-40	MS-60	MS-63	Proof
1867-1967	62,998,215	—	—	—	—	BV	2.50	—
ND1867-1967	—	—	—	—	—	—	—	2.50

KM# 67a 2.3328 g. 0.5000 Silver 0.0375 oz. ASW 18.03 mm.
Subject: Confederation Centennial **Obv:** Young bust right **Rev:** Atlantic mackerel left, denomination above, dates below

Date	Mintage	VG-8	F-12	VF-20	XF-40	MS-60	MS-63	Proof
1867-1967	Inc. above	—	—	—	—	BV	2.00	—

Ottawa

KM# 72 2.3328 g. 0.5000 Silver 0.0375 oz. ASW 18.03 mm.   **Obv:** Bust right **Obv. Designer:** Arnold Machin **Rev:** Bluenose sailing left, date at right, denomination below **Rev. Designer:** Emanuel Hahn **Note:** Ottawa Mint reeding has pointed deep areas in the edge reeding.

Date	Mintage	VG-8	F-12	VF-20	XF-40	MS-60	MS-63	Proof
1968	70,460,000	—	—	—	—	BV	0.45	—

Ottawa

KM# 72a Nickel 18.03 mm.   **Obv:** Young bust right **Obv. Designer:** Arnold Machin **Rev:** Bluenose sailing left, date at right, denomination below **Rev. Designer:** Emanuel Hahn **Note:** Ottawa Mint reeding has pointed deep areas in the edge reeding.

Date	Mintage	VG-8	F-12	VF-20	XF-40	MS-60	MS-63	Proof
1968	87,412,930	—	—	—	0.10	0.15	0.40	—

Philadelphia

KM# 73 2.3300 g. Nickel 18.03 mm.   **Obv:** Young bust right **Obv. Designer:** Arnold Machin **Rev:** Bluenose sailing left, date at right, denomination below **Rev. Designer:** Emanuel Hahn **Note:** Philadelphia Mint reeding has flat deep areas in the edge reeding.

Date	Mintage	VG-8	F-12	VF-20	XF-40	MS-60	MS-63	Proof
1968	85,170,000	—	—	—	0.10	0.15	0.40	—
1969	—	—	10,000	12,000	16,000	25,000	—	—

Note: *Large date, large ship, 10-20 known*

KM# 77.1 2.0700 g. Nickel 18.03 mm.   **Obv:** Young bust right **Obv. Designer:** Arnold Machin **Rev:** Redesigned smaller Bluenose sailing left, date at right, denomination below **Rev. Designer:** Emanuel Hahn **Edge:** Reeded

Date	Mintage	MS-63	Proof
1969	55,833,929	0.50	—
1970	5,249,296	1.00	—
1971	41,016,968	0.50	—
1972	60,169,387	0.50	—
1973	167,715,435	0.50	—
1974	201,566,565	0.50	—
1975	207,680,000	0.50	—
1976	95,018,533	0.50	—
1977	128,452,206	0.50	—
1978	170,366,431	0.50	—

KM# 77.2 2.0700 g. Nickel 18.03 mm. **Obv:** Smaller young bust right **Obv. Designer:** Arnold Machin **Rev:** Redesigned smaller Bluenose sailing left, denomination below, date at right **Rev. Designer:** Emanuel Hahn **Edge:** Reeded

Date	Mintage	MS-63	Proof
1979	237,321,321	0.35	—
1980	170,111,533	0.35	—
1981	123,912,900	0.35	—
1981 Proof	199,000	—	1.50
1982	93,475,000	0.35	—
1982 Proof	180,908	—	1.50
1983	111,065,000	0.35	—
1983 Proof	168,000	—	1.50
1984	121,690,000	0.35	—
1984 Proof	161,602	—	1.50
1985	143,025,000	0.35	—
1985 Proof	157,037	—	1.50
1986	168,620,000	0.35	—
1986 Proof	175,745	—	1.50
1987	147,309,000	0.35	—
1987 Proof	179,004	—	1.50
1988	162,998,558	0.35	—
1988 Proof	175,259	—	1.50
1989	199,104,414	0.35	—
1989 Proof	170,528	—	1.50

KM#183 2.1400 g. Nickel 18.03 mm. **Obv:** Crowned head right **Obv. Designer:** Dora dePedery-Hunt **Rev:** Bluenose sailing left, date at right, denomination below **Rev. Designer:** Emanuel Hahn **Edge:** Reeded

Date	Mintage	MS-63	Proof
1990	65,023,000	0.35	—
1990 Proof	140,649	—	2.50
1991	50,397,000	0.45	—
1991 Proof	131,888	—	4.00
1993	135,569,000	0.35	—
1993 Proof	143,065	—	2.00
1994	145,800,000	0.35	—
1994 Proof	146,424	—	2.50
1995	123,875,000	0.35	—
1995 Proof	50,000	—	2.50
1996	51,814,000	0.35	—
1996 Proof	—	—	2.50
1997	43,126,000	0.35	—

Date	Mintage	MS-63	Proof
1997 Proof	—	—	2.50
1998	203,514,000	0.35	—
1998 Proof	—	—	2.50
1998W	—	1.50	—
1999	258,462,000	0.35	—
1999 Proof	—	—	2.50
2000	159,125,000	0.35	—
2000 Proof	—	—	2.50
2000W	—	1.50	—

KM#206 Nickel 18.03 mm. **Subject:** Confederation 125 **Obv:** Crowned head right **Rev:** Bluenose sailing left, date at right, denomination below

Date	Mintage	MS-63	Proof
1867-1992	174,476,000	0.35	—
1867-1992 Proof	147,061	—	3.00

KM# 183a 2.4000 g. 0.9250 Silver 0.0714 oz. ASW 18.03 mm. **Obv:** Crowned head right **Rev:** Bluenose sailing left, date at right, denomination below

Date	Mintage	MS-63	Proof
1996 Proof	—	—	5.50
1997 Proof	—	—	5.50
1998 Proof	—	—	4.00
1998O Proof	—	—	4.00
1999 Proof	—	—	5.00
2000 Proof	—	—	5.00
2001 Proof	—	—	5.00
2002 Proof	—	—	7.50
2003 Proof	—	—	7.50

KM# 299 2.4000 g. 0.9250 Silver 0.0714 oz. ASW 18.03 mm. **Subject:** John Cabot **Obv:** Crowned head right **Rev:** Ship with full sails divides dates, denomination below **Rev. Designer:** Donald H. Curley

Date	Mintage	MS-63	Proof
1997 Proof	49,848	—	17.50

KM# 311 2.3200 g. 0.9250 Silver 0.0690 oz. ASW 18.03 mm. **Subject:** 90th Anniversary Royal Canadian Mint **Obv:** Crowned head right **Rev:** Denomination and date within wreath, crown above

Date	Mintage	MS-63	Proof
1908-1998 Matte	25,000	—	10.00
1908-1998 Proof	25,000	—	10.00

KM# 183b 1.7700 g. Nickel Plated Steel 18.03 mm. **Obv:** Crowned head right **Obv. Designer:** Dora dePedery-Hunt **Rev:** Bluenose sailing left, date at right, denomination below **Rev. Designer:** Emanuel Hahn **Edge:** Reeded

Date	Mintage	MS-63	Proof
1999 P	Est. 20,000	15.00	—
2000 P	Est. 200	1,000	—
2001 P	266,000,000	0.45	—
2003 P	162,398,000	0.20	—

KM# 409 2.4000 g. 0.9250 Silver 0.0714 oz. ASW 18.03 mm. **Subject:** First Canadian Credit Union **Obv:** Crowned head right **Rev:** Alphonse Desjardins' house (founder of the first credit union in Canada), dates at right, denomination below **Edge:** Reeded

Date	Mintage	MS-63	Proof
2000 Proof	66,336	—	8.00

KM# 412a 2.4000 g. 0.9250 Silver 0.0714 oz. ASW 18 mm. **Subject:** Year of the Volunteer **Obv:** Crowned head right **Rev:** Three portraits left above banner, radiant sun below **Edge:** Reeded

Date	Mintage	MS-63	Proof
2001P Proof	40,634	—	9.00

KM# 412 1.7700 g. Nickel Plated Steel 18 mm. **Subject:** Year of the Volunteer **Obv:** Crowned head right **Rev:** Three portraits left and radiant sun **Edge:** Reeded

Date	Mintage	MS-63	Proof
2001P	224,714,000	4.50	—

KM# 447 1.7700 g. Nickel Plated Steel 18 mm. **Subject:** Elizabeth II Golden Jubilee **Obv:** Crowned head right, Jubilee commemorative dates 1952-2002

Date	Mintage	MS-63	Proof
1952-2002P	252,563,000	1.00	—
1952-2002 Proof	32,642	—	2.50

KM# 447a 2.3200 g. 0.9250 Silver 0.0690 oz. ASW 18 mm. **Subject:** Elizabeth II Golden Jubilee **Obv:** Crowned head right, Jubilee commemorative dates 1952-2002

Date	Mintage	MS-63	Proof
2002 Proof	21,537	—	12.50

KM# 492 1.7700 g. Nickel Plated Steel 18 mm. **Obv:** Head right **Obv. Designer:** Susanna Blunt **Rev:** Bluenose sailing left

Date	Mintage	MS-63	Proof
2003P	—	1.25	—
2004P	211,924,000	0.60	—
2004P Proof	—	—	2.50
2005P	212,175,000	0.60	—
2005P Proof	—	—	2.50
2006P	312,122,000	0.60	—

Date	Mintage	MS-63	Proof
2006P Proof	—	—	2.50
2007(ml) Straight 7	304,110,000	0.60	—
2007(ml) Curved 7	Inc. above	0.60	—
2007(ml) Proof	—	—	2.50
2008(ml)	467,495,000	0.60	—
2008(ml) Proof	—	—	2.50
2009(ml)	370,700,000	0.60	—
2009(ml) Proof	—	—	2.50
2010(ml)	—	0.60	—
2010(ml) Proof	—	—	2.50
2011(ml)	—	0.60	—
2011(ml) Proof	—	—	2.50
2012(ml)	—	0.60	—
2012(ml) Proof	—	—	2.50

KM# 470 2.3200 g. 0.9250 Silver 0.0690 oz. ASW **Subject:** 50th Anniversary of the Coronation of Elizabeth II **Obv:** Head right **Rev:** Bluenose sailing left

Date	Mintage	MS-63	Proof
1953-2003 Proof	21,537	—	12.00

KM# 492a 2.4000 g. 0.9250 Silver 0.0714 oz. ASW 18 mm.   **Obv:** Bare head right **Obv. Designer:** Susanna Blunt **Rev:** Sailboat **Edge:** Reeded

Date	Mintage	MS-63	Proof
2004 Proof	—	—	5.00

KM# 524 2.4000 g. 0.9250 Silver 0.0714 oz. ASW 18 mm.   **Subject:** Golf, Championship of Canada, Centennial. **Obv:** Head right

Date	Mintage	MS-63	Proof
2004	39,486	12.50	—

KM# 1025 Silver 18.03 mm.   **Obv:** George V bust left **Rev:** Value within wreath, dual dates below

Date	Mintage	MS-63	Proof
1935-2010 Proof	—	—	20.00

KM# 1155 Silver 18.03 mm.

Date	Mintage	MS-63	P/L	Proof
1911-2011 Proof	—	—	—	20.00

20 CENTS

KM# 4 4.6480 g. 0.9250 Silver 0.1382 oz. ASW   **Obv:** Head left **Obv. Legend:** VICTORIA DEI GRATIA REGINA. CANADA **Rev:** Denomination and date within wreath, crown above

Date	Mintage	VG-8	F-12	VF-20	XF-40	MS-60	MS-63	Proof
1858	750,000	60.00	100.00	125	225	900	2,500	—

25 CENTS

KM# 5 5.8100 g. 0.9250 Silver 0.1728 oz. ASW 23.88 mm.   **Obv:** Crowned head

left **Obv. Legend:** VICTORIA DEI GRATIA REGINA. CANADA **Obv. Designer:** Leonard C. Wyon **Rev:** Denomination and date within wreath, crown above

Date	Mintage	VG-8	F-12	VF-20	XF-40	MS-60	MS-63	Proof
1870	900,000	22.00	45.00	85.00	200	750	2,000	—
1871	400,000	27.00	50.00	125	250	1,000	2,400	—
1871H	748,000	35.00	60.00	150	300	1,100	2,100	—
1872H	Inc. above	—	—	—	—	2,500	6,000	—
Note: Inverted "A" for "V" in Victoria								
1872H	2,240,000	13.00	25.00	45.00	125	550	1,800	—
1874H	1,600,000	13.00	25.00	45.00	125	450	1,400	—
1875H	1,000,000	400	700	1,700	3,000	20,000	35,000	—
1880H Narrow 0	400,000	60.00	125	300	600	1,700	3,500	—
1880H Wide 0	Inc. above	150	350	600	1,400	4,500	8,000	—
1880H Narrow/wide 0	Inc. above	100.00	225	400	950	2,800	—	—
1881H	820,000	30.00	55.00	125	300	1,300	4,000	—
1882H	600,000	30.00	65.00	125	300	1,200	3,000	—
1883H	960,000	20.00	40.00	85.00	200	600	1,700	—
1885	192,000	150	300	5,500	1,100	4,000	10,000	—
1886/3	540,000	90.00	200	400	750	2,400	4,500	—
1886	Inc. above	45.00	90.00	200	450	1,700	4,500	—
1887	100,000	150	300	550	1,200	7,500	12,500	—
1888	400,000	26.00	40.00	90.00	200	750	2,200	—
1889	66,324	175	350	650	1,400	4,500	13,000	—
1890H	200,000	30.00	60.00	150	300	1,000	2,300	—
1891	120,000	125	225	400	750	1,800	3,500	—
1892	510,000	20.00	40.00	85.00	200	750	2,300	—
1893	100,000	150	300	550	1,000	2,000	3,000	—
1894	220,000	30.00	65.00	150	300	850	2,000	—
1899	415,580	12.00	25.00	60.00	150	600	1,500	—
1900	1,320,000	11.00	20.00	50.00	125	550	1,200	—
1901	640,000	15.00	24.00	65.00	200	650	1,400	—

KM# 11 5.8100 g. 0.9250 Silver 0.1728 oz. ASW 23.4 mm.   **Obv:** Crowned bust right **Obv. Designer:** G. W. DeSaulles **Rev:** Denomination and date within wreath, crown above

Date	Mintage	VG-8	F-12	VF-20	XF-40	MS-60	MS-63	Proof
1902	464,000	16.00	35.00	85.00	250	1,000	2,600	—
1902H	800,000	11.00	22.50	65.00	150	350	700	—
1903	846,150	20.00	40.00	100.00	300	1,100	2,600	—
1904	400,000	28.00	75.00	200	500	2,250	7,000	—
1905	800,000	20.00	45.00	150	400	2,000	6,000	—
1906 Large crown	1,237,843	14.00	30.00	75.00	250	800	2,400	—
1906 Small crown, Rare	Inc. above	3,500	5,500	100,000	19,000	30,000	40,000	—
1907	2,088,000	11.00	22.50	70.00	175	600	1,700	—

Date	Mintage	VG-8	F-12	VF-20	XF-40	MS-60	MS-63	Proof
1908	495,016	24.00	50.00	100.00	250	550	1,000	—
1909	1,335,929	16.00	40.00	100.00	250	850	2,400	—

KM# 11a 5.8319 g. 0.9250 Silver 0.1734 oz. ASW **Obv:** Crowned bust right **Rev:** Denomination and date within wreath, crown above

Date	Mintage	VG-8	F-12	VF-20	XF-40	MS-60	MS-63	Proof
1910	3,577,569	10.00	22.50	55.00	100.00	350	850	—

KM# 18 5.8319 g. 0.9250 Silver 0.1734 oz. ASW **Obv:** Crowned bust left **Obv. Legend:** GEORGIVS V REX ET IND IMP **Obv. Designer:** E. B. MacKennal **Rev:** Denomination and date within wreath, crown above

Date	Mintage	VG-8	F-12	VF-20	XF-40	MS-60	MS-63	Proof
1911	1,721,341	18.00	20.00	55.00	125	350	650	—

KM# 24 5.8319 g. 0.9250 Silver 0.1734 oz. ASW 23.5 mm. **Obv:** Crowned bust left **Obv. Legend:** GEORGIVS V DEI GRA REX ET IND IMP **Obv. Designer:** E. B. MacKennal **Rev:** Denomination and date within wreath, crown above

Date	Mintage	VG-8	F-12	VF-20	XF-40	MS-60	MS-63	Proof
1912	2,544,199	9.00	15.00	30.00	70.00	400	1,500	—
1913	2,213,595	7.00	14.00	30.00	65.00	350	1,250	—
1914	1,215,397	9.00	17.00	40.00	80.00	650	2,100	—
1915	242,382	28.00	70.00	225	600	3,500	8,500	—
1916	1,462,566	BV	12.00	25.00	50.00	250	800	—
1917	3,365,644	BV	9.00	18.00	40.00	150	300	—
1918	4,175,649	BV	9.00	14.00	35.00	125	225	—
1919	5,852,262	BV	9.00	14.00	35.00	125	225	—

Dot below wreath

KM# 24a 5.8319 g. 0.8000 Silver 0.1500 oz. ASW **Obv:** Crowned bust left **Obv. Designer:** E. B. MacKennal **Rev:** Denomination and date within wreath, crown below

Date	Mintage	VG-8	F-12	VF-20	XF-40	MS-60	MS-63
1920	1,975,278	BV	9.00	18.00	40.00	200	550
1921	597,337	17.00	35.00	125	300	1,450	3,500

Date	Mintage	VG-8	F-12	VF-20	XF-40	MS-60	MS-63
1927	468,096	40.00	70.00	125	300	1,000	2,100
1928	2,114,178	BV	9.00	18.00	50.00	175	450
1929	2,690,562	BV	9.00	18.00	45.00	150	400
1930	968,748	BV	9.00	27.00	50.00	250	650
1931	537,815	BV	10.00	30.00	65.00	300	650
1932	537,994	BV	10.00	30.00	65.00	300	650
1933	421,282	BV	10.00	35.00	85.00	250	450
1934	384,350	BV	12.00	45.00	90.00	350	650
1935	537,772	BV	10.00	35.00	65.00	200	400
1936	972,094	BV	8.00	14.00	28.00	100.00	225
1936 Dot below wreath	153,322	40.00	95.00	225	450	1,050	2,400

Note: *David Akers John Jay Pittman sale Part Three, 10-99, nearly Choice Unc. realized $6,900; considered a possible specimen example*

Maple leaf after date

KM# 35 5.8320 g. 0.8000 Silver 0.1500 oz. ASW 23.5 mm.   **Obv:** Head left **Obv. Designer:** T. H. Paget **Rev:** Caribou left, denomination above, date at right **Rev. Designer:** Emanuel Hahn

Date	Mintage	VG-8	F-12	VF-20	XF-40	MS-60	MS-63
1937	2,690,176	—	BV	6.00	9.00	20.00	40.00
1938	3,149,245	—	BV	8.00	15.00	80.00	150
1939	3,532,495	—	BV	8.00	11.00	65.00	125
1940	9,583,650	—	—	BV	5.00	20.00	40.00
1941	6,654,672	—	—	BV	6.00	23.00	45.00
1942	6,935,871	—	—	BV	6.00	24.00	45.00
1943	13,559,575	—	—	BV	6.00	23.00	45.00
1944	7,216,237	—	—	BV	6.00	30.00	65.00
1945	5,296,495	—	—	BV	6.00	23.00	55.00
1946	2,210,810	—	BV	6.00	12.00	55.00	100.00
1947	1,524,554	—	BV	6.00	12.00	65.00	100.00
1947 Dot after 7	Inc. above	65.00	90.00	125	225	450	900
1947 Maple leaf after 7	4,393,938	—	—	BV	6.00	20.00	30.00

KM# 44 5.8319 g. 0.8000 Silver 0.1500 oz. ASW 23.5 mm.   **Obv:** Head left, modified legend **Obv. Designer:** T. H. Paget **Rev:** Caribou left, denomination above, date at right **Rev. Designer:** Emanuel Hahn

Date	Mintage	VG-8	F-12	VF-20	XF-40	MS-60	MS-63	Proof
1948	2,564,424	—	—	BV	12.00	70.00	125	—
1949	7,988,830	—	—	BV	12.00	15.00	30.00	—

Date	Mintage	VG-8	F-12	VF-20	XF-40	MS-60	MS-63	Proof
1950	9,673,335	—	—	BV	12.00	12.00	23.00	—
1951	8,290,719	—	—	BV	12.00	11.00	18.00	—
1952	8,859,642	—	—	BV	12.00	10.00	17.00	—

 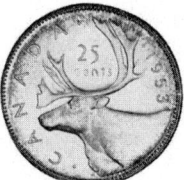

KM# 52 5.8319 g. 0.8000 Silver 0.1500 oz. ASW 23.8 mm.   **Obv:** Laureate bust right **Obv. Designer:** Mary Gillick **Rev:** Caribou left, denomination above, date at right **Rev. Designer:** Emanuel Hahn

Date	Mintage	VG-8	F-12	VF-20	XF-40	MS-60	MS-63	Proof
1953 Without strap	10,546,769	—	—	—	BV	8.00	15.00	—
1953 With strap	Inc. above	—	—	BV	6.00	11.00	27.50	—
1954	2,318,891	—	—	BV	11.00	30.00	60.00	—
1955	9,552,505	—	—	BV	6.00	9.00	17.00	—
1956	11,269,353	—	—	—	BV	8.00	12.00	—
1957	12,770,190	—	—	—	BV	8.00	10.00	—
1958	9,336,910	—	—	—	BV	8.00	10.00	—
1959	13,503,461	—	—	—	—	BV	8.00	—
1960	22,835,327	—	—	—	—	BV	8.00	—
1961	18,164,368	—	—	—	—	BV	8.00	—
1962	29,559,266	—	—	—	—	BV	8.00	—
1963	21,180,652	—	—	—	—	BV	8.00	—
1964	36,479,343	—	—	—	—	BV	8.00	—

KM# 62 5.8319 g. 0.8000 Silver 0.1500 oz. ASW 23.8 mm.   **Obv:** Young bust right **Obv. Designer:** Arnold Machin **Rev:** Caribou left, denomination above, date at right **Rev. Designer:** Emanuel Hahn

Date	Mintage	VG-8	F-12	VF-20	XF-40	MS-60	MS-63	Proof
1965	44,708,869	—	—	—	—	BV	8.00	—
1966	25,626,315	—	—	—	—	BV	8.00	—

KM#68 5.8319 g. 0.8000 Silver 0.1500 oz. ASW 23.8 mm.   **Subject:** Confederation Centennial **Obv:** Young bust right **Rev:** Lynx striding left divides dates and

denomination **Rev. Designer:** Alex Colville

Date	Mintage	VG-8	F-12	VF-20	XF-40	MS-60	MS-63	Proof
1867-1967	48,855,500	—	—	—	—	BV	6.00	—

KM# 68a 5.8319 g. 0.5000 Silver 0.0937 oz. ASW 23.8 mm.   **Subject:** Confederation Centennial **Obv:** Young bust right **Rev:** Lynx striding left divides dates and denomination

Date	Mintage	VG-8	F-12	VF-20	XF-40	MS-60	MS-63	Proof
1867-1967	Inc. above	—	—	—	BV	3.25	4.50	—

KM# 62a 5.8319 g. 0.5000 Silver 0.0937 oz. ASW 23.8 mm.   **Obv:** Young bust right **Obv. Designer:** Machin **Rev:** Caribou left, denomination above, date at right

Date	Mintage	MS-63	Proof
1968	71,464,000	4.50	—

KM# 62b 5.0600 g. Nickel 23.8 mm. **Obv:** Young bust right **Obv. Designer:** Machin **Rev:** Caribou left, denomination above, date at right

Date	Mintage	MS-63	Proof
1968	88,686,931	0.80	—
1969	133,037,929	0.80	—
1970	10,302,010	2.00	—
1971	48,170,428	0.80	—
1972	43,743,387	0.80	—
1974	192,360,598	0.80	—
1975	141,148,000	0.80	—
1976	86,898,261	0.80	—
1977	99,634,555	0.80	—
1978	176,475,408	0.80	—

KM# 81.1 Nickel 23.8 mm.   **Subject:** Royal Candian Mounted Police Centennial **Obv:** Young bust right **Rev:** Mountie divides dates, denomination above **Rev. Designer:** Paul Cedarberg **Note:** 120 beads.

Date	Mintage	MS-63	Proof
1873-1973	134,958,587	1.25	—

KM# 81.2 Nickel 23.8 mm.   **Subject:** RCMP Centennial **Obv:** Young bust right **Rev:** Mountie divides dates, denomination above **Note:** Large bust, 132 beads.

Date	Mintage	MS-63	Proof
1873-1973	Inc. above	750	—

KM# 74 5.0700 g. Nickel 23.88 mm. **Obv:** Small young bust right **Obv. Designer:** Machin **Rev. Designer:** Emanuel Hahn

Date	Mintage	MS-63	Proof
1979	131,042,905	0.75	—
1980	76,178,000	0.75	—
1981	131,580,272	0.75	—
1981 Proof	199,000	—	2.00
1982	171,926,000	0.75	—
1982 Proof	180,908	—	2.00
1983	13,162,000	1.50	—
1983 Proof	168,000	—	3.00
1984	121,668,000	0.75	—
1984 Proof	161,602	—	2.00
1985	158,734,000	0.75	—
1985 Proof	157,037	—	2.00
1986	132,220,000	0.75	—
1986 Proof	175,745	—	2.00
1987	53,408,000	1.25	—
1987 Proof	179,004	—	2.00
1988	80,368,473	0.95	—
1988 Proof	175,259	—	2.00
1989	119,796,307	0.75	—
1989 Proof	170,928	—	2.00

KM# 184 5.0700 g. Nickel 23.88 mm. **Obv:** Crowned head right **Obv. Designer:** Dora dePedery-Hunt **Rev:** Caribou left, denomination above, date at right **Rev. Designer:** Emanuel Hahn

Date	Mintage	MS-63	Proof
1990	31,258,000	0.90	—

Date	Mintage	MS-63	Proof
1990 Proof	140,649	—	2.50
1991	459,000	12.00	—
1991 Proof	131,888	—	20.00
1993	73,758,000	0.70	—
1993 Proof	143,065	—	2.00
1994	77,670,000	0.70	—
1994 Proof	146,424	—	3.00
1995	89,210,000	0.70	—
1995 Proof	50,000	—	3.00
1996	28,106,000	0.70	—
1996 Proof	—	—	6.00
1997	—	0.70	—
1997 Proof	—	—	6.00
1998W	—	5.00	—
1999	258,888,000	0.75	—
1999 Proof	—	—	6.00
2000	434,087,000	0.75	—
2000 Proof	—	—	6.00
2000W	—	5.00	—
2001	8,415,000	5.00	—
2001 Proof	—	—	7.50

KM# 203 5.0000 g. Nickel 23.9 mm. **Series:** 125th Anniversary of Confederation **Subject:** New Brunswick **Obv:** Crowned head right **Rev:** Covered bridge in Newton, denomination below **Rev. Designer:** Ronald Lambert

Date	Mintage	MS-63	Proof
1992	12,174,000	0.70	—

KM# 203a 5.8319 g. 0.9250 Silver 0.1734 oz. ASW 23.8 mm. **Series:** 125th Anniversary of Confederation **Subject:** New Brunswick **Obv:** Crowned head right **Rev:** Covered bridge in Newton, denomination below

Date	Mintage	MS-63	Proof
1992 Proof	149,579	—	8.50

KM# 207 Nickel 23.8 mm.   **Subject:**

Confederation 125 **Obv:** Crowned head right **Obv. Designer:** Dora dePedery-Hunt **Rev:** Caribou left, denomination above, date at right **Rev. Designer:** Emanuel Hahn

Date	Mintage	MS-63	Proof
1867-1992	442,986	12.50	—
1867-1992 Proof	147,061	—	20.00

KM# 212 Nickel 23.8 mm.   **Series:** 125th Anniversary of Confederation **Subject:** Northwest Territories **Obv:** Crowned head right **Rev. Designer:** Beth McEachen

Date	Mintage	MS-63	Proof
1992	12,582,000	0.70	—

KM# 212a 5.8319 g. 0.9250 Silver 0.1734 oz. ASW 23.8 mm.   **Series:** 125th Anniversary of Confederation **Subject:** Northwest Territories **Obv:** Crowned head right

Date	Mintage	MS-63	Proof
1992 Proof	149,579	—	8.50

KM# 213 Nickel 23.8 mm.   **Series:** 125th Anniversary of Confederation **Subject:** Newfoundland **Rev:** Fisherman rowing a dory, denomination below **Rev. Designer:** Christopher Newhook

Date	Mintage	MS-63	Proof
1992	11,405,000	0.70	—

KM# 213a 5.8319 g. 0.9250 Silver 0.1734 oz. ASW 23.8 mm.   **Series:** 125th Anniversary of Confederation **Subject:** Newfoundland **Rev:** Fisherman rowing a dory, denomination below

Date	Mintage	MS-63	Proof
1992 Proof	149,579	—	8.50

KM# 214 Nickel 23.8 mm.   **Series:** 125th Anniversary of Confederation **Subject:** Manitoba **Obv:** Crowned head right **Rev. Designer:** Muriel Hope

Date	Mintage	MS-63	Proof
1992	11,349,000	0.70	—

KM# 214a 5.8319 g. 0.9250 Silver 0.1734 oz. ASW 23.8 mm.   **Series:** 125th Anniversary of Confederation **Subject:** Manitoba **Obv:** Crowned head right

Date	Mintage	MS-63	Proof
1992 Proof	149,579	—	8.50

KM# 220 Nickel 23.8 mm.   **Series:** 125th Anniversary of Confederation **Subject:** Yukon **Obv:** Crowned head right **Rev. Designer:** Libby Dulac

Date	Mintage	MS-63	Proof
1992	10,388,000	0.70	—

KM# 220a 5.8319 g. 0.9250 Silver 0.1734 oz. ASW 23.8 mm.   **Series:** 125th Anniversary of Confederation **Subject:** Yukon **Obv:** Crowned head right

Date	Mintage	MS-63	Proof
1992 Proof	149,579	—	8.50

KM# 221 Nickel 23.8 mm.   **Series:** 125th Anniversary of Confederation **Subject:** Alberta **Obv:** Crowned head right **Rev:** Rock formations in the badlands near Drumhelter, denomination below **Rev. Designer:** Mel Heath

Date	Mintage	MS-63	Proof
1992	12,133,000	0.70	—

KM# 221a 5.8319 g. 0.9250 Silver 0.1734 oz. ASW 23.8 mm.   **Series:** 125th Anniversary of Confederation **Subject:** Alberta **Obv:** Crowned head right **Rev:** Rock formations in the

badlands near Drumhelter, denomination below **Rev. Designer:** Mel Heath

Date	Mintage	MS-63	Proof
1992 Proof	—	—	5.50

KM# 222 Nickel 23.8 mm. **Series:** 125th Anniversary of Confederation **Subject:** Prince Edward Island **Obv:** Crowned head right **Rev. Designer:** Nigel Roe

Date	Mintage	MS-63	Proof
1992	13,001,000	0.70	—

KM# 222a 5.8319 g. 0.9250 Silver 0.1734 oz. ASW 23.8 mm. **Series:** 125th Anniversary of Confederation **Subject:** Prince Edward Island **Obv:** Crowned head right **Rev. Designer:** Nigel Roe

Date	Mintage	MS-63	Proof
1992 Proof	149,579	—	8.50

KM# 223 Nickel 23.8 mm.   **Series:** 125th Anniversary of Confederation **Subject:** Ontario **Obv:** Crowned head right **Rev:** Jack pine, denomination below **Rev. Designer:** Greg Salmela

Date	Mintage	MS-63	Proof
1992	14,263,000	0.70	—

KM# 223a 5.8319 g. 0.9250 Silver 0.1734 oz. ASW 23.8 mm.   **Series:** 125th Anniversary of Confederation **Subject:** Ontario **Obv:** Crowned head right **Rev:** Jack pine, denomination below **Rev. Designer:** Greg Salmela

Date	Mintage	MS-63	Proof
1992 Proof	149,579	—	8.50

KM# 231 5.0300 g. Nickel 23.8 mm.
Series: 125th Anniversary of
Confederation **Subject:** Nova Scotia
Obv: Crowned head right
Rev: Lighthouse, denomination below
Rev. Designer: Bruce Wood

Date	Mintage	MS-63	Proof
1992	13,600,000	0.70	—

KM# 231a 5.8319 g. 0.9250 Silver
0.1734 oz. ASW 23.8 mm.   **Series:**
125th Anniversary of Confederation
Subject: Nova Scotia **Obv:** Crowned
head right **Rev:** Lighthouse,
denomination below
Rev. Designer: Bruce Wood

Date	Mintage	MS-63	Proof
1992 Proof	149,579	—	8.50

KM# 232 Nickel 23.8 mm.
Series: 125th Anniversary of
Confederation **Subject:** British
Columbia **Obv:** Crowned head right,
dates below **Rev:** Large rock, whales,
denomination below **Rev. Designer:**
Carla Herrera Egan

Date	Mintage	MS-63	Proof
1992	14,001,000	0.70	—

KM# 232a 5.8319 g. 0.9250 Silver
0.1734 oz. ASW 23.8 mm.   **Series:**
125th Anniversary of Confederation
Subject: British Columbia **Obv:**
Crowned head right, dates below **Rev:**
Large rock, whales, denomination
below **Rev. Designer:** Carla Herrera
Egan

Date	Mintage	MS-63	Proof
1992 Proof	149,579	—	8.50

KM# 233   Nickel 23.8 mm.   **Series:**
125th Anniversary of Confederation
Subject: Saskatchewan **Obv:** Crowned
head right **Rev:** Buildings behind wall,
grain stalks on right, denomination
below **Rev. Designer:** Brian Cobb

Date	Mintage	MS-63	Proof
1992	14,165,000	0.70	—

KM# 233a 5.8319 g. 0.9250 Silver
0.1734 oz. ASW 23.8 mm.   **Series:**
125th Anniversary of Confederation
Subject: Saskatchewan **Obv:** Crowned
head right **Rev:** Buildings behind wall,
grain stalks on right, denomination
below **Rev. Designer:** Brian Cobb

Date	Mintage	MS-63	Proof
1992 Proof	149,579	—	8.50

KM# 234   Nickel 23.8 mm.   **Series:**
125th Anniversary of Confederation
Subject: Quebec **Obv:** Crowned head
right **Rev:** Boats on water, large rocks
in background, denomination below
Rev. Designer: Romualdas Bukauskas

Date	Mintage	MS-63	Proof
1992	13,607,000	0.70	—

KM# 234a 5.8319 g. 0.9250 Silver
0.1734 oz. ASW 23.8 mm.   **Series:**
125th Anniversary of Confederation
Subject: Quebec **Obv:** Crowned head
right **Rev:** Boats on water, large rocks
in background, denomination below
Rev. Designer: Romualdas Bukauskas

Date	Mintage	MS-63	Proof
1992 Proof	149,579	—	8.50

KM# 184a 5.9000 g. 0.9250 Silver 0.1755 oz. ASW 23.88 mm.　Obv: Crowned head right Rev: Caribou left, denomination above, date at right

Date	Mintage	MS-63	Proof
1996 Proof	—	—	9.50
1997 Proof	—	—	9.50
1998 Proof	—	—	8.50
1998O Proof	—	—	8.50
1999 Proof	—	—	8.50
2001 Proof	—	—	9.50
2003 Proof	—	—	9.50

KM# 312　23.8 mm.　Subject: 90th Anniversary Royal Canadian Mint Obv: Crowned head right Rev: Denomination and date within wreath, crown above

Date	Mintage	MS-63	Proof
1998 Matte	25,000	—	15.00
1998 Proof	—	—	15.00

KM# 184b 4.4000 g. Nickel Plated Steel 23.88 mm.　Obv: Crowned head right Rev: Caribou left, denomination above, date at right

Date	Mintage	MS-63	Proof
1999 P	Est. 20,000	20.00	—
2000 P	—	5,500	—
Note: 3-5 known			
2001 P	55,773,000	0.95	—
2001 P Proof	—	—	5.00
2002 P	156,105,000	2.50	—
2002 P Proof	—	—	5.00
2003 P	87,647,000	2.50	—
2003 P Proof	—	—	5.00

KM# 342 5.0700 g. Nickel 23.8 mm. Series: Millennium Subject: January - A Country Unfolds Obv: Crowned

head right Rev: Totem pole, portraits Rev. Designer: P. Ka-Kin Poon

Date	Mintage	MS-63	Proof
1999	12,181,200	0.65	—

KM# 342a 5.8319 g. 0.9250 Silver 0.1734 oz. ASW 23.8 mm.　Series: Millennium Subject: January Obv: Crowned head right Rev: Totem pole, portraits Rev. Designer: P. Ka-kin Poon

Date	Mintage	MS-63	Proof
1999 Proof	113,645	—	9.50

KM# 343 5.0900 g. Nickel 23.8 mm. Series: Millennium Subject: February - Etched in Stone Obv: Crowned head right Rev: Native petroglyphs Rev. Designer: L. Springer

Date	Mintage	MS-63	Proof
1999	14,469,250	0.65	—

KM# 343a 5.8319 g. 0.9250 Silver 0.1734 oz. ASW 23.8 mm.　Series: Millennium Subject: February Obv: Crowned head right Rev: Native petroglyphs Rev. Designer: L. Springer

Date	Mintage	MS-63	Proof
1999 Proof	113,645	—	9.50

KM# 344 5.0700 g. Nickel 23.8 mm. Series: Millennium Subject: March - The Log Drive Obv: Crowned head right Rev: Lumberjack Rev. Designer: M. Lavoie

Date	Mintage	MS-63	Proof
1999	15,033,500	0.65	—

KM# 344a 5.8319 g. 0.9250 Silver 0.1734 oz. ASW 23.8 mm.　Series: Millennium Subject: March Obv: Crowned head right Rev: Lumberjack Rev. Designer: M. Lavoie

Date	Mintage	MS-63	Proof
1999 Proof	113,645	—	9.50

KM# 345 5.0700 g. Nickel 23.8 mm.
Series: Millennium Subject: April - Our
Northern Heritage Obv: Crowned head
right Rev: Owl, polar bear Rev.
Designer: Ken Ojnak Ashevac

Date	Mintage	MS-63	Proof
1999	15,446,000	0.65	—

KM# 345a 5.8319 g. 0.9250 Silver
0.1734 oz. ASW 23.8 mm.   Series:
Millennium Subject: April Obv:
Crowned head right Rev: Owl, polar bear
Rev. Designer: Ken Ojnak Ashevac

Date	Mintage	MS-63	Proof
1999 Proof	113,645	—	9.50

KM# 346 5.0700 g. Nickel 23.8 mm.
Series: Millennium Subject: May - The
Voyageures Obv: Crowned head right
Rev: Voyageurs in canoe Rev.
Designer: S. Mineok

Date	Mintage	MS-63	Proof
1999	15,566,100	0.65	—

KM# 346a 5.8319 g. 0.9250 Silver
0.1734 oz. ASW 23.8 mm.   Series:
Millennium Subject: May Obv:
Crowned head right Rev: Voyageurs in
canoe Rev. Designer: S. Mineok

Date	Mintage	MS-63	Proof
1999 Proof	113,645	—	9.50

KM# 347 5.0300 g. Nickel 23.8 mm.

Series: Millennium Subject: June -
From Coast to Coast Obv: Crowned
head right Rev: 19th-century
locomotive Rev. Designer: G. Ho Edge:
Reeded

Date	Mintage	MS-63	Proof
1999	20,432,750	0.65	—

KM# 347a 5.8319 g. 0.9250 Silver
0.1734 oz. ASW 23.8 mm.   Series:
Millennium Subject: June Obv:
Crowned head right Rev: 19th-century
locomotive Rev. Designer: G. Ho Edge:
Reeded

Date	Mintage	MS-63	Proof
1999 Proof	113,645	—	9.50

KM# 348 5.0700 g. Nickel 23.8 mm.
Series: Millennium Subject: July - A
Nation of People Obv: Crowned head
right Rev: 6 stylized portraits Rev.
Designer: M. H. Sarkany

Date	Mintage	MS-63	Proof
1999	17,321,000	0.65	—

KM# 348a 5.8319 g. 0.9250 Silver
0.1734 oz. ASW 23.8 mm.   Series:
Millennium Subject: July Obv:
Crowned head right Rev: 6 stylized
portraits Rev. Designer: M.H. Sarkany

Date	Mintage	MS-63	Proof
1999 Proof	113,645	—	9.50

KM# 349 5.0700 g. Nickel 23.8 mm.
Series: Millennium Subject: August -
The Pioneer Spirit Obv: Crowned head
right Rev: Hay harvesting Rev.
Designer: A. Botelho

Date	Mintage	MS-63	Proof
1999	18,153,700	0.65	—

KM# 349a 5.8319 g. 0.9250 Silver 0.1734 oz. ASW 23.8 mm.   **Series:** Millennium **Subject:** August **Obv:** Crowned head right **Rev:** Hay harvesting **Rev. Designer:** A. Botelho

Date	Mintage	MS-63	Proof
1999 Proof	113,645	—	9.50

KM# 350 5.0700 g. Nickel 23.8 mm. **Series:** Millennium **Subject:** September - Canada Through a Child's Eye **Obv:** Crowned head right **Rev:** Childlike artwork **Rev. Designer:** Claudia Bertrand

Date	Mintage	MS-63	Proof
1999	31,539,350	0.65	—

KM# 350a 5.8319 g. 0.9250 Silver 0.1734 oz. ASW 23.8 mm.   **Series:** Millennium **Subject:** September **Obv:** Crowned head right **Rev:** Childlike artwork **Rev. Designer:** Claudia Bertrand

Date	Mintage	MS-63	Proof
1999 Proof	113,645	—	9.50

KM# 351 5.0700 g. Nickel 23.8 mm. **Series:** Millennium **Subject:** October - Tribute to the First Nations **Obv:** Crowned head right **Rev:** Aboriginal artwork **Rev. Designer:** J. E. Read

Date	Mintage	MS-63	Proof
1999	32,136,650	0.65	—

KM# 351a 5.8319 g. 0.9250 Silver 0.1734 oz. ASW 23.8 mm.   **Series:** Millennium **Subject:** October **Obv:** Crowned head right **Rev:** Aboriginal artwork **Rev. Designer:** J.E. Read

Date	Mintage	MS-63	Proof
1999 Proof	113,645	—	9.50

KM# 352 5.0700 g. Nickel 23.8 mm. **Series:** Millennium **Subject:** November - The Airplane Opens the North **Obv:** Crowned head right **Rev:** Bush plane with landing skis **Rev. Designer:** B. R. Brown

Date	Mintage	MS-63	Proof
1999	27,162,800	0.65	—

KM# 352a 5.8319 g. 0.9250 Silver 0.1734 oz. ASW 23.8 mm.   **Series:** Millennium **Subject:** November **Obv:** Crowned head right **Rev:** Bush plane with landing skis **Rev. Designer:** B.R. Brown

Date	Mintage	MS-63	Proof
1999 Proof	113,645	—	9.50

KM# 353 5.0700 g. Nickel 23.8 mm. **Series:** Millennium **Subject:** December - This is Canada **Obv:** Crowned head right **Rev:** Eclectic geometric design **Rev. Designer:** J. L. P. Provencher

Date	Mintage	MS-63	Proof
1999	43,339,200	0.70	—

KM# 353a 5.1000 g. 0.9250 Silver 0.1517 oz. ASW 23.8 mm.   **Series:** Millennium **Subject:** December **Obv:** Crowned head right **Rev:** Eclectic geometric design **Rev. Designer:** J.L.P. Provencher

Date	Mintage	MS-63	Proof
1999 Proof	113,645	—	9.50

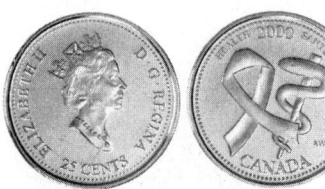

KM# 373 Nickel 23.8 mm.   **Subject:** Health **Obv:** Crowned head right, denomination below **Rev:** Ribbon and caduceus, date above **Rev. Designer:** Anny Wassef

Date	Mintage	MS-63	Proof
2000	35,470,900	0.65	—

KM# 373a 0.9250 Silver 23.8 mm. **Subject:** Health **Obv:** Crowned head right, denomination below **Rev:** Ribbon and caduceus, date above **Rev. Designer:** Anny Wassef

Date	Mintage	MS-63	Proof
2000 Proof	76,956	—	9.50

KM# 374 5.1000 g. Nickel 23.85 mm. **Subject:** Freedom **Obv:** Crowned head right, denomination below **Rev:** 2 children on maple leaf and rising sun, date above **Rev. Designer:** Kathy Vinish

Date	Mintage	MS-63	Proof
2000	35,188,900	0.65	—

KM# 374a 0.9250 Silver 23.8 mm. **Subject:** Freedom **Obv:** Crowned head right, denomination below **Rev:** 2 children on maple leaf and rising sun, date above **Rev. Designer:** Kathy Vinish

Date	Mintage	MS-63	Proof
2000 Proof	76,956	—	9.00

KM# 375 Nickel 23.8 mm.   **Subject:** Family **Obv:** Crowned head right, denomination below **Rev:** Wreath of native carvings, date above **Rev. Designer:** Wade Stephen Baker

Date	Mintage	MS-63	Proof
2000	35,107,700	0.65	—

KM# 375a 0.9250 Silver 23.8 mm. **Subject:** Family **Obv:** Crowned head right, denomination below **Rev:** Wreath of native carvings, date above **Rev. Designer:** Wade Stephen Baker

Date	Mintage	MS-63	Proof
2000 Proof	76,956	—	9.00

KM# 376 5.0800 g. Nickel 23.8 mm. **Subject:** Community **Obv:** Crowned head right, denomination below **Rev:** Map on globe, symbols surround, date above **Rev. Designer:** Michelle Thibodeau

Date	Mintage	MS-63	Proof
2000	35,155,400	0.65	—

KM# 376a 0.9250 Silver 23.8 mm. **Subject:** Community **Obv:** Crowned head right, denomination below **Rev:** Map on globe, symbols surround, date above **Rev. Designer:** Michelle Thibodeau

Date	Mintage	MS-63	Proof
2000 Proof	76,956	—	9.00

KM# 377 Nickel 23.8 mm.   **Subject:** Harmony **Obv:** Crowned **Rev:** Maple leaf, date above **Rev. Designer:** Haver Demirer

Date	Mintage	MS-63	Proof
2000	35,184,200	0.65	—

KM# 377a 0.9250 Silver 23.8 mm.
Subject: Harmony **Obv:** Crowned
head right, denomination below **Rev:**
Maple leaf **Rev. Designer:** Haver
Demirer

Date	Mintage	MS-63	Proof
2000 Proof	76,956	—	9.00

KM# 378 Nickel 23.8 mm. **Subject:**
Wisdom **Obv:** Crowned head right,
denomination below **Rev:** Man with
young child, date above **Rev. Designer:**
Cezar Serbanescu

Date	Mintage	MS-63	Proof
2000	35,123,950	0.65	—

KM# 378a 0.9250 Silver 23.8 mm.
Subject: Wisdom **Obv:** Crowned head
right, denomination below **Rev:** Man
with young child **Rev. Designer:** Cezar
Serbanescu

Date	Mintage	MS-63	Proof
2000 Proof	76,956	—	9.00

KM# 379 Nickel 23.8 mm. **Subject:**
Creativity **Obv:** Crowned head right,
denomination below **Rev:** Canoe full of
children, date above **Rev. Designer:**
Kong Tat Hui

Date	Mintage	MS-63	Proof
2000	35,316,770	0.65	—

KM# 379a 0.9250 Silver 23.8 mm.
Subject: Creativity **Obv:** Crowned
head right, denomination below **Rev:**
Canoe full of children **Rev. Designer:**
Kong Tat Hui

Date	Mintage	MS-63	Proof
2000 Proof	76,956	—	9.00

KM# 380 Nickel 23.8 mm. **Subject:**
Ingenuity **Obv:** Crowned head right,
denomination below **Rev:** Crescent-
shaped city views, date above **Rev.
Designer:** John Jaciw

Date	Mintage	MS-63	Proof
2000	36,078,360	0.65	—

KM# 380a 0.9250 Silver 23.8 mm.
Subject: Ingenuity **Obv:** Crowned
head right, denomination below **Rev:**
Crescent-shaped city views **Rev.
Designer:** John Jaciw

Date	Mintage	MS-63	Proof
2000 Proof	76,956	—	9.00

KM# 381 Nickel 23.8 mm. **Subject:**
Achievement **Obv:** Crowned head
right, denomination below **Rev:** Rocket
above jagged design, date above **Rev.
Designer:** Daryl Dorosz

Date	Mintage	MS-63	Proof
2000	35,312,750	0.65	—

KM# 381a 0.9250 Silver 23.8 mm.
Subject: Achievement **Obv:** Crowned
head right, denomination below **Rev:**
Rocket above jagged design **Rev.
Designer:** Daryl Dorosz

Date	Mintage	MS-63	Proof
2000 Proof	76,956	—	9.00

KM# 382 Nickel 23.8 mm. **Subject:**
Natural legacy **Obv:** Crowned head
right, denomination below **Rev:**
Environmental elements, date above
Rev. Designer: Randy Trantau

Date	Mintage	MS-63	Proof
2000	36,236,900	0.65	—

KM# 382a 0.9250 Silver 23.8 mm.
Subject: Natural legacy **Obv:** Crowned head right, denomination below **Rev:** Environmental elements **Rev. Designer:** Randy Trantau

Date	Mintage	MS-63	Proof
2000 Proof	76,956	—	9.00

KM# 383 Nickel 23.8 mm.   **Subject:** Celebration **Obv:** Crowned head right, denomination below **Rev:** Fireworks, children behind flag, date above **Rev. Designer:** Laura Paxton

Date	Mintage	MS-63	Proof
2000	35,144,100	0.65	—

KM# 383a 0.9250 Silver 23.8 mm.
Subject: Celebration **Obv:** Crowned head right, denomination below **Rev:** Fireworks, children behind flag **Rev. Designer:** Laura Paxton

Date	Mintage	MS-63	Proof
2000 Proof	76,956	—	9.00

KM# 384.1 Nickel 23.8 mm.
Subject: Pride **Obv:** Crowned head right, denomination below **Rev:** Large ribbon 2 in red with 3 small red maple leaves on large maple leaf, date above **Rev. Designer:** Donald F. Warkentin **Edge:** Reeded **Note:** Colorized version.

Date	Mintage	MS-63	Proof
2000	49,399	6.50	—

KM# 384.2 Nickel 23.8 mm.

Subject: Pride **Obv:** Crowned head right, denomination below **Rev:** Large ribbon 2 with three small maple leaves on large maple leaf, date above **Rev. Designer:** Donald F. Warkentin

Date	Mintage	MS-63	Proof
2000	50,666,800	0.65	—

KM# 384.2a 0.9250 Silver 23.8 mm.
Subject: Pride **Obv:** Crowned head right, denomination below **Rev:** Ribbon 2 with 3 small maple leaves on large maple leaf **Rev. Designer:** Donald F. Warkentin

Date	Mintage	MS-63	Proof
2000 Proof	76,956	—	9.00

KM# 419 4.4000 g. Nickel Plated Steel 23.9 mm.   **Subject:** Canada Day **Obv:** Crowned head right **Rev:** Maple leaf at center, children holding hands below **Rev. Designer:** Silke Ware **Edge:** Reeded

Date	Mintage	MS-63	Proof
2001	96,352	7.00	—

KM# 448 4.4000 g. Nickel Plated Steel 23.9 mm.   **Subject:** Elizabeth II Golden Jubilee **Obv:** Crowned head right **Rev:** Caribou left

Date	Mintage	MS-63	Proof
1952-2002P	152,485,000	2.00	—
1952-2002P Proof	32,642	—	6.00

KM# 448a 5.9000 g. 0.9250 Silver 0.1755 oz. ASW 23.9 mm.   **Subject:** Elizabeth II Golden Jubilee **Obv:** Crowned head right, Jubilee commemorative dates 1952-2002

Date	Mintage	MS-63	Proof
1952-2002 Proof	100,000	—	12.50

KM# 451 4.4000 g. Nickel Plated Steel 23.9 mm.   **Rev:** Small human figures supporting large maple leaf

Date	Mintage	MS-63	Proof
2002P	30,627,000	5.00	—

KM# 451a 4.4000 g. Nickel Plated Steel 23.9 mm. **Subject:** Canada Day **Obv:** Crowned head right **Rev:** Human figures supporting large red maple leaf **Edge:** Reeded

Date	Mintage	MS-63	Proof
2002P	49,901	6.00	—

KM# 493 4.4000 g. Nickel Plated Steel 23.9 mm. **Obv:** Bare head right **Obv. Designer:** Susanna Blunt **Rev:** Caribou left, denomination above, date at right

Date	Mintage	MS-63	Proof
2003P	66,861,633	2.00	—
2003P W	—	—	—
2004P	177,466,000	2.50	—
2004P Proof	—	—	5.00
2005P	206,346,000	2.50	—
2005P Proof	—	—	5.00
2006P	423,189,000	2.50	—
2006P Proof	—	—	5.00
2007(ml)	386,763,000	2.50	—
2007(ml) Proof	—	—	5.00
2008(ml)	387,222,000	2.50	—
2008(ml) Proof	—	—	5.00
2009(ml)	266,766,000	2.50	—
2009(ml) Proof	—	—	5.00
2010(ml)	—	2.50	—
2010(ml) Proof	—	—	5.00
2011(ml)	—	2.50	—
2011(ml) Proof	—	—	5.00
2012(ml)	—	2.50	—
2012(ml) Proof	—	—	5.00

KM# 471 5.9000 g. 0.9250 Silver 0.1755 oz. ASW 23.9 mm. **Subject:** 50th Anniversary of the Coronation of Elizabeth II **Obv:** 1953 Effigy of the Queen, Coronation Jubilee dates 1953-2003 **Obv. Designer:** Mary Gillick

Date	Mintage	MS-63	Proof
1953-2003 Proof	21,537	—	12.50

KM# 474 4.4000 g. 0.9250 Silver 0.1308 oz. ASW 23.9 mm. **Subject:** Canada Day **Obv:** Queen's head right **Rev:** Polar bear and red colored maple leaves

Date	Mintage	MS-63	Proof
2003 Proof	63,511	—	12.00

KM# 493a 5.9000 g. 0.9250 Silver 0.1755 oz. ASW 23.9 mm. **Obv:** Bare head right **Obv. Designer:** Suanne Blunt **Rev:** Caribou **Edge:** Reeded

Date	Mintage	MS-63	Proof
2004 Proof	—	—	6.50

KM# 510 4.4000 g. Nickel Plated Steel 23.9 mm. **Obv:** Bare head right **Rev:** Red poppy in center of maple leaf **Edge:** Reeded

Date	Mintage	MS-63	Proof
2004	28,500,000	5.00	—

KM# 510a 5.9000 g. 0.9250 Silver 0.1755 oz. ASW 23.9 mm. **Obv:** Bare head right **Rev:** Poppy at center of maple leaf, selectively gold plated **Edge:** Reeded **Note:** Housed in Annual Report.

Date	Mintage	MS-63	Proof
2004 Proof	12,677	—	20.00

KM# 525 4.4000 g. Nickel Plated Steel 23.9 mm. **Obv:** Bare head right **Rev:** Maple leaf, colorized

Date	Mintage	MS-63	Proof
2004	16,028	8.00	—

KM# 628 4.4000 g. Nickel Plated Steel 23.9 mm. **Subject:** First Settlement, Ile Ste Croix 1604-2004 **Obv:** Bare head right **Rev:** Sailing ship Bonne-Renommee

Date	Mintage	MS-63	Proof
2004P	15,400,000	5.00	—

KM# 698 4.4000 g. Nickel Plated Steel **Rev:** Santa, colorized

Date	Mintage	MS-63	Proof
2004	62,777	5.00	—

KM# 699 4.4000 g. Nickel Plated Steel 23.9 mm. **Series:** Canada Day **Rev:** Moose head, humorous

Date	Mintage	MS-63	Proof
2004	44,752	5.00	—

KM# 529 4.4000 g. Nickel Plated Steel 23.9 mm. **Subject:** WWII, 60th Anniversary **Obv:** Head right **Rev:** Three soldiers and flag

Date	Mintage	MS-63	Proof
1945-2005	3,500	20.00	—

KM# 530 4.4000 g. Nickel Plated Steel 23.9 mm. **Subject:** Alberta **Obv:** Head right

Date	Mintage	MS-63	Proof
2005P	20,640,000	7.00	—

KM# 531 4.4000 g. Nickel Plated Steel 23.9 mm. **Subject:** Canada Day **Obv:** Head right **Rev:** Beaver, colorized

Date	Mintage	MS-63	Proof
2005P	58,370	8.50	—

KM# 532 4.4000 g. Nickel Plated Steel 23.9 mm. **Subject:** Saskatchewan **Obv:** Head right

Date	Mintage	MS-63	Proof
2005P	19,290,000	7.00	—

KM# 533 4.4000 g. Nickel Plated Steel 23.9 mm. **Obv:** Head right **Rev:** Stuffed bear in Christmas stocking, colorized

Date	Mintage	MS-63	Proof
2005P	72,831	10.00	—

KM# 535 4.4000 g. Nickel Plated Steel 23.9 mm. **Subject:** Year of the Veteran **Obv:** Head right **Rev:** Conjoined busts of young and veteran left **Edge:** Reeded

Date	Mintage	MS-63	Proof
2005P	29,390,000	7.00	—

KM# 576 4.4000 g. Nickel Plated Steel 23.9 mm. **Subject:** Quebec Winter Carnival **Obv:** Head right **Rev:** Snowman, colorized

Date	Mintage	MS-63	Proof
2006	8,200	10.00	—

KM# 534 4.4000 g. Nickel Plated Steel 23.9 mm. **Subject:** Toronto Maple Leafs **Obv:** Head right **Rev:** Colorized team logo

Date	Mintage	MS-63	Proof
2006P	11,765	12.50	—

KM# 575 4.4000 g. Nickel Plated Steel 23.9 mm. **Subject:** Montreal Canadiens **Obv:** Head right **Rev:** Colorized logo

Date	Mintage	MS-63	Proof
2006P	11,765	12.50	—

KM# 629 4.4000 g. Nickel Plated Steel
23.9 mm. **Obv:** Head right **Rev:**
Medal of Bravery **Edge:** Reeded

Date	Mintage	MS-63	Proof
2006(ml)	20,040,000	2.50	—

KM# 632 12.6100 g. Nickel Plated Steel
35 mm. **Subject:** Queen Elizabeth II
80th Birthday **Rev:** Crown, colorized

Date	Mintage	MS-63	Proof
1926-2006 Specimen	24,977	—	25.00

KM# 633 4.4300 g. Nickel Plated Steel
23.9 mm. **Subject:** Canada Day **Obv:**
Crowned head right **Rev:** Boy
marching with flag, colorized

Date	Mintage	MS-63	Proof
2006P	30,328	6.00	—

KM# 634 4.4300 g. Nickel Plated
Steel **Subject:** Breast Cancer **Rev:**

Four ribbons, all colorized **Note:** Sold
housed in a bookmark.

Date	Mintage	MS-63	Proof
2006P	40,911	10.00	—

KM# 636 4.4000 g. Nickel Plated Steel
Obv: Head right **Obv. Designer:** Susana
Blunt **Rev:** Medal of Bravery design
(maple leaf within wreath)

Date	Mintage	MS-63	Proof
2006	20,045,111	7.00	—

KM# 637 4.4300 g. Nickel Plated
Steel **Subject:** Wedding **Rev:**
Colorized bouquet of flowers

Date	Mintage	MS-63	Proof
2007(ml)	10,318	5.00	—

KM# 642 4.4300 g. Nickel Plated
Steel **Subject:** Ottawa Senators **Obv:**
Head right **Rev:** Logo

Date	Mintage	MS-63	Proof
2006P	11,765	12.50	—

KM# 644 4.4300 g. Nickel Plated
Steel **Subject:** Calgary Flames **Obv:**
Head right **Rev:** Logo

Date	Mintage	MS-63	Proof
2007(ml)	1,082	12.50	—

KM# 645 4.4300 g. Nickel Plated
Steel **Subject:** Edmonton Oilers **Obv:**
Head right **Rev:** Logo

Date	Mintage	MS-63	Proof
2007(ml)	2,214	12.50	—

KM# 647 4.4300 g. Nickel Plated
Steel **Subject:** Santa and Rudolph
Rev: Colorized Santa in sled lead by
Rudolph

Date	Mintage	MS-63	Proof
2006P	99,258	5.00	—

KM# 682 4.4300 g. Nickel Plated Steel
Subject: Curling **Obv:** Head right

Date	Mintage	MS-63	Proof
2007	22,400,000	7.50	—
2008 Mule	—	—	—

KM# 683 4.4300 g. Nickel Plated Steel **Subject:** Ice Hockey **Obv:** Head right

Date	Mintage	MS-63	Proof
2007	22,400,000	7.50	—
2008 Mule	—	—	—

KM# 684 4.4300 g. Nickel Plated Steel 23.8 mm. **Subject:** Paraolympic Winter Games **Obv:** Head right **Rev:** Wheelchair curling

Date	Mintage	MS-63	Proof
2007	22,400,000	7.50	—
2008 Mule	—	—	—

KM#685 4.4300 g. Nickel Plated Steel **Subject:** Biathlon **Obv:** Head right

Date	Mintage	MS-63	Proof
2007	22,400,000	7.50	—
2008 Mule	—	—	—

KM# 638 4.4300 g. Nickel Plated Steel **Subject:** Birthday **Rev:** Colorized baloons

Date	Mintage	MS-63	Proof
2007(ml)	24,531	5.00	—

KM# 639 4.4300 g. Nickel Plated Steel **Subject:** Baby birth **Rev:** Colorized baby rattle **Edge:** Reeded

Date	Mintage	MS-63	Proof
2007(ml)	30,090	5.00	—

KM# 640 4.4300 g. Nickel Plated Steel **Subject:** Oh Canada **Obv:** Head right **Rev:** Maple leaf, colorized

Date	Mintage	MS-63	Proof
2006(ml)	23,582	8.50	—

KM# 641 4.4300 g. Nickel Plated Steel **Subject:** Congratulations **Obv:** Head right **Rev:** Fireworks, colorized

Date	Mintage	MS-63	Proof
2006(ml)	9,671	8.00	—

KM# 643 4.4300 g. Nickel Plated Steel **Subject:** Vancouver Canucks **Obv:** Head right **Rev:** Logo

Date	Mintage	MS-63	Proof
2007(ml)	1,526	12.50	—

KM# 686 4.4300 g. Nickel Plated Steel 23.8 mm. **Subject:** Alpine Skiing **Obv:** Head right

Date	Mintage	MS-63	Proof
2007	22,400,000	7.50	—
2008 Mule	—	—	—

KM# 701 4.4300 g. Nickel Plated Steel **Subject:** Birthday **Rev:** Party hat, multicolor

Date	Mintage	MS-63	Proof
2007	11,376	8.00	—

KM# 702 4.4300 g. Nickel Plated Steel **Subject:** Congratulations **Rev:** Trophy, multicolor

Date	Mintage	MS-63	Proof
2007	—	8.00	—

KM# 703 4.4300 g. Nickel Plated Steel **Subject:** Wedding **Rev:** Cake, multicolor

Date	Mintage	MS-63	Proof
2007	—	8.00	—

KM# 704 4.4300 g. Nickel Plated

Steel   **Subject:** Canada Day **Rev:**
Mountie, colorized

Date	Mintage	MS-63	Proof
2007(ml)	27,743	8.00	—

KM# 705 4.4300 g. Nickel Plated
Steel   **Subject:** Christmas **Rev:**
Multicolor tree

Date	Mintage	MS-63	Proof
2007	66,267	8.00	—

KM# 706 12.6100 g. Nickel Plated
Steel 35.0 mm.   **Subject:** Red-
breasted Nuthatch **Obv:** Head right
Obv. Legend: ELIZABETH II - D • G •
REGINA **Obv. Designer:** Susanna
Blunt **Rev:** Nuthatch perched on pine
branch multicolor **Rev. Legend:**
CANADA **Rev. Designer:** Arnold
Nogy **Edge:** Plain

Date	Mintage	MS-63	Proof
2007(ml) Specimen	11,909	25.00	—

KM# 707 12.6100 g. Nickel Plated
Steel 35 mm.   **Obv:** Elizabeth II **Rev:**
Multicolor ruby-throated
hummingbird and flower **Edge:** Plain

Date	Mintage	MS-63	Proof
2007 Specimen	17,174	—	25.00

KM# 708 12.6100 g. Nickel Plated
Steel   **Subject:** Queen's 60th Wedding
Anniversary **Rev:** Royal carriage in
color

Date	Mintage	MS-63	Proof
1947-2007 Specimen	15,235	—	24.00

KM# 713 4.4000 g. Nickel Plated
Steel   **Rev:** Toronto Maple Leaf logo,
colorized

Date	Mintage	MS-63	Proof
2007(ml)	5,365	5.00	—

KM# 714 4.4000 g. Nickel Plated
Steel   **Rev:** Ottawa Senators logo,
colorized

Date	Mintage	MS-63	Proof
2007(ml)	2,474	5.00	—

KM# 723 4.4000 g. Nickel Plated
Steel   **Rev:** Montreal Canadiens logo,
colorized

Date	Mintage	MS-63	Proof
2007(ml)	4,091	5.00	—

KM# 1039 4.4300 g. Nickel Plated Steel 23.9 mm. **Subject:** Canada Day **Rev:** Colorized moose head

Date	Mintage	MS-63	Proof
2008	11,538	12.50	—

KM# 760 4.4300 g. Nickel Plated Steel **Subject:** Baby **Rev:** Multicolor blue teddy bear

Date	Mintage	MS-63	Proof
2008	29,639	8.00	—

KM# 761 4.4300 g. Nickel Plated Steel **Subject:** Birthday **Rev:** Multicolor party hat

Date	Mintage	MS-63	Proof
2008	11,376	8.00	—

KM# 762 4.4300 g. Nickel Plated Steel **Subject:** Congratulations **Rev:** Multicolor trophy

Date	Mintage	MS-63	Proof
2008	6,821	8.00	—

KM# 763 4.4300 g. Nickel Plated Steel **Subject:** Wedding

Rev: Multicolor wedding cake

Date	Mintage	MS-63	Proof
2008	7,407	8.00	—

KM# 764 4.4300 g. Nickel Plated Steel **Subject:** Santa Claus **Rev:** Multicolor Santa

Date	Mintage	MS-63	Proof
2008	42,344	8.00	—

KM# 765 4.4300 g. Nickel Plated Steel 23.9 mm. **Subject:** Vancouver Olympics **Rev:** Freestyle skiing

Date	Mintage	MS-63	Proof
2008	—	2.00	—

KM# 766 4.4300 g. Nickel Plated Steel 23.8 mm. **Subject:** Vancouver Olympics **Rev:** Figure skating

Date	Mintage	MS-63	Proof
2008	—	2.00	—

KM# 768 4.4300 g. Nickel Plated Steel 23.9 mm. **Subject:** Vancouver Olympics **Rev:** Snow boarding

Date	Mintage	MS-63	Proof
2008	—	2.00	—

KM# 769 4.4300 g. Nickel Plated Steel **Subject:** Vancouver Olympics **Rev:** Olympic mascott - Miga

Date	Mintage	MS-63	Proof
2008	—	3.00	—

KM# 770 4.4300 g. Nickel Plated Steel **Subject:** Vancouver Olympics **Rev:** Olympic mascott - Quatchi

Date	Mintage	MS-63	Proof
2008	—	3.00	—

KM# 771 4.4300 g. Nickel Plated Steel **Subject:** Vancouver Olympics **Rev:** Olympic mascott - Sumi

Date	Mintage	MS-63	Proof
2008	—	3.00	—

KM# 772 4.4300 g. Nickel Plated Steel **Subject:** Oh Canada **Rev:** Multicolor red flag

Date	Mintage	MS-63	Proof
2008	—	8.00	—

KM# 773 12.6100 g. Nickel Plated Steel 35 mm. **Obv:** Bust right **Obv. Designer:** Susanna Blunt **Rev:** Downy woodpecker in tree, multicolor **Rev. Designer:** Arnold Nogy **Edge:** Plain **Note:** Prev. KM#717.

Date	Mintage	MS-63	Proof
2008(ml)	14,282	24.00	—

KM# 774 12.6100 g. Nickel Plated Steel 35 mm. **Obv:** Bust right **Obv. Designer:** Susanna Blunt **Rev:** Northern cardinal perched on branch - multicolor **Rev. Designer:** Arnold Nogy **Edge:** Plain **Note:** Prev. KM#718.

Date	Mintage	MS-63	Proof
2008(ml)	11,604	25.00	—

KM# 775 4.4300 g. Nickel Plated Steel 23.8 mm. **Subject:** End of WWI, 90th Anniversary **Rev:** Multicolor poppy

Date	Mintage	MS-63	Proof
1918-2008	10,167	8.00	—

KM# 776 12.6100 g. Nickel Plated Steel 35 mm. **Subject:** Anne of Green Gables **Rev:** Image of young girl, multicolor **Rev. Designer:** Ben Stahl

Date	Mintage	MS-63	Proof
1908-2008	32,795	20.00	—

KM# 841 4.4300 g. Nickel Plated Steel **Subject:** Vancouver Olympics **Rev:** Bobsleigh **Shape:** 23.8

Date	Mintage	MS-63	Proof
2008	—	3.00	—

KM# 885 4.4000 g. Nickel Plated Steel 35 mm.   **Subject:** Canada Day **Rev:** Animals in boat with flag **Rev. Legend:** Canada 25 cents

Date	Mintage	MS-63	Proof
2009	11,091	5.00	—

KM# 1041 4.4300 g. Nickel Plated Steel   **Subject:** WWI **Rev:** Three military men standing over tomb

Date	Mintage	MS-63	Proof
2008(ml)	10,167	12.50	—

KM# 840 4.4300 g. Nickel Plated Steel 23.8 mm.   **Subject:** Valcouver 2010 Olympics **Rev:** Cross-country skiing

Date	Mintage	MS-63	Proof
2009	—	3.00	—

KM# 886 12.6100 g. Nickel Plated Steel 35 mm.   **Subject:** Notre-Dame-Du-Saguenay **Obv:** Bust right **Obv. Legend:** Elizabeth II DG Regina **Obv. Designer:** Susanna Blunt **Rev:** Color photo of fjord and statue **Rev. Legend:** Canada 25 cents

Date	Mintage	MS-63	Proof
2009 Specimen	16,653	—	25.00

KM# 842 4.4300 g. Nickel Plated Steel 23.9 mm.   **Subject:** Edmonton Olympics **Rev:** Speed skating

Date	Mintage	MS-63	Proof
2009	—	3.00	—

KM# 915 4.4300 g. Nickel Plated Steel 23.9 mm.   **Subject:** Surprise Birthday **Obv:** Bust right **Obv. Designer:** Susanna Blunt **Rev:** Colorized

Date	Mintage	MS-63	Proof
2009	9,663	12.50	—

KM# 916 4.4300 g. Nickel Plated Steel
23.9 mm.   **Subject:** Share the
Excitement **Obv:** Bust right **Obv.**
Designer: Susanna Blunt **Rev:** Colorized

Date	Mintage	MS-63	Proof
2009	4,126	12.50	—

KM# 917 4.4300 g. Nickel Plated Steel
23.9 mm.   **Subject:** Share the Love
Obv: Bust right **Obv. Designer:**
Susanna Blunt **Rev:** Two doves, coolored

Date	Mintage	MS-63	Proof
2009	7,571	12.50	—

KM#918 4.4300 g. Nickel Plated Steel
23.9 mm.   **Subject:** Thank You **Obv:**
Bust right **Obv. Designer:** Susanna
Blunt **Rev:** Colorized

Date	Mintage	MS-63	Proof
2009	4,415	12.50	—

KM# 933 4.4000 g. Nickel Plated Steel
23.9 mm.   **Rev:** Santa Claus, multicolor

Date	Mintage	MS-63	Proof
2009	933	16.50	—

KM# 934 4.4000 g. Nickel Plated Steel
23.9 mm.   **Rev:** Multicolor teddy bear,
crescent moon

Date	Mintage	MS-63	Proof
2009	25,182	16.50	—

KM# 935 4.4000 g. Nickel Plated Steel
23.9 mm.   **Subject:** Oh Canada **Rev:**
Maple leaves, yellow color

Date	Mintage	MS-63	Proof
2009	14,451	16.50	—

KM# 952 4.4000 g. Nickel Plated Steel
23.9 mm.   **Rev:** Sledge hockey

Date	Mintage	MS-63	Proof
2009	—	3.00	—

KM# 1063 Nickel Plated Steel
Subject: Men's Hockey **Rev:** Hockey
player and maple leaf outline

Date	Mintage	MS-63	Proof
2009	—	2.50	—

KM# 1063a Nickel Plated Steel
Subject: Men's Hockey **Rev:** Hockey
player and maple leaf outline in red

Date	Mintage	MS-63	Proof
2009	—	7.50	—

KM# 1064 Nickel Plated Steel
Subject: Women's Hockey **Rev:**
Hockey player and maple leaf outline

Date	Mintage	MS-63	Proof
2009	—	2.50	—

KM# 1064a Nickel Plated Steel
Subject: Women's Hockey **Rev:**
Hockey player and male leaf outline in
red

Date	Mintage	MS-63	Proof
2009	—	7.50	—

KM# 1065 Nickel Plated Steel
Subject: Klassen - Female hockey
player **Rev:** Skater and maple leaf
outline

Date	Mintage	MS-63	Proof
2009	—	2.50	—

KM# 1065a Nickel Plated Steel
Subject: Klassen - female skater **Rev:**
Skater and maple leaf outline in red

Date	Mintage	MS-63	Proof
2009	—	7.50	—

KM# 880 4.4000 g. Nickel Plated Steel
23.88 mm.   **Subject:** Miga Mascot
Vancouver Olympics **Rev:** Mica Mascot
- color **Rev. Legend:** Vancouver 2010 25
cents

Date	Mintage	MS-63	Proof
2010	14,654	3.00	—

KM# 881 4.4000 g. Nickel Plated Steel
23.88 mm.   **Subject:** Quatchi Mascot -
Vancouver Olympics **Obv:** Bust right
Rev: Quatchi Mascot color **Rev.
Legend:** Vancouver 2010 25 cents

Date	Mintage	MS-63	Proof
2010	15,310	3.00	—

KM# 882 4.4000 g. Nickel Plated Steel
23.88 mm.   **Subject:** Sumi Mascot
Rev: Sumi Mascot color **Rev. Legend:**
Vancouver 2010 25 cents

Date	Mintage	MS-63	Proof
2010	15,333	3.00	—

KM# 953 4.4000 g. Nickel Plated Steel
23.9 mm.   **Rev:** Ice hockey

Date	Mintage	MS-63	Proof
2010	—	3.00	—

KM# 953a 4.4000 g. Nickel Plated
Steel 23.9 mm.   **Rev:** Ice Hockey - red
enamel

Date	Mintage	MS-63	Proof
2010	—	8.00	—

KM# 954 4.4000 g. Nickel Plated Steel
23.9 mm.   **Rev:** Curling

Date	Mintage	MS-63	Proof
2010	—	3.00	—

KM# 954a 4.4000 g. Nickel Plated
Steel 23.9 mm.   **Rev:** Curling red
enamel

Date	Mintage	MS-63	Proof
2010	—	8.00	—

KM# 955 4.4000 g. Nickel Plated Steel 23.9 mm.   **Rev:** Wheelchair curling

Date	Mintage	MS-63	Proof
2010	—	3.00	—

KM# 955a 4.4000 g. Nickel Plated Steel 23.9 mm.   **Rev:** Wheelchair curling - red enamel

Date	Mintage	MS-63	Proof
2010	—	8.00	—

KM# 956 4.4000 g. Nickel Plated Steel 23.9 mm.   **Rev:** Biathlon

Date	Mintage	MS-63	Proof
2010	—	3.00	—

KM# 956a 4.4000 g. Nickel Plated Steel 23.9 mm.   **Rev:** Biathlon - red enamel

Date	Mintage	MS-63	Proof
2010	—	8.00	—

KM# 957 4.4000 g. Nickel Plated Steel 23.9 mm.   **Rev:** Alpine skiing

Date	Mintage	MS-63	Proof
2010	—	3.00	—

KM# 957a 4.4000 g. Nickel Plated Steel 23.9 mm.   **Rev:** Alpine skiing - red enamel

Date	Mintage	MS-63	Proof
2010	—	8.00	—

KM# 958 4.4000 g. Nickel Plated Steel 23.9 mm.   **Rev:** Snowboarding

Date	Mintage	MS-63	Proof
2010	—	3.00	—

KM# 958a 4.4000 g. Nickel Plated Steel 23.9 mm.   **Rev:** Snowboarding - red enamel

Date	Mintage	MS-63	Proof
2010	—	8.00	—

KM# 959 23.9000 g. Nickel Plated Steel 23.9 mm.   **Rev:** Free-style skiing

Date	Mintage	MS-63	Proof
2010	—	3.00	—

KM# 959a 4.4000 g. Nickel Plated Steel 23.9 mm.   **Rev:** Free-style skiing - red enamel

Date	Mintage	MS-63	Proof
2010	—	8.00	—

KM# 960 4.4000 g. Nickel Plated Steel 23.9 mm.   **Rev:** Alpine skiing

Date	Mintage	MS-63	Proof
2010	—	3.00	—

KM# 960a 4.4000 g. Nickel Plated Steel 23.9 mm.   **Rev:** Alpine skiing - red enamel

Date	Mintage	MS-63	Proof
2010	—	8.00	—

KM# 988 4.4000 g. Multi-Ply Plated Steel 23.88 mm.   **Rev:** Blue baby carriage

Date	Mintage	MS-63	Proof
2010	—	10.00	—

KM# 989 4.4000 g. Nickel Plated Steel 23.9 mm.   **Rev:** Purple gift box

Date	Mintage	MS-63	Proof
2010	—	10.00	—

KM# 991 4.4000 g. Nickel Plated Steel 23.9 mm.   **Rev:** Three maple leaves

Date	Mintage	MS-63	Proof
2010	—	12.50	—

KM# 992 4.4000 g. Nickel Plated Steel 23.9 mm.   **Rev:** Three zinnias

Date	Mintage	MS-63	Proof
2010	—	12.50	—

KM# 993 23.9000 g. Nickel Plated Steel 23.9 mm.   **Rev:** Pink hearts and roses

Date	Mintage	MS-63	Proof
2010	—	10.00	—

KM# 994 12.6100 g. Nickel Plated Steel 35 mm.   **Rev:** Goldfinch, multicolor **Rev. Designer:** Arnold Nogy

Date	Mintage	MS-63	Proof
2010 Proof	Est. 14,000	—	25.00

KM# 1001 12.6100 g. Nickel Plated Steel 35 mm.   **Subject:** Blue Jay **Rev:** Multicolor blue jay on yellow maple leaves

Date	Mintage	MS-63	Proof
2010	Est. 14,000	—	25.00

KM# 1006 0.5000 g. 0.9990 Gold 0.0161 oz. AGW 11 mm.   **Rev:** Caribou head left

Date	Mintage	MS-63	Proof
2010 Proof	15,000	—	80.00

KM# 1021   Nickel Plated Steel 23.9 mm.   **Rev:** Santa Claus in color

Date	Mintage	MS-63	Proof
2010	—	15.00	—

KM# 1026   Silver 23.8 mm.   **Obv:** George V bust left **Rev:** Value within wreath, dual dates below

Date	Mintage	MS-63	Proof
1935-2010 Proof	—	—	25.00

KM# 1028 4.4000 g. Nickel Plated Steel 23.9 mm.   **Rev:** Soldier standing, two red poppies, large maple leaf behind

Date	Mintage	MS-63	Proof
2010	—	15.00	—

KM# 1110 12.6100 g. Nickel Plated Steel 35 mm.   **Subject:** Royal Wedding **Rev:** Colored portraits left of William and Katherine

Date	Mintage	MS-63	Proof
2011 Proof	—	—	25.00

KM# 1156 Silver 23.8 mm.

Date	Mintage	MS-63	P/L	Proof
1911-2011	—	—	—	25.00

KM# 1079 12.6100 g. Nickel Plated Steel 35 mm.   **Rev:** Barn Swallow in color **Rev. Designer:** Arnold Nagy

Date	Mintage	MS-63	Proof
2011	Est. 14,000	—	25.00

KM# 1080 4.4300 g. Nickel Plated Steel 23.88 mm.   **Subject:** Oh Canada! **Rev:** Maple leaf and circular legend

Date	Mintage	MS-63	Proof
2011	—	2.50	—

KM# 1081 4.4300 g. Nickel Plated Steel 23.88 mm.   **Subject:** Wedding **Rev:** Two rings

Date	Mintage	MS-63	Proof
2011	—	2.50	—

KM# 1082 4.4300 g. Nickel Plated Steel 23.88 mm.   **Subject:** Birthday **Rev:** Year in four baloons

Date	Mintage	MS-63	Proof
2011	—	2.50	—

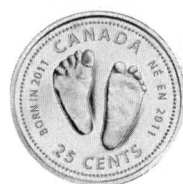

KM# 1083 4.4300 g. Nickel Plated Steel 23.88 mm.   **Subject:** New Baby! **Rev:** Baby's feet

Date	Mintage	MS-63	Proof
2011	—	2.50	—

KM# 1084 4.4300 g. Nickel Plated Steel 23.88 mm.   **Rev:** Tooth Fairy

Date	Mintage	MS-63	Proof
2011	—	2.50	—

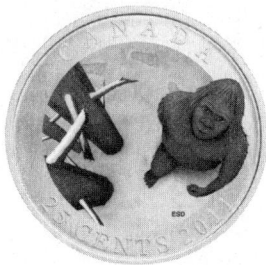

KM# 1113 12.6100 g. Nickel Plated Steel 35 mm. **Rev:** Fantasy Furry Woods creature in color

Date	Mintage	MS-63	Proof
2011	—	20.00	—

KM# 1116 12.6100 g. Nickel Plated Steel 35 mm. **Rev:** Black capped chickadee in color

Date	Mintage	MS-63	Proof
2011 Proof	—	—	25.00

KM# 1114 12.6100 g. Nickel Plated Steel 35 mm. **Rev:** Fantasy sea serpent in color

Date	Mintage	MS-63	Proof
2011	—	20.00	—

KM# 1148 4.4300 g. Nickel Plated Steel 23.9 mm. **Obv:** Bust right **Rev:** Snowflake

Date	Mintage	MS-63	Proof
2011	—	7.50	—

KM# 1168 4.4000 g. Nickel Plated Steel 23.9 mm. **Obv:** Bust right **Rev:** Stylized bison

Date	Mintage	MS-63	Proof
2011	—	2.50	—

KM# 1168a 4.4000 g. Nickel Plated Steel with color 23.9 mm. **Obv:** Bust right **Rev:** Stylized bison, green circle in background

Date	Mintage	MS-63	Proof
2011	—	9.50	—

KM# 1169 4.4000 g. Nickel Plated Steel 23.9 mm. **Obv:** Bust right **Rev:** Stylized falcon

Date	Mintage	MS-63	Proof
2011	—	2.50	—

KM# 1169a 4.4000 g. Nickel Plated Steel with color 23.9 mm. **Obv:** Bust right **Rev:** Stylized falcon with yellow circle in background

Date	Mintage	MS-63	Proof
2011	—	9.50	—

KM# 1115 12.6100 g. Nickel Plated Steel 35 mm. **Rev:** Tulip and ladybug in color

Date	Mintage	MS-63	Proof
2011	—	25.00	—

KM# 1170 4.4000 g. Nickel Plated Steel 23.9 mm.   **Obv:** Bust right **Rev:** Stylized orca whale

Date	Mintage	MS-63	Proof
2011	—	2.50	—

KM# 1170a 4.4000 g. Nickel Plated Steel with color 23.9 mm.   **Obv:** Bust right **Rev:** Stylized orca whale with blue circle in background

Date	Mintage	MS-63	Proof
2011	—	9.50	—

KM# 1171 0.5000 g. 0.9990 Gold 0.0161 oz. AGW 11 mm.   **Obv:** Bust right **Rev:** Cougar head left

Date	Mintage	MS-63	Proof
2011 Proof	—	—	80.00

KM# 1172 12.6100 g. Copper Plated Silver gold plated 35 mm.   **Obv:** Bust right **Rev:** Wayne Greskey in hockey helmet left

Date	Mintage	MS-63	Proof
2011 Proof	—	—	35.00

KM# 1192 4.4300 g. Nickel Plated Steel 23.9 mm.   **Subject:** Canadian Broadcasting Company, 75th Anniversary **Obv:** Bust right **Rev:** Old-time radio microphone

Date	Mintage	MS-63	Proof
2011	—	2.50	—

KM# 1193 12.6100 g. Nickel Plated Steel 35 mm.   **Subject:** Mythical Creature - Mishepishu **Obv:** Bust right **Rev:** Horned lizard in color

Date	Mintage	MS-63	Proof
2011	—	15.00	—

KM# 1227 4.4300 g. Nickel Plated Steel 23.9 mm.   **Obv:** Bust right **Rev:** Tooth Fairy in flight

Date	Mintage	MS-63	Proof
2012	—	2.50	—

KM# 1228 4.4300 g. Nickel Plated Steel 23.9 mm.   **Subject:** Baby **Rev:** Baby's mobile

Date	Mintage	MS-63	Proof
2012	—	2.50	—

KM# 1229 4.4300 g. Nickel Plated Steel 23.9 mm.   **Subject:** Wedding **Rev:** Two wedding rings with small feet

Date	Mintage	MS-63	Proof
2012	—	2.50	—

KM# 1230 4.4300 g. Nickel Plated Steel 23.9 mm.   **Subject:** Birthday **Rev:** Cone with character face

Date	Mintage	MS-63	Proof
2012	—	2.50	—

KM# 1231 4.4300 g. Nickel Plated Steel 23.9 mm.   **Subject:** Oh, Canada ! **Rev:** Maple leaves with character faces

Date	Mintage	MS-63	Proof
2012	—	2.50	—

50 CENTS

KM# 6 11.6200 g. 0.9250 Silver 0.3456 oz. ASW 29.72 mm.   **Obv:** VICTORIA DEI GRATIA REGINA. CANADA **Obv. Designer:** Leonard C. Wyon **Rev:** Denomination and date within wreath, crown above **Edge:** Reeded

Date	Mintage	VG-8	F-12	VF-20	XF-40	MS-60	MS-63
1870	450,000	900	1,400	2,400	5,000	25,000	40,000
1870 LCW	Inc. above	45.00	75.00	175	400	3,500	10,000
1871	200,000	75.00	150	350	650	7,000	15,000
1871H	45,000	150	225	450	1,100	8,500	22,000
1872H	80,000	55.00	95.00	200	450	4,000	10,500

Date	Mintage	VG-8	F-12	VF-20	XF-40	MS-60	MS-63
1872H Inverted A for V in Victoria	Inc. above	500	700	1,900	5,000	25,000	—
1881H	150,000	60.00	125	225	550	5,500	16,000
1888	60,000	225	400	750	1,400	9,500	22,000
1890H	20,000	1,200	1,900	3,500	6,000	30,000	65,000
1892	151,000	70.00	125	350	650	9,000	21,000
1894	29,036	500	900	1,500	2,500	14,000	35,000
1898	100,000	75.00	150	350	750	9,000	26,000
1899	50,000	200	350	700	1,600	14,000	35,000
1900	118,000	60.00	100.00	200	500	5,000	10,500
1901	80,000	80.00	150	300	750	7,000	17,500

Victorian leaves

KM#12 11.6200 g. 0.9250 Silver 0.3456 oz. ASW 29.72 mm.   **Obv:** Crowned bust right **Obv. Designer:** G. W. DeSaulles **Rev:** Denomination and date within wreath, crown above **Edge:** Reeded

Date	Mintage	VG-8	F-12	VF-20	XF-40	MS-60	MS-63
1902	120,000	28.00	55.00	150	350	1,950	4,500
1903H	140,000	35.00	70.00	225	550	2,100	5,500
1904	60,000	175	300	750	1,500	5,000	14,500
1905	40,000	225	450	950	2,100	9,000	22,500
1906	350,000	24.00	45.00	150	400	1,950	4,500
1907	300,000	24.00	50.00	125	350	1,900	5,000
1908	128,119	40.00	95.00	250	600	1,500	2,800
1909	302,118	28.00	90.00	250	750	3,000	12,000
1910 Victoria leaves	649,521	35.00	70.00	175	550	2,400	7,500

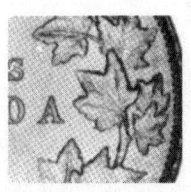

Edwardian leaves

KM#12a 11.6200 g. 0.9250 Silver 0.3456 oz. ASW 29.72 mm.   **Obv:** Crowned bust right **Obv. Designer:** G. W. DeSaulles **Rev:** Denomination and date within wreath **Edge:** Reeded

Date	Mintage	VG-8	F-12	VF-20	XF-40	MS-60	MS-63	Proof
1910 Edwardian leaves	Inc. above	23.00	40.00	100.00	400	1,550	4,500	—

KM# 19 11.6200 g. 0.9250 Silver 0.3456 oz. ASW 29.72 mm. **Obv:** Crwned bust left **Obv. Designer:** E. B. MacKennal **Rev:** Denomination and date within wreath, crown above **Edge:** Reeded

Date	Mintage	VG-8	F-12	VF-20	XF-40	MS-60	MS-63	Proof
1911	209,972	25.00	100.00	350	800	1,950	4,000	—

KM# 25 11.6200 g. 0.9250 Silver 0.3456 oz. ASW 29.72 mm. **Obv:** Crowned bust left, modified legend **Obv. Designer:** E. B. MacKennal **Rev:** Denomination and date within wreath, crown above **Edge:** Reeded

Date	Mintage	VG-8	F-12	VF-20	XF-40	MS-60	MS-63	Proof
1912	285,867	16.00	40.00	150	350	1,650	4,000	—
1913	265,889	16.00	40.00	175	400	1,900	6,500	—
1914	160,128	40.00	100.00	300	850	4,000	11,500	—
1916	459,070	14.00	24.00	75.00	200	950	2,900	—
1917	752,213	14.00	22.00	55.00	150	700	1,650	—
1918	754,989	14.00	20.00	40.00	125	600	1,400	—
1919	1,113,429	14.00	20.00	40.00	125	550	1,400	—

KM#25a 11.6638 g. 0.8000 Silver 0.3000 oz. ASW 29.72 mm. **Obv:** Crowned bust left **Obv. Designer:** E. B. MacKennal **Rev:** Denomination and date within wreath, crown below **Edge:** Reeded

Date	Mintage	VG-8	F-12	VF-20	XF-40	MS-60	MS-63	Proof
1920	584,691	14.00	22.00	55.00	200	850	2,100	—
1921	—	35,000	40,000	50,000	55,000	70,000	125,000	—

Note: *75 to 100 known; David Akers John Jay Pittman sale, Part Three, 10-99, Gem Unc. realized $63,250*

Date	Mintage	VG-8	F-12	VF-20	XF-40	MS-60	MS-63	Proof
1929	228,328	14.00	22.00	50.00	150	700	1,650	—
1931	57,581	20.00	40.00	100.00	300	1,200	2,400	—
1932	19,213	150	250	500	1,100	5,000	9,500	—
1934	39,539	28.00	40.00	125	300	950	1,950	—
1936	38,550	24.00	45.00	100.00	300	750	1,400	—

KM# 36 11.6638 g. 0.8000 Silver 0.3000 oz. ASW 29.72 mm.   **Obv:** Head left **Obv. Designer:** T. H. Paget **Rev:** Crowned arms with supporters, denomination above, date below **Rev. Designer:** George E. Kruger-Gray **Edge:** Reeded

Date	Mintage	VG-8	F-12	VF-20	XF-40	MS-60	MS-63
1937	192,016	BV	12.00	14.00	18.00	40.00	95.00
1938	192,018	BV	14.00	20.00	40.00	175	450
1939	287,976	BV	12.00	15.00	28.00	100.00	300
1940	1,996,566	—	—	BV	28.00	35.00	75.00
1941	1,714,874	—	—	BV	28.00	35.00	75.00
1942	1,974,164	—	—	BV	28.00	35.00	75.00
1943	3,109,583	—	—	BV	28.00	35.00	75.00
1944	2,460,205	—	—	BV	28.00	35.00	75.00
1945	1,959,528	—	—	BV	28.00	35.00	95.00
1946	950,235	—	BV	13.00	18.00	80.00	175
1946 hoof in 6	Inc. above	28.00	40.00	60.00	225	1,650	4,500
1947 straight 7	424,885	—	BV	13.00	20.00	95.00	250
1947 curved 7	Inc. above	—	BV	13.00	30.00	125	350
1947 maple leaf, straight 7	38,433	28.00	40.00	55.00	100.00	250	400
1947 maple leaf, curved 7	Inc. above	1,500	1,950	2,500	3,000	6,000	12,000

KM# 45 11.6638 g. 0.8000 Silver 0.3000 oz. ASW 29.72 mm.   **Obv:** Head left, modified legend **Obv. Designer:** T. H. Paget **Rev:** Crowned arms with supporters, denomination above, date below **Rev. Designer:** George E. Kruger-Gray **Edge:** Reeded

Date	Mintage	VG-8	F-12	VF-20	XF-40	MS-60	MS-63
1948	37,784	90.00	125	150	175	300	450
1949	858,991	—	—	BV	13.00	55.00	125
1949 hoof over 9	Inc. above	20.00	22.50	45.00	90.00	500	1,150

Date	Mintage	VG-8	F-12	VF-20	XF-40	MS-60	MS-63
1950 no lines in 0	2,384,179	14.00	16.00	18.00	45.00	200	350
1950 lines in 0	Inc. above	—	—	BV	12.00	16.00	45.00
1951	2,421,730	—	—	—	BV	14.00	30.00
1952	2,596,465	—	—	—	BV	14.00	24.00

KM# 53 11.6638 g. 0.8000 Silver 0.3000 oz. ASW 29.72 mm. **Obv:** Laureate bust right **Obv. Designer:** Mary Gillick **Rev:** Crowned arms with supporters, denomination above, date below **Edge:** Reeded

Date	Mintage	VG-8	F-12	VF-20	XF-40	MS-60	MS-63	Proof
1953	1,630,429	—	—	—	BV	13.00	22.50	—
Note: small date								
1953	Inc. above	—	—	BV	12.00	28.00	55.00	—
Note: large date, straps								
1953	Inc. above	—	BV	12.00	20.00	95.00	225	—
Note: large date without straps								
1954	506,305	—	—	BV	14.00	28.00	50.00	—
1955	753,511	—	—	BV	12.00	19.00	30.00	—
1956	1,379,499	—	—	—	BV	12.00	20.00	—
1957	2,171,689	—	—	—	BV	12.00	15.00	—
1958	2,957,266	—	—	—	BV	12.00	13.00	—

KM# 56 11.6638 g. 0.8000 Silver 0.3000 oz. ASW 29.7 mm. **Obv:** Luareate bust right **Obv. Designer:** Mary Gillick **Rev:** Crown divides date above arms with supporters, denomination at right **Rev. Designer:** Thomas Shingles **Edge:** Reeded

Date	Mintage	VG-8	F-12	VF-20	XF-40	MS-60	MS-63	Proof
1959	3,095,535	—	—	—	—	BV	12.00	—
Note: horizontal shading								
1960	3,488,897	—	—	—	—	BV	12.00	—
1961	3,584,417	—	—	—	—	BV	12.00	—
1962	5,208,030	—	—	—	—	BV	12.00	—
1963	8,348,871	—	—	—	—	BV	12.00	—
1964	9,377,676	—	—	—	—	BV	12.00	—

KM# 63 11.6638 g. 0.8000 Silver 0.3000 oz. ASW 29.72 mm.   **Obv:** Young bust right **Obv. Designer:** Arnold Machin **Rev:** Crown divides date above arms with supporters, denomination at right **Rev. Designer:** Thomas Shingles **Edge:** Reeded

Date	Mintage	VG-8	F-12	VF-20	XF-40	MS-60	MS-63	Proof
1965	12,629,974	—	—	—	—	BV	12.00	—
1966	7,920,496	—	—	—	—	BV	12.00	—

KM# 69 11.6638 g. 0.8000 Silver 0.3000 oz. ASW 29.72 mm.   **Subject:** Confederation Centennial **Obv:** Young bust right **Rev:** Seated wolf howling divides denomination at top, dates at bottom **Rev. Designer:** Alex Colville **Edge:** Reeded

Date	Mintage	VG-8	F-12	VF-20	XF-40	MS-60	MS-63	Proof
1867-1967	4,211,392	—	—	—	—	BV	12.00	14.00

KM# 75.1 8.1000 g. Nickel 27.13 mm.   **Obv:** Young bust right **Obv. Designer:** Arnold Machin **Rev:** Crown divides date above arms with supporters, denomination at right **Rev. Designer:** Thomas Shingles **Edge:** Reeded

Date	Mintage	VG-8	F-12	VF-20	XF-40	MS-60	MS-63	Proof
1968	3,966,932	—	—	—	0.50	0.80	1.25	—
1969	7,113,929	—	—	—	0.50	0.80	1.25	—
1970	2,429,526	—	—	—	0.50	0.80	1.25	—
1971	2,166,444	—	—	—	0.50	0.80	1.25	—
1972	2,515,632	—	—	—	0.50	0.80	1.25	—
1973	2,546,096	—	—	—	0.50	0.80	1.25	—
1974	3,436,650	—	—	—	0.50	0.80	1.25	—
1975	3,710,000	—	—	—	0.50	0.80	1.25	—
1976	2,940,719	—	—	—	0.50	0.80	1.25	—

KM# 75.2 8.1000 g. Nickel 27.13 mm.   **Obv:** Small young bust right **Obv.**

Designer: Arnold Machin **Rev:** Crown divides date above arms with supporters, denomination at right **Rev. Designer:** Thomas Shingles **Edge:** Reeded

Date	Mintage	VG-8	F-12	VF-20	XF-40	MS-60	MS-63	Proof
1977	709,839	—	—	0.50	0.75	1.25	2.00	—

KM# 75.3 8.1000 g. Nickel 27.13 mm.   **Obv:** Young bust right **Obv. Designer:** Arnold Machin **Rev:** Crown divides date above arms with supporters, denomination at right, redesigned arms **Rev. Designer:** Thomas Shingles **Edge:** Reeded

Date	Mintage	VG-8	F-12	VF-20	XF-40	MS-60	MS-63	Proof
1978	3,341,892	—	—	—	0.50	0.65	1.00	—
Note: *square jewels*								
1978	Inc. above	—	—	1.00	2.50	4.50	6.00	—
Note: *round jewels*								
1979	3,425,000	—	—	—	0.50	0.65	1.00	—
1980	1,574,000	—	—	—	0.50	0.65	1.00	—
1981	2,690,272	—	—	—	0.50	0.65	1.00	—
1981 Proof	199,000	—	—	—	—	—	—	3.00
1982	2,236,674	—	—	—	30.00	65.00	95.00	—
Note: *small beads*								
1982 Proof	180,908	—	—	—	—	—	—	3.00
Note: *small beads*								
1982	Inc. above	—	—	—	0.50	0.65	1.00	—
Note: *large beads*								
1983	1,177,000	—	—	—	0.50	0.65	1.00	—
1983 Proof	168,000	—	—	—	—	—	—	3.00
1984	1,502,989	—	—	—	0.50	0.65	1.00	—
1984 Proof	161,602	—	—	—	—	—	—	3.00
1985	2,188,374	—	—	—	0.50	0.65	1.00	—
1985 Proof	157,037	—	—	—	—	—	—	3.00
1986	781,400	—	—	—	0.50	0.80	1.00	—
1986 Proof	175,745	—	—	—	—	—	—	3.00
1987	373,000	—	—	—	0.50	0.80	1.00	—
1987 Proof	179,004	—	—	—	—	—	—	3.50
1988	220,000	—	—	—	0.50	0.80	1.00	—
1988 Proof	175,259	—	—	—	—	—	—	3.00
1989	266,419	—	—	—	0.50	0.80	1.00	—
1989 Proof	170,928	—	—	—	—	—	—	3.00

KM# 185 8.1000 g. Nickel 27.13 mm.   **Obv:** Crowned head right **Obv. Designer:** Dora dePedery-Hunt **Rev:** Crown divides date above arms with supporters, denomination at right **Rev. Designer:** Thomas Shingles **Edge:** Reeded

Date	Mintage	VG-8	F-12	VF-20	XF-40	MS-60	MS-63	Proof
1990	207,000	—	—	—	0.50	0.80	1.00	—
1990 Proof	140,649	—	—	—	—	—	—	5.00
1991	490,000	—	—	—	0.50	0.85	1.00	—
1991 Proof	131,888	—	—	—	—	—	—	7.00
1993	393,000	—	—	—	0.50	0.85	1.00	—
1993 Proof	143,065	—	—	—	—	—	—	3.00
1994	987,000	—	—	—	0.50	0.75	1.00	—
1994 Proof	146,424	—	—	—	—	—	—	4.00
1995	626,000	—	—	—	0.50	0.75	1.00	—
1995 Proof	50,000	—	—	—	—	—	—	4.00
1996 Proof	—	—	—	—	—	—	—	4.00
1996	458,000	—	—	—	0.50	0.65	1.00	—

KM# 208 8.1000 g. Nickel 27.1 mm. **Subject:** Confederation 125 **Obv:** Crowned head right **Obv. Designer:** Dora dePedery-Hunt **Rev:** Crown divides date above arms with supporters, denomination at right **Rev. Designer:** Thomas Shingles **Edge:** Reeded

Date	Mintage	MS-63	Proof
1992	445,000	1.00	—
1992 Proof	147,061	—	5.00

KM# 261 11.6638 g. 0.9250 Silver 0.3469 oz. ASW   **Obv:** Crowned head right **Rev:** Atlantic Puffin, denomination and date at right **Rev. Designer:** Sheldon Beveridge

Date	Mintage	MS-63	Proof
1995 Proof	—	—	24.00

KM# 262 11.6638 g. 0.9250 Silver 0.3469 oz. ASW   **Obv:** Crowned head

right **Rev:** Whooping crane left, denomination and date at right **Rev. Designer:** Stan Witten

Date	Mintage	MS-63	Proof
1995 Proof	—	—	24.00

KM# 263 11.6638 g. 0.9250 Silver 0.3469 oz. ASW **Obv:** Crowned head right **Rev:** Gray Jays, denomination and date at right **Rev. Designer:** Sheldon Beveridge

Date	Mintage	MS-63	Proof
1995 Proof	—	—	24.00

KM# 264 11.6638 g. 0.9250 Silver 0.3469 oz. ASW **Obv:** Crowned head right **Rev:** White-tailed ptarmigans, date and denomination at right **Rev. Designer:** Cosme Saffioti

Date	Mintage	MS-63	Proof
1995 Proof	—	—	22.00

KM# 283 11.6638 g. 0.9250 Silver 0.3469 oz. ASW 27 mm. **Obv:** Crowned head right **Rev:** Moose calf left, denomination and date at right **Rev. Designer:** Ago Aarand

Date	Mintage	MS-63	Proof
1996 Proof	—	—	20.00

KM# 284 11.6638 g. 0.9250 Silver 0.3469 oz. ASW 27 mm. **Obv:** Crowned head right **Rev:** Wood ducklings, date and denomination at right **Rev. Designer:** Sheldon Beveridge

Date	Mintage	MS-63	Proof
1996 Proof	—	—	20.00

KM# 285 11.6638 g. 0.9250 Silver 0.3469 oz. ASW 27 mm. **Obv:** Crowned head right **Rev:** Cougar kittens, date and denomination at right **Rev. Designer:** Stan Witten

Date	Mintage	MS-63	Proof
1996 Proof	—	—	20.00

KM# 286 11.6638 g. 0.9250 Silver 0.3469 oz. ASW 27 mm. **Obv:** Crowned head right **Rev:** Bear cubs standing, date and denomination at right **Rev. Designer:** Sheldon Beveridge

Date	Mintage	MS-63	Proof
1996 Proof	—	—	20.00

KM# 185a 11.6380 g. 0.9250 Silver
0.3461 oz. ASW   **Obv:** Crowned head
right **Obv. Designer:** Dora dePedery-
Hunt **Rev:** Crown divides date above
arms with supporters, denomination at
right **Rev. Designer:** Thomas Shingles

Date	Mintage	MS-63	Proof
1996 Proof	—	—	12.00

KM# 290 8.1000 g. Nickel 27.1 mm.
Obv: Crowned head right **Obv.
Designer:** Dora dePedery-Hunt **Rev:**
Redesigned arms **Rev. Designer:** Cathy
Bursey-Sabourin **Edge:** Reeded

Date	Mintage	MS-63	Proof
1997	387,000	1.00	—
1997 Proof	—	—	5.00
1998	308,000	1.00	—
1998 Proof	—	—	—
1998W	—	2.00	—
1999	496,000	1.00	—
1999 Proof	—	—	5.00
2000	559,000	1.00	—
2000 Proof	—	—	5.00
2000W	—	1.50	—
2001P	—	1.50	—
2001P Proof	—	—	5.00
2003P	—	1.50	—
2003P Proof	—	—	5.00

KM# 292 11.6638 g. 0.9250 Silver
0.3469 oz. ASW 27 mm.   **Obv:**
Crowned head right **Rev:** Duck Toling
Retriever, date and denomination at
right **Rev. Designer:** Stan Witten

Date	Mintage	MS-63	Proof
1997 Proof	—	—	17.00

KM# 293 11.6638 g. 0.9250 Silver
0.3469 oz. ASW   **Obv:** Crowned head
right **Rev:** Labrador leaping left, date
and denomination at right **Rev.
Designer:** Sheldon Beveridge

Date	Mintage	MS-63	Proof
1997 Proof	—	—	17.00

KM# 294 11.6638 g. 0.9250 Silver
0.3469 oz. ASW   **Obv:** Crowned head
right **Rev:** Newfoundland right, date
and denomination at right **Rev.
Designer:** William Woodruff

Date	Mintage	MS-63	Proof
1997 Proof	—	—	17.00

KM# 295 11.6638 g. 0.9250 Silver
0.3469 oz. ASW 27.1 mm.   **Obv:**
Crowned head right **Rev:** Eskimo dog
leaping forward, date and
denomination at right **Rev. Designer:**
Cosme Saffioti

Date	Mintage	MS-63	Proof
1997 Proof	—	—	17.00

KM# 290a 11.6640 g. 0.9250 Silver
0.3469 oz. ASW 27.13 mm.   **Obv:**
Crowned head right **Obv. Designer:**
Dora dePedery-Hunt **Rev:** Redesigned

arms **Rev. Designer:** Cathy Bursey-Sabourin **Edge:** Reeded

Date	Mintage	MS-63	Proof
1997 Proof	—	—	12.00
1998 Proof	—	—	12.00
1999 Proof	—	—	12.00
2000 Proof	—	—	12.00
2001 Proof	—	—	12.00
2003 Proof	—	—	12.00

KM# 313 11.6638 g. 0.9250 Silver 0.3469 oz. ASW   **Subject:** 90th Anniversary Royal Canadian Mint **Obv:** Crowned head right **Rev:** Denomination and date within wreath, crown above **Rev. Designer:** W. H. J. Blakemore

Date	Mintage	MS-63	Proof
1908-1998 Matte	25,000	—	15.00
1908-1998 Proof	25,000	—	15.00

KM# 318 11.6638 g. 0.9250 Silver 0.3469 oz. ASW   **Obv:** Crowned head right **Rev:** Killer Whales, date and denomination at right **Rev. Designer:** William Woodruff

Date	Mintage	MS-63	Proof
1998 Proof	—	—	17.00

KM# 319 11.6638 g. 0.9250 Silver 0.3469 oz. ASW 27 mm.   **Obv:**

Crowned head right **Rev:** Humpback whale, date and denomination at right **Rev. Designer:** Sheldon Beveridge

Date	Mintage	MS-63	Proof
1998 Proof	—	—	17.00

KM# 320 11.6638 g. 0.9250 Silver 0.3469 oz. ASW   **Obv:** Crowned head right **Rev:** Beluga whales, date and denomination at right **Rev. Designer:** Cosme Saffioti

Date	Mintage	MS-63	Proof
1998 Proof	—	—	17.00

KM# 321 11.6638 g. 0.9250 Silver 0.3469 oz. ASW 27 mm.   **Obv:** Crowned head right **Rev:** Blue whale, date and denomination at right **Rev. Designer:** Stan Witten

Date	Mintage	MS-63	Proof
1998 Proof	—	—	17.00

KM# 327 11.6638 g. 0.9250 Silver 0.3469 oz. ASW   **Subject:** 110 Years Canadian Soccer **Obv:** Crowned head right **Rev:** Soccer players, dates above, denomination at right **Rev. Designer:** Stan Witten

Date	Mintage	MS-63	Proof
1998 Proof	—	—	12.00

KM# 314 11.6638 g. 0.9250 Silver 0.3469 oz. ASW **Subject:** 110 Years Canadian Speed and Figure Skating **Obv:** Crowned head right **Rev:** Speed skaters, dates below, denomination above **Rev. Designer:** Sheldon Beveridge

Date	Mintage	MS-63	Proof
1998 Proof	—	—	12.00

KM# 315 11.6638 g. 0.9250 Silver 0.3469 oz. ASW **Subject:** 100 Years Canadian Ski Racing **Obv:** Crowned head right **Rev:** Skiers, dates below, denomination upper left **Rev. Designer:** Ago Aarand

Date	Mintage	MS-63	Proof
1998 Proof	—	—	12.00

KM# 328 11.6638 g. 0.9250 Silver 0.3469 oz. ASW **Subject:** 20 Years Canadian Auto Racing **Obv:** Crowned head right **Rev:** Race car divides date and denomination **Rev. Designer:** Cosme Saffioti

Date	Mintage	MS-63	Proof
1998 Proof	—	—	12.00

KM# 290b 6.9000 g. Nickel Plated Steel 27.13 mm. **Obv:** Crowned head right **Obv. Designer:** Dora dePedery-Hunt **Rev:** Redesigned arms **Rev. Designer:** Cathy Bursey-Sabourin **Edge:** Reeded

Date	Mintage	MS-63	Proof
1999 P	Est. 20,000	15.00	—
2000 P	Est. 50	3,500	—
Note: Available only in RCM presentation coin clocks			
2001 P	389,000	1.50	—
2003 P	—	5.00	—

KM# 335 11.6638 g. 0.9250 Silver 0.3469 oz. ASW **Series:** Canadian Cats **Obv:** Crowned head right **Rev:** Cymric cat, date below, denomination at bottom **Rev. Designer:** Susan Taylor

Date	Mintage	MS-63	Proof
1999 Proof	—	—	35.00

KM# 336 11.6638 g. 0.9250 Silver 0.3469 oz. ASW **Series:** Canadian Cats **Obv:** Crowned head right **Rev:** Tonkinese cat, date below, denomination at bottom **Rev. Designer:** Susan Taylor

Date	Mintage	MS-63	Proof
1999 Proof	—	—	35.00

KM# 337 11.6638 g. 0.9250 Silver 0.3469 oz. ASW **Series:** Canadian Cats **Obv:** Crowned head right **Rev:** Cougar, date and denomination below **Rev. Designer:** Susan Taylor

Date	Mintage	MS-63	Proof
1999 Proof	—	—	35.00

KM# 334 11.6638 g. 0.9250 Silver 0.3469 oz. ASW **Subject:** First U.S.-Canadian Yacht Race **Obv:** Crowned head right **Rev:** Yachts, dates at left, denomination below **Rev. Designer:** Stan Witten

Date	Mintage	MS-63	Proof
1999 Proof	—	—	12.00

KM# 371 9.3600 g. 0.9250 Silver 0.2783 oz. ASW 27.1 mm. **Subject:** Basketball **Obv:** Crowned head right **Rev:** Basketball players **Rev. Designer:** Sheldon Beveridge **Edge:** Reeded

Date	Mintage	MS-63	Proof
1999 Proof	—	—	10.00

KM# 372 9.3600 g. 0.9250 Silver 0.2783 oz. ASW 27.1 mm. **Obv:** Crowned head right **Rev:** Football players **Rev. Designer:** Cosme Saffioti **Edge:** Reeded

Date	Mintage	MS-63	Proof
1999 Proof	—	—	11.00

KM# 338 11.6638 g. 0.9250 Silver 0.3469 oz. ASW **Series:** Canadian Cats **Obv:** Crowned head right **Rev:** Lynx, date and denomination below **Rev. Designer:** Susan Taylor

Date	Mintage	MS-63	Proof
1999 Proof	—	—	35.00

KM# 389 9.3500 g. 0.9250 Silver 0.2781 oz. ASW **Obv:** Crowned head right **Rev:** Great horned owl, facing, date and denomination at right **Rev. Designer:** Susan Taylor

Date	Mintage	MS-63	Proof
2000 Proof	—	—	20.00

KM# 333 11.6638 g. 0.9250 Silver 0.3469 oz. ASW **Subject:** 1904 Canadian Open **Obv:** Crowned head right **Rev:** Golfers, date at right, denomination below **Rev. Designer:** William Woodruff

Date	Mintage	MS-63	Proof
1999 Proof	—	—	15.00

KM# 390 9.3500 g. 0.9250 Silver
0.2781 oz. ASW   **Obv:** Crowned head
right **Rev:** Red-tailed hawk, dates and
denomination at right

Date	Mintage	MS-63	Proof
2000 Proof	—	—	20.00

KM# 391 9.3500 g. 0.9250 Silver
0.2781 oz. ASW   **Obv:** Crowned head
right **Rev:** Osprey, dates and
denomination at right **Rev. Designer:**
Susan Taylor

Date	Mintage	MS-63	Proof
2000 Proof	—	—	20.00

KM# 392 9.3500 g. 0.9250 Silver
0.2781 oz. ASW   **Obv:** Crowned head
right **Rev:** Bald eagle, dates and
denomination at right **Rev. Designer:**
William Woodruff

Date	Mintage	MS-63	Proof
2000 Proof	—	—	20.00

KM# 393 9.3500 g. 0.9250 Silver
0.2781 oz. ASW   **Subject:**
Steeplechase **Obv:** Crowned head right
Rev: Steeplechase, dates and
denomination below **Rev. Designer:**
Susan Taylor

Date	Mintage	MS-63	Proof
1840-2000 Proof	—	—	12.00

KM# 394 9.3500 g. 0.9250 Silver
0.2781 oz. ASW   **Subject:** Bowling
Obv: Crowned head right **Rev.
Designer:** William Woodruff

Date	Mintage	MS-63	Proof
2000 Proof	—	—	12.00

KM# 385 9.3500 g. 0.9250 Silver
0.2781 oz. ASW   **Subject:** Ice Hockey
Obv: Crowned head right **Rev:** 4
hockey players **Rev. Designer:** Stanley
Witten

Date	Mintage	MS-63	Proof
2000 Proof	—	—	12.00

KM# 386 9.3500 g. 0.9250 Silver
0.2781 oz. ASW   **Subject:** Curling
Obv: Crowned head right **Rev:** Motion
study of curlers, dates and
denomination below **Rev. Designer:**
Cosme Saffioti

Date	Mintage	MS-63	Proof
1910-2000 Proof	—	—	12.00

KM# 420 9.3000 g. 0.9250 Silver 0.2766 oz. ASW 27.13 mm.   **Series:** Festivals - Quebec **Obv:** Crowned head right **Rev:** Snowman and Chateau Frontenac **Rev. Designer:** Sylvie Daigneault **Edge:** Reeded

Date	Mintage	MS-63	Proof
2001 Proof	58,123	—	8.50

KM# 423 9.3000 g. 0.9250 Silver 0.2766 oz. ASW 27.13 mm.   **Series:** Festivals - Prince Edward Island **Obv:** Crowned head right **Rev:** Family, juggler and building **Rev. Designer:** Brenda Whiteway **Edge:** Reeded

Date	Mintage	MS-63	Proof
2001 Proof	58,123	—	8.50

KM# 421 9.3000 g. 0.9250 Silver 0.2766 oz. ASW 27.13 mm.   **Series:** Festivals - Nunavut **Obv:** Crowned head right **Rev:** Dancer, dog sled and snowmobiles **Rev. Designer:** John Mardon **Edge:** Reeded

Date	Mintage	MS-63	Proof
2001 Proof	58,123	—	8.50

KM# 424 9.3000 g. 0.9250 Silver 0.2766 oz. ASW 27.13 mm.   **Series:** Folklore - The Sled **Obv:** Crowned head right **Rev:** Family scene **Rev. Designer:** Valentina Hotz-Entin **Edge:** Reeded

Date	Mintage	MS-63	Proof
2001 Proof	28,979	—	9.00

KM# 422 9.3000 g. 0.9250 Silver 0.2766 oz. ASW 27.13 mm.   **Series:** Festivals - Newfoundland **Obv:** Crowned head right **Rev:** Sailor and musical people **Rev. Designer:** David Craig **Edge:** Reeded

Date	Mintage	MS-63	Proof
2001 Proof	58,123	—	8.50

KM# 425 9.3000 g. 0.9250 Silver 0.2766 oz. ASW 27.13 mm.   **Series:** Folklore - The Maiden's Cave **Obv:** Crowned head right **Rev:** Woman shouting **Rev. Designer:** Peter Kiss **Edge:** Reeded

Date	Mintage	MS-63	Proof
2001 Proof	28,979	—	9.00

KM# 426 9.3000 g. 0.9250 Silver 0.2766 oz. ASW 27.13 mm. **Series:** Folklore - The Small Jumpers **Obv:** Crowned head right **Rev:** Jumping children on seashore **Rev. Designer:** Miynki Tanobe **Edge:** Reeded

Date	Mintage	MS-63	Proof
2001 Proof	28,979	—	9.00

KM# 509 6.9000 g. Nickel Plated Steel 27.13 mm. **Obv:** Crowned head right **Rev:** National arms **Edge:** Reeded

Date	Mintage	MS-63	Proof
2001 P	—	1.50	—

KM# 444 6.9000 g. Nickel Plated Steel 27.13 mm. **Subject:** Queen's Golden Jubilee **Obv:** Coronation crowned head right and monogram **Rev:** Canadian arms **Rev. Designer:** Bursey Sabourin **Edge:** Reeded

Date	Mintage	MS-63	Proof
1952-2002P	14,440,000	2.50	—

KM# 444a 9.3000 g. 0.9250 Silver 0.2766 oz. ASW 27.13 mm. **Subject:** Elizabeth II Golden Jubilee **Obv:** Crowned head right, Jubilee commemorative dates 1952-2002

Date	Mintage	MS-63	Proof
1952-2002 Proof	100,000	—	17.50

KM# 444b 9.3000 g. 0.9250 Silver Gilt 0.2766 oz. ASW 27.13 mm. **Subject:** Queen's Golden Jubilee **Obv:** Crowned head right and monogram **Rev:** Canadian arms **Edge:** Reeded **Note:** Special 24 karat gold-plated issue of KM#444.

Date	Mintage	MS-63	Proof
1952-2002 Proof	32,642	—	35.00

KM# 454 9.3000 g. 0.9250 Silver 0.2766 oz. ASW 27.13 mm. **Subject:** Nova Scotia Annapolis Valley Apple Blossom Festival **Obv:** Crowned head right **Rev. Designer:** Bonnie Ross

Date	Mintage	MS-63	Proof
2002 Proof	59,998	—	8.50

KM# 455 9.3000 g. 0.9250 Silver 0.2766 oz. ASW 27.13 mm. **Subject:** Stratford Festival **Obv:** Crowned head right **Rev:** Couple with building in background **Rev. Designer:** Laurie McGaw

Date	Mintage	MS-63	Proof
2002 Proof	59,998	—	8.50

KM# 456 9.3000 g. 0.9250 Silver 0.2766 oz. ASW 27.13 mm. **Subject:** Folklorama **Obv:** Crowned head right **Rev. Designer:** William Woodruff

Date	Mintage	MS-63	Proof
2002 Proof	59,998	—	8.50

KM# 457 9.3000 g. 0.9250 Silver 0.2766 oz. ASW 27.13 mm. **Subject:** Calgary Stampede **Obv:** Crowned head right **Rev. Designer:** Stan Witten

Date	Mintage	MS-63	Proof
2002 Proof	59,998	—	8.50

KM# 458 9.3000 g. 0.9250 Silver 0.2766 oz. ASW 27.13 mm. **Subject:** Squamish Days Logger Sports **Obv:** Crowned head right **Rev. Designer:** Jose Osio

Date	Mintage	MS-63	Proof
2002 Proof	59,998	—	8.50

KM# 459 9.3000 g. 0.9250 Silver 0.2766 oz. ASW 27.13 mm. **Series:** Folklore and Legends **Obv:** Crowned head right **Rev:** The Shoemaker in Heaven **Rev. Designer:** Francine Gravel

Date	Mintage	MS-63	Proof
2002 Proof	19,267	—	9.50

KM# 460 9.3000 g. 0.9250 Silver 0.2766 oz. ASW 27.13 mm. **Series:** Folklore and Legends **Subject:** The

Ghost Ship **Obv:** Crowned head right
Rev. Designer: Colette Boivin

Date	Mintage	MS-63	Proof
2002 Proof	19,267	—	9.50

KM# 461 9.3000 g. 0.9250 Silver
0.2766 oz. ASW 27.13 mm. **Series:**
Folklore and Legends **Subject:** The Pig
That Wouldn't Get Over the Stile **Obv:**
Crowned head right **Rev. Designer:**
Laura Jolicoeur

Date	Mintage	MS-63	Proof
2002 Proof	19,267	—	9.50

KM#494 6.9000 g. Nickel Plated Steel
27.13 mm. **Obv:** Crowned head right
Obv. Designer: Susanna Blunt **Rev:**
National arms **Rev. Designer:** Cathy
Bursey-Sabourin **Edge:** Reeded

Date	Mintage	MS-63	Proof
2003P W	—	5.00	—
2003P W Proof	—	—	7.50
2004P	—	5.00	—
2004P Proof	—	—	7.50
2005P	200,000	1.50	—
2005P Proof	—	—	5.00
2006P	98,000	1.50	—
2006P Proof	—	—	5.00
2007(ml)	250,000	1.50	—
2007(ml) Proof	—	—	5.00
2008(ml)	211,000	1.50	—
2008(ml) Proof	—	—	5.00
2009(ml)	150,000	1.50	—
2009(ml) Proof	—	—	5.00
2010(ml)	—	1.50	—
2010(ml) Proof	—	—	5.00
2011(ml)	—	1.50	—
2011(ml) Proof	—	—	5.00
2012(ml)	—	1.50	—
2012(ml) Proof	—	—	5.00

KM# 472 11.6200 g. 0.9250 Silver
0.3456 oz. ASW 27.13 mm. **Subject:**
50th Anniversary of the Coronation of
Elizabeth II **Obv:** Crowned head right,
Jubilee commemorative dates 1952-
2002 **Obv. Designer:** Mary Gillick

Date	Mintage	MS-63	Proof
2003 Proof	30,000	—	15.00

KM# 475 9.3000 g. 0.9250 Silver
0.2766 oz. ASW 27.13 mm. **Obv:**
Crowned head right **Obv. Designer:**
Dora dePédery-Hunt **Rev:** Golden
daffodil **Rev. Designer:** Christie
Paquet, Stan Witten

Date	Mintage	MS-63	Proof
2003 Proof	36,293	—	25.00

KM# 476 9.3000 g. 0.9250 Silver
0.2766 oz. ASW 27.13 mm. **Subject:**
Yukon International Storytelling
Festival **Obv:** Crowned head right **Obv.
Designer:** Dora dePédery-Hunt **Rev.
Designer:** Ken Anderson, Jose Oslo

Date	Mintage	MS-63	Proof
2003 Proof	—	—	11.00

KM# 477 9.3000 g. 0.9250 Silver
0.2766 oz. ASW 27.13 mm. **Subject:**
Festival Acadien de Caraquet **Obv:**
Crowned head right **Obv. Designer:**
Dora dePédery-Hunt **Rev:** Sailboat and
couple **Rev. Designer:** Susan Taylor,
Hudson Design Group

Date	Mintage	MS-63	Proof
2003 Proof	—	—	11.00

KM# 478 9.3000 g. 0.9250 Silver
0.2766 oz. ASW 27.13 mm. **Subject:**

Back to Batoche **Obv:** Crowned head right **Obv. Designer:** Dora dePédery-Hunt **Rev. Designer:** David Hannan, Stan Witten

Date	Mintage	MS-63	Proof
2003 Proof	—	—	11.00

KM# 479 9.3000 g. 0.9250 Silver 0.2766 oz. ASW 27.13 mm. **Subject:** Great Northern Arts Festival **Obv:** Crowned head right **Obv. Designer:** Dora dePédery-Hunt **Rev. Designer:** Dawn Oman, Susan Taylor

Date	Mintage	MS-63	Proof
2003 Proof	—	—	11.00

KM# 494a 9.3000 g. 0.9250 Silver 0.2766 oz. ASW 27.13 mm. **Obv:** Crowned head right **Obv. Designer:** Susanna Blunt **Rev:** Canadian coat of arms **Edge:** Reeded

Date	Mintage	MS-63	Proof
2004 Proof	—	—	7.50

KM# 526 1.2700 g. 0.9999 Gold 0.0408 oz. AGW 14 mm. **Subject:** Moose **Obv:** Head right **Rev:** Moose head facing right

Date	Mintage	MS-63	Proof
2004 Proof	—	—	85.00

KM# 606 9.3000 g. 0.9250 Silver 0.2766 oz. ASW 27.13 mm. **Obv:** Head right **Obv. Designer:** Susanna Blunt **Rev:** Clouded Sulphur Butterfly, hologram **Rev. Designer:** Susan Taylor

Date	Mintage	MS-63	Proof
2004 Proof	15,281	—	30.00

KM# 712 9.3000 g. 0.9250 Silver 0.2766 oz. ASW 27.13 mm. **Rev:** Hologram of Tiger Swallowtail butterfly

Date	Mintage	MS-63	Proof
2004 Proof	20,462	—	30.00

KM# 536 9.3000 g. 0.9250 Silver 0.2766 oz. ASW with partial gold plating 27.13 mm. **Subject:** Golden rose **Obv:** Head right **Obv. Designer:** Susanna Blunt **Rev. Designer:** Christie Paquet

Date	Mintage	MS-63	Proof
2005 Proof	17,418	—	19.00

KM# 537 9.3000 g. 0.9250 Silver 0.2766 oz. ASW 27.13 mm. **Obv:** Head right **Obv. Designer:** Susanna Blunt **Rev:** Great Spangled Fritillary butterfly, hologram **Rev. Designer:** Jianping Yan

Date	Mintage	MS-63	Proof
2005 Proof	20,000	—	35.00

KM# 538 9.3000 g. 0.9250 Silver 0.2766 oz. ASW 27.13 mm. **Subject:** Toronto Maple Leafs **Obv:** Head right **Obv. Designer:** Susanna Blunt **Rev:** Darryl Sittler

Date	Mintage	MS-63	Proof
2005 Specimen	25,000	—	16.00

KM# 539 9.3000 g. 0.9250 Silver 0.2766 oz. ASW 27.13 mm. **Subject:** Toronto Maple Leafs **Obv:** Head right **Obv. Designer:** Susanna Blunt **Rev:** Dave Keon

Date	Mintage	MS-63	Proof
2005 Specimen	25,000	—	16.00

KM# 540 9.3000 g. 0.9250 Silver 0.2766 oz. ASW 27.13 mm. **Subject:** Toronto Maple Leafs **Obv:** Head right **Obv. Designer:** Susanna Blunt **Rev:** Jonny Bover

Date	Mintage	MS-63	Proof
2005 Specimen	25,000	—	16.00

KM# 541 9.3000 g. 0.9250 Silver 0.2766 oz. ASW 27.13 mm.   **Subject:** Toronto Maple Leafs **Obv:** Head right **Obv. Designer:** Susanna Blunt **Rev:** Tim Horton

Date	Mintage	MS-63	Proof
2005 Specimen	25,000	—	16.00

KM# 543 9.3000 g. 0.9250 Silver 0.2766 oz. ASW   **Subject:** WWII - Battle of Britain **Obv:** Head right **Rev:** Fighter plane in sky

Date	Mintage	MS-63	Proof
2005 Specimen	20,000	—	22.50

KM# 544 9.3000 g. 0.9250 Silver 0.2766 oz. ASW 27.13 mm.   **Subject:** WWII - Battle of Scheldt **Obv:** Head right **Obv. Designer:** Susanna Blunt **Rev:** Four soldiers walking down road **Rev. Designer:** Peter Mossman

Date	Mintage	MS-63	Proof
2005 Specimen	20,000	—	19.00

KM# 545 9.3000 g. 0.9250 Silver 0.2766 oz. ASW 27.13 mm.   **Subject:** WWII - Battle of the Atlantic **Obv:** Head right **Obv. Designer:** Susanna Blunt **Rev:** Merchant ship sinking **Rev. Designer:** Peter Mossman

Date	Mintage	MS-63	Proof
2005 Specimen	20,000	—	19.00

KM# 546 9.3000 g. 0.9250 Silver 0.2766 oz. ASW 27.13 mm.   **Subject:** WWII - Conquest of Sicily **Obv:** Head right **Obv. Designer:** Susanna Blunt **Rev:** Tank among town ruins **Rev. Designer:** Peter Mossman

Date	Mintage	MS-63	Proof
2005 Specimen	20,000	—	19.00

KM# 547 9.3000 g. 0.9250 Silver 0.2766 oz. ASW 27.13 mm.   **Subject:** WWII - Liberation of the Netherlands **Obv:** Head right **Obv. Designer:** Susanna Blunt **Rev:** Soldiers in parade, one holding flag **Rev. Designer:** Peter Mossman

Date	Mintage	MS-63	Proof
2005 Specimen	20,000	—	19.00

KM# 548 9.3000 g. 0.9250 Silver 0.2766 oz. ASW 27.13 mm.   **Subject:** WWII - Raid of Dieppe **Obv:** Head right **Obv. Designer:** Susanna Blunt **Rev:** Three soldiers exiting landing craft **Rev. Designer:** Peter Mossman

Date	Mintage	MS-63	Proof
2005 Specimen	20,000	—	19.00

KM# 577 9.3000 g. 0.9250 Silver 0.2766 oz. ASW 27.13 mm.   **Subject:** Montreal Canadiens **Obv:** Head right **Obv. Designer:** Susanna Blunt **Rev:** Guy LaFleur

Date	Mintage	MS-63	Proof
2005 Specimen	25,000	—	17.50

KM# 578 9.3000 g. 0.9250 Silver 0.2766 oz. ASW 27.13 mm.   **Subject:** Montreal Canadiens **Obv:** Head right **Obv. Designer:** Susanna Blunt **Rev:** Jaque Plante

Date	Mintage	MS-63	Proof
2005 Specimen	25,000	—	17.50

KM# 579 9.3000 g. 0.9250 Silver 0.2766 oz. ASW 27.13 mm.   **Subject:** Montreal Canadiens **Obv:** Head right **Obv. Designer:** Susanna Blunt **Rev:** Jean Beliveau

Date	Mintage	MS-63	Proof
2005 Specimen	25,000	—	17.50

KM# 580 9.3000 g. 0.9250 Silver 0.2766 oz. ASW 27.13 mm.   **Subject:** Montreal Canadiens **Obv:** Head right **Obv. Designer:** Susanna Blunt **Rev:** Maurice Richard

Date	Mintage	MS-63	Proof
2005 Specimen	25,000	—	17.50

KM# 599 9.3000 g. 0.9250 Silver 0.2766 oz. ASW 27.13 mm.   **Obv:** Head right **Obv. Designer:** Susanna Blunt **Rev:** Monarch butterfly, colorized **Rev. Designer:** Susan Taylor

Date	Mintage	MS-63	Proof
2005 Proof	20,000	—	35.00

KM# 542 1.2700 g. 0.9990 Gold 0.0408 oz. AGW 13.92 mm.   **Rev:** Voyagers with northern lights above **Rev. Designer:** Emanuel Hahn

Date	Mintage	MS-63	Proof
2005 Proof	Est. 25,000	—	100

KM# 648 9.3000 g. 0.9250 Silver
0.2766 oz. ASW With Partial Gold
Plating   **Subject:** Golden Daisy **Obv:**
Head right

Date	Mintage	MS-63	Proof
2006	18,190	22.00	—

KM# 649 9.3000 g. 0.9250 Silver
0.2766 oz. ASW   **Subject:** Short-tailed
swallowtail **Obv:** Head right **Rev:**
Colorized butterfly

Date	Mintage	MS-63	Proof
2006	24,568	25.00	—

KM# 650 9.3000 g. 0.9250 Silver
0.2766 oz. ASW   **Obv:** Head right **Rev:**
Silvery blue hologram

Date	Mintage	MS-63	Proof
2006	16,000	25.00	—

KM# 651 9.3000 g. 0.9250 Silver
0.2766 oz. ASW   **Subject:** Cowboy
Obv: Head right

Date	Mintage	MS-63	Proof
2006	—	17.50	—

KM# 494b 6.9000 g. Nickel Plated
Steel partially gilt 27.13 mm.   **Rev:**
State Arms, gilt **Note:** Housed in Mint
Annual Report

Date	Mintage	MS-63	Proof
2006	—	15.00	—

KM# 716 9.3000 g. 0.9250 Silver
0.2766 oz. ASW   **Rev:** Multicolor
holiday ornaments

Date	Mintage	MS-63	Proof
2006	16,989	17.50	—

KM# 717 1.2400 g. 0.9990 Gold
0.0398 oz. AGW 13.9 mm.   **Rev:** Wolf

Date	Mintage	MS-63	Proof
2006 Proof	—	—	100

KM# 926 1.2400 g. 0.9990 Gold
0.0398 oz. AGW 13.9 mm.   **Rev:**
Cowboy and bronco rider

Date	Mintage	MS-63	Proof
2006 Proof	—	—	100

KM# 715 9.3000 g. 0.9250 Silver
0.2766 oz. ASW with partial gold
plating 27.12 mm.   **Rev:** Forget-me-
not flower

Date	Mintage	MS-63	Proof
2007 Proof	22,882	—	29.00

KM# 927 1.2400 g. 0.9990 Gold
0.0398 oz. AGW 13.9 mm.   **Subject:**
Gold Louis

Date	Mintage	MS-63	Proof
2007 Proof	—	—	100

KM# 777 1.2400 g. 0.9990 Gold
0.0398 oz. AGW 13.9 mm.   **Subject:**
DeHavilland beaver

Date	Mintage	MS-63	Proof
2008 Proof	20,000	—	100

KM# 778 20.0000 g. 0.9250 Silver 0.5948 oz. ASW colorized green 34.06 mm.   **Subject:** Milk delivery **Obv:** Bust right **Rev:** Cow head and milk can **Shape:** Triangle

Date	Mintage	MS-63	Proof
2008 Proof	24,448	—	35.00

KM# 846 9.3000 g. 0.9250 Silver 0.2766 oz. ASW 27.13 mm.   **Rev:** Edmonton Oiler's lenticular design, old and new logos

Date	Mintage	MS-63	Proof
2009	—	15.00	—

KM# 779 9.3000 g. 0.9250 Silver 0.2766 oz. ASW 35 mm.   **Rev:** Multicolor snowman

Date	Mintage	MS-63	Proof
2008	21,679	17.50	—

KM# 780 9.3000 g. 0.9250 Silver 0.2766 oz. ASW   **Subject:** Ottawa Mint Centennial 1908-2008

Date	Mintage	MS-63	Proof
2008 Proof	3,248	—	20.00

KM# 847 9.3000 g. 0.9250 Silver 0.2766 oz. ASW 27.13 mm.   **Rev:** Montreal Canadiens lenticular design, old and new logos

Date	Mintage	MS-63	Proof
2009	—	15.00	—

KM# 848 9.3000 g. 0.9250 Silver 0.2766 oz. ASW 27.13 mm.   **Rev:** Ottawa Senators lenticular design, old and new logos

Date	Mintage	MS-63	Proof
2009	—	15.00	—

KM# 845 9.3000 g. 0.9250 Silver 0.2766 oz. ASW 27.13 mm.   **Rev:** Calgary Flames lenticular design, old and new logos

Date	Mintage	MS-63	Proof
2009	—	15.00	—

KM# 849 9.3000 g. 0.9250 Silver

0.2766 oz. ASW 27.13 mm.   **Rev:**
Toronto Maple Leafs lenticular design,
old and new logos

Date	Mintage	MS-63	Proof
2009	—	15.00	—

KM# 850 9.3000 g. 0.9250 Silver
0.2766 oz. ASW 27.13 mm.   **Rev:**
Vancouver Canucks lenticular design,
old and new logos

Date	Mintage	MS-63	Proof
2009	—	15.00	—

KM# 857 6.9000 g. Nickel Plated Steel
35 mm.   **Rev:** Calgary Flames
lenticular old and new logos

Date	Mintage	MS-63	Proof
2009	—	25.00	—

KM# 858 6.9000 g. Nickel Plated Steel
35 mm.   **Rev:** Edmonton Oilers
lenticular old and new logos

Date	Mintage	MS-63	Proof
2009	—	25.00	—

KM# 859 35.0000 g. Nickel Plated
Steel 35 mm.   **Rev:** Montreal
Canadians lenticular old and new logo

Date	Mintage	MS-63	Proof
2009	—	25.00	—

KM# 860 6.9000 g. Nickel Plated Steel
35 mm.   **Rev:** Ottawa Senators
lenticular old and new logos

Date	Mintage	MS-63	Proof
2009	—	25.00	—

KM# 861 6.9000 g. Nickel Plated Steel
35 mm.   **Rev:** Toronto Maple Leafs
lenticular old and new logos

Date	Mintage	MS-63	Proof
2009	—	25.00	—

KM# 862 6.9000 g. Nickel Plated Steel
35 mm.   **Rev:** Vancouver Canucks
lenticular old and new logos

Date	Mintage	MS-63	Proof
2009	—	25.00	—

KM# 887 19.1000 g. Copper-Nickel
34.06 mm.   **Subject:** Six-string
national guitar **Obv:** Bust right **Obv.
Legend:** Elizabeth II DG Regina **Obv.
Designer:** Susanna Blunt **Rev:**
Hologram with 6 "strings" **Rev.
Legend:** 50 CENTS Canada **Shape:**
Triangle

Date	Mintage	MS-63	Proof
2009 Proof	13,602	—	50.00

KM# 936 9.3000 g. Nickel   **Rev:**
Vancouver Canucks goalie jersey

Date	Mintage	MS-63	Proof
2009	3,563	15.00	—

KM# 937 6.9000 g. Nickel Plated Steel
35 mm.   **Rev:** Calgary Flames player -
colorized

Date	Mintage	MS-63	Proof
2009	3,518	15.00	—

KM# 938 6.9000 g. Nickel Plated Steel
35 mm.   **Rev:** Edmonton Oilers player

Date	Mintage	MS-63	Proof
2009	3,562	15.00	—

KM# 939 6.9000 g. Nickel Plated Steel
35 mm.   **Rev:** Toronto Maple Leafs
player

Date	Mintage	MS-63	Proof
2009	5,918	15.00	—

KM# 940 6.9000 g. Nickel Plated Steel
35 mm.   **Rev:** Montreal Canadiens
player

Date	Mintage	MS-63	Proof
2009	9,865	15.00	—

KM# 941 6.9000 g. Nickel Plated Steel
35 mm.   **Rev:** Ottawa Senators player

Date	Mintage	MS-63	Proof
2009	3,293	15.00	—

KM# 1035 12.6100 g. Brass Plated Steel

35 mm.   **Subject:** Christmas toy train
Rev: movement from far to close

Date	Mintage	MS-63	Proof
2009	19,103	17.50	—

KM# 961 6.9000 g. Nickel Plated Steel 35 mm.   **Rev:** Bob sleigh

Date	Mintage	MS-63	Proof
2010	—	15.00	—

KM# 961a 6.9000 g. Nickel Plated Steel 35 mm.   **Rev:** Bob sleigh - red enamel

Date	Mintage	MS-63	Proof
2010	—	15.00	—

KM# 962 6.9000 g. Nickel Plated Steel 35 mm.   **Rev:** Speed skating

Date	Mintage	MS-63	Proof
2010	—	15.00	—

KM# 962a 6.9000 g. Nickel Plated Steel 35 mm.   **Rev:** Speed skating - red enamel

Date	Mintage	MS-63	Proof
2010	—	15.00	—

KM# 963 6.9000 g. Nickel Plated Steel 35 mm.   **Rev:** Miga in bob sleigh

Date	Mintage	MS-63	Proof
2010	2,119	15.00	—

KM# 964 6.9000 g. Nickel Plated Steel 35 mm.   **Rev:** Miga in hockey

Date	Mintage	MS-63	Proof
2010	5,275	15.00	—

KM# 965 6.9000 g. Nickel Plated Steel 35 mm.   **Rev:** Quatchi in ice hockey

Date	Mintage	MS-63	Proof
2010	5,614	15.00	—

KM# 966 6.9000 g. Nickel Plated Steel 35 mm.   **Rev:** Sumi Para Sledge

Date	Mintage	MS-63	Proof
2010	3,707	15.00	—

KM# 967 6.9000 g. Nickel Plated Steel 35 mm.   **Rev:** Figure-skating mascot
Edge: Reeded

Date	Mintage	MS-63	Proof
2010	2,981	15.00	—

KM# 968 6.9000 g. Nickel Plated Steel 35 mm.   **Rev:** Free-style mascot

Date	Mintage	MS-63	Proof
2010	2,114	15.00	—

KM# 969 6.9000 g. Nickel Plated Steel 35 mm.   **Rev:** Skeleton mascot

Date	Mintage	MS-63	Proof
2010	1,672	15.00	—

KM# 970 6.9000 g. Nickel Plated Steel 35 mm.   **Rev:** Parallel giant slalom mascot

Date	Mintage	MS-63	Proof
2010	1,730	15.00	—

KM# 971 6.9000 g. Nickel Plated Steel 35 mm.   **Rev:** Alpine skiing mascot

Date	Mintage	MS-63	Proof
2010	2,309	15.00	—

KM# 972 6.9000 g. Nickel Plated Steel 35 mm.   **Rev:** Para Olympic alpine skiing mascott

Date	Mintage	MS-63	Proof
2010	1,902	15.00	—

KM# 973 6.9000 g. Nickel Plated Steel 35 mm.   **Rev:** Snowboard mascot

Date	Mintage	MS-63	Proof
2010	2,090	15.00	—

KM# 974 6.9000 g. Nickel Plated Steel 35 mm.   **Rev:** Speed-skating mascott

Date	Mintage	MS-63	Proof
2010	1,825	15.00	—

KM# 986 12.6100 g. Brass Plated Steel   **Rev:** Dasplerosaurus Torosus - 3-D lenticular movement

Date	Mintage	MS-63	Proof
2010	—	—	40.00

KM# 1015 12.6100 g. Brass Plated Steel 35 mm.   **Rev:** Sinosauropteryx

Date	Mintage	MS-63	Proof
2010	—	25.00	—

KM#1016 12.6100 g. Brass Plated Steel
35 mm.   **Rev:** Albertosaurus

Date	Mintage	MS-63	Proof
2010	—	25.00	—

KM# 1043   Nickel Plated Steel 34 mm.   **Rev:** Santa Claus transforms into Rudolf the red-nosed reindeer

Date	Mintage	MS-63	Proof
2010	—	17.50	—

KM# 1157   Silver

Date	Mintage	MS-63	Proof
1911-2011	—	—	45.00

KM# 1180 6.9000 g. Nickel Plated Steel 27.13 mm.   **Obv:** Bust right **Rev:** Winnipeg Jets Logo, jet over maple leaf **Edge:** Reeded

Date	Mintage	MS-63	Proof
2011	—	15.00	—

KM# 1191 12.6100 g. Copper Plated Steel 35 mm.   **Obv:** Bust right **Rev:** Santa Claus checking list, and in sled over house

Date	Mintage	MS-63	Proof
2011	—	27.50	—

KM# 1202 1.2700 g. 0.9999 Gold 0.0408 oz. AGW 13.92 mm.   **Rev:** Wood Bison **Rev. Designer:** Corrine Hunt **Edge:** Reeded

Date	Mintage	MS-63	Proof
2011 Proof	Est. 2,500	—	100

KM# 1204 1.2700 g. 0.9999 Gold 0.0408 oz. AGW 13.92 mm.   **Subject:** Boreal Forest **Rev:** Bird and tree **Rev. Designer:** Corrine Hunt **Edge:** Reeded

Date	Mintage	MS-63	Proof
2011 Proof	Est. 2,500	—	100

KM# 1206 1.2700 g. 0.9999 Gold 0.0408 oz. AGW 13.92 mm.   **Rev:** Peregrine Falcon perched on branch **Rev. Designer:** Corrine Hunt

Date	Mintage	MS-63	Proof
2011 Proof	Est. 2,500	—	100

KM# 1208 1.2700 g. 0.9999 Gold 0.0408 oz. AGW 13.92 mm.   **Rev:** Orca Whale **Rev. Designer:** Corrine Hunt **Edge:** Reeded

Date	Mintage	MS-63	Proof
2011 Proof	Est. 2,500	—	100

DOLLAR

KM# 30 23.3276 g. 0.8000 Silver 0.6000 oz. ASW 36 mm.   **Subject:** Silver Jubilee **Obv:** Bust left **Obv. Designer:** Percy Metcalfe **Rev:** Voyager, date and denomination below **Rev. Designer:** Emanuel Hahn

Date	Mintage	F-12	VF-20	XF-40	AU-50	MS-60	MS-63	Proof
1935	428,707	23.00	27.00	35.00	40.00	45.00	70.00	4,500

KM# 31 23.3276 g. 0.8000 Silver 0.6000 oz. ASW 36 mm.   **Obv:** Crowned bust left **Obv. Designer:** E. B. MacKennal **Rev:** Voyageur, date and denomination below **Rev. Designer:** Emanuel Hahn

Date	Mintage	F-12	VF-20	XF-40	AU-50	MS-60	MS-63	Proof
1936	339,600	23.00	26.00	30.00	35.00	50.00	100.00	4,500

Pointed 7   Blunt 7

Maple leaf

KM# 37 23.3276 g. 0.8000 Silver 0.6000 oz. ASW 36 mm.   **Obv:** Head left **Obv. Designer:** T. H. Paget **Rev:** Voyageur, date and denomination below **Rev. Designer:** Emanuel Hahn

Date	Mintage	F-12	VF-20	XF-40	AU-50	MS-60	MS-63	Proof
1937	207,406	23.00	26.00	30.00	35.00	40.00	95.00	—
1937 Mirror Proof	1,295	—	—	—	—	—	—	1,050

Date	Mintage	F-12	VF-20	XF-40	AU-50	MS-60	MS-63	Proof
1937 Matte Proof	Inc. above	—	—	—	—	—	—	350
1938	90,304	35.00	45.00	70.00	85.00	100.00	250	8,000
1945	38,391	125	175	225	300	350	750	2,900
1946	93,055	26.00	40.00	55.00	70.00	100.00	400	2,400
1947 Pointed 7		80.00	125	175	200	400	2,000	4,500
1947 Blunt 7	65,595	60.00	90.00	125	150	175	400	5,000
1947 Maple leaf	21,135	150	200	225	300	400	800	2,900

KM# 38 23.3276 g. 0.8000 Silver 0.6000 oz. ASW 36 mm.   **Subject:** Royal Visit
Obv: Head left **Obv. Designer:** T. H. Paget **Rev:** Tower at center of building, date and denomination below **Rev. Designer:** Emanuel Hahn

Date	Mintage	F-12	VF-20	XF-40	AU-50	MS-60	MS-63	Proof
1939	1,363,816	—	—	BV	23.00	24.00	35.00	—
1939	—	—	—	—	—	—	—	800
Note: Matte specimen								
1939 Proof	—	—	—	—	—	—	—	1,350
Note: Mirror specimen								

KM# 46 23.3276 g. 0.8000 Silver 0.6000 oz. ASW 36 mm.   **Obv:** Head left, modified left legend **Obv. Designer:** T. H. Paget **Rev:** Voyageur, date and denomination below **Rev. Designer:** Emanuel Hahn

Date	Mintage	F-12	VF-20	XF-40	AU-50	MS-60	MS-63	Proof
1948	18,780	750	950	1,300	1,400	1,700	3,000	5,000
1950	261,002	—	23.00	24.00	25.00	30.00	75.00	1,800
Note: With 3 water lines								
1950 Matte Proof	—	—	—	—	—	—	—	—
Note: With 4 water lines, 1 known								
1950	Inc. above	23.00	28.00	35.00	40.00	55.00	125	2,600
Note: Arnprior with 2-1/2 water lines								
1951	416,395	—	—	BV	22.00	25.00	40.00	1,000
Note: With 3 water lines								

Date	Mintage	F-12	VF-20	XF-40	AU-50	MS-60	MS-63	Proof
1951	Inc. above	40.00	60.00	90.00	125	225	450	3,000
Note: Arnprior with 1-1/2 water lines								
1952	406,148	—	—	BV	22.00	24.00	35.00	1,500
Note: With 3 water lines								
1952	Inc. above	BV	23.00	30.00	35.00	55.00	100.00	1,900
Note: Short water links								
1952	Inc. above	—	BV	22.00	24.00	26.00	60.00	—
Note: Without water lines								

KM#47 23.3276 g. 0.8000 Silver 0.6000 oz. ASW 36 mm. **Subject:** Newfoundland **Obv:** Head left **Obv. Designer:** T. H. Paget **Rev:** "The Matthew", John Cabot's ship, date and denomination below **Rev. Designer:** Thomas Shingles

Date	Mintage	F-12	VF-20	XF-40	AU-50	MS-60	MS-63	Proof
1949	672,218	BV	23.00	25.00	27.50	30.00	35.00	400
1949 Proof	—	—	—	—	—	—	—	2,600

KM#54 23.3276 g. 0.8000 Silver 0.6000 oz. ASW 36 mm. **Obv:** Laureate bust right **Obv. Designer:** Mary Gillick **Rev:** Voyageur, date and denomination below **Rev. Designer:** Emanuel Hahn **Note:** All genuine circulation strike 1955 Arnprior dollars have a die break running along the top of TI in the word GRATIA on the obverse.

Date	Mintage	F-12	VF-20	XF-40	AU-50	MS-60	MS-63	Proof
1953	1,074,578	—	—	—	BV	23.00	30.00	1,600
Note: Without strap, wire rim								
1953	Inc. above	—	—	—	BV	23.00	30.00	—
Note: With strap, flat rim								
1954	246,606	—	BV	23.00	25.00	30.00	50.00	—
1955	268,105	—	BV	23.00	24.00	30.00	50.00	—
Note: With 3 water lines								
1955	Inc. above	85.00	95.00	100.00	125	150	300	—
Note: Arnprior with 1-1/2 water lines* and die break								

Date	Mintage	F-12	VF-20	XF-40	AU-50	MS-60	MS-63	Proof
1956	209,092	BV	22.00	24.00	26.00	35.00	85.00	—
1957	496,389	—	—	—	BV	23.00	26.00	—
Note: With 3 water lines								
1957	Inc. above	—	BV	24.00	26.00	28.00	50.00	—
Note: With 1 water line								
1959	1,443,502	—	—	—	—	BV	24.00	—
1960	1,420,486	—	—	—	—	BV	24.00	—
1961	1,262,231	—	—	—	—	BV	24.00	—
1962	1,884,789	—	—	—	—	BV	24.00	—
1963	4,179,981	—	—	—	—	BV	24.00	—

KM# 55 23.3276 g. 0.8000 Silver 0.6000 oz. ASW 36 mm.   **Subject:** British Columbia **Obv:** Laureate bust right **Obv. Designer:** Mary Gillick **Rev:** Totem Pole, dates at left, denomination below **Rev. Designer:** Stephan Trenka

Date	Mintage	F-12	VF-20	XF-40	AU-50	MS-60	MS-63	Proof
1858-1958	3,039,630	—	—	—	BV	23.00	26.00	—

KM# 58 23.3276 g. 0.8000 Silver 0.6000 oz. ASW 36 mm.   **Subject:** Charlottetown **Obv:** Laureate bust right **Rev:** Design at center, dates at outer edges, denomination below **Rev. Designer:** Dinko Voldanovic

Date	Mintage	F-12	VF-20	XF-40	AU-50	MS-60	MS-63	Proof
1864-1964	7,296,832	—	—	—	—	BV	24.00	—
1864-1964 Specimen proof	Inc. above	—	—	—	—	—	—	300

| Large beads | Medium beads | Small beads |

KM#64.1 23.3276 g. 0.8000 Silver 0.6000 oz. ASW 36 mm.   **Obv:** Young bust right **Obv. Designer:** Arnold Machin **Rev:** Voyageur, date and denomination below **Rev. Designer:** Emanual Hahn

Date	Mintage	F-12	VF-20	XF-40	AU-50	MS-60	MS-63	Proof
1965	10,768,569	—	—	—	—	BV	24.00	400
Note: Small beads, pointed 5								
1965	Inc. above	—	—	—	—	BV	24.00	400
Note: Small beads, blunt 5								
1965	Inc. above	—	—	—	—	BV	24.00	—
Note: Large beads, blunt 5								
1965	Inc. above	—	—	—	BV	23.00	28.00	—
Note: Large beads, pointed 5								
1965	Inc. above	—	—	BV	23.00	26.00	45.00	—
Note: Medium beads, pointed 5								
1966	9,912,178	—	—	—	—	BV	24.00	—
Note: Large beads								
1966	485	—	—	2,400	2,600	2,900	4,000	—
Note: Small beads								

KM#70 23.3280 g. 0.8000 Silver 0.6000 oz. ASW 36 mm.   **Subject:** Confederation Centennial **Obv:** Young bust right **Obv. Designer:** Arnold Machin **Rev:** Goose left, dates below, denomination above **Rev. Designer:** Alex Colville

Date	Mintage	MS-63	Proof
1867-1967	6,767,496	24.00	24.00

KM# 76.1 15.6400 g. Nickel 32 mm.
Obv: Young bust right **Obv. Designer:**
Arnold Machin **Rev:** Voyageur, date
and denomination below **Rev.**
Designer: Emanuel Hahn

Date	Mintage	MS-63	P/L	Proof
1968 Small island	—	10.00	7.50	—
1968	1,408,143	2.50	1.75	—
1968 No Island	—	12.00	4.50	—
1968	—	—	30.00	—
Note: Doubled die; exhibits extra water lines				
1968	5,579,714	2.00	—	—
1969	4,809,313	2.50	—	—
1969	594,258	—	1.75	125
1972	2,676,041	3.50	—	—
1972	405,865	—	2.25	—

KM# 78 15.6000 g. Nickel 32 mm.
Subject: Manitoba **Obv:** Young bust
right **Rev:** Pasque flower divides dates
and denomination **Rev. Designer:**
Raymond Taylor

Date	Mintage	MS-63	P/L	Proof
1870-1970	4,140,058	3.50	—	—
1870-1970	645,869	—	2.25	80.00

KM# 79 15.7000 g. Nickel 32.1 mm.
Subject: British Columbia **Obv:** Young
bust right **Rev:** Shield divides dates,
denomination below, flowers above
Rev. Designer: Thomas Shingles

Date	Mintage	MS-63	P/L	Proof
1871-1971	4,260,781	3.50	—	—
1871-1971	468,729	—	2.25	125

KM# 80 23.3276 g. 0.5000 Silver
0.3750 oz. ASW 36 mm.   **Subject:**
British Columbia **Obv:** Young bust
right **Rev:** Crowned arms with
supporters divide dates, maple at top
divides denomination, crowned lion
atop crown on shield **Rev. Designer:**
Patrick Brindley

Date	Mintage	MS-63	P/L	Proof
1871-1971 Specimen	585,674	—	13.00	—

KM# 64.2a 23.3276 g. 0.5000 Silver
0.3750 oz. ASW 36 mm.   **Obv:** Smaller
young bust right **Obv. Designer:**
Arnold Machin **Rev:** Voyageur **Rev.**
Designer: Emanuel Hahn

Date	Mintage	MS-63	P/L	Proof
1972 Specimen	341,598	—	12.00	—
1972 Proof	Inc. above	—	—	14.00

KM# 82 Nickel 32 mm. **Subject:**
Prince Edward Island **Obv:** Young bust
right **Rev:** Building, inscription below
divides dates, denomination above
Rev. Designer: Terry Manning

Date	Mintage	MS-63	P/L	Proof
1873-1973	3,196,452	2.00	—	—
1873-1973 (c)	466,881	—	2.50	—

KM# 83 23.3276 g. 0.5000 Silver
0.3750 oz. ASW 36 mm. **Obv:** Young
bust right **Rev:** Mountie left, dates
below, denomination at right **Rev.
Designer:** Paul Cedarberg

Date	Mintage	MS-63	P/L	Proof
1873-1973 Specimen	1,031,271	—	14.00	—
1873-1973 Specimen	—	—	25.00	—

Note: Dollar housed in special blue case with
RCMP crest.

KM# 88 Nickel 32 mm. **Subject:**
Winnipeg Centennial **Obv:** Young bust
right **Rev:** Zeros frame pictures, dates
below, denomination at bottom **Rev.
Designer:** Paul Pederson and Patrick
Brindley

Date	Mintage	MS-63	P/L	Proof
1874-1974	2,799,363	2.00	—	—
1874-1974 (c)	363,786	—	2.50	—

KM# 88a 23.3276 g. 0.5000 Silver
0.3750 oz. ASW 36 mm. **Subject:**
Winnipeg Centennial **Obv:** Young bust
right **Rev:** Zeros frame pictures, dates
below, denomination at bottom **Rev.
Designer:** Paul Pederson and Patrick
Brindley

Date	Mintage	MS-63	P/L	Proof
1974-1974 Specimen	728,947	—	14.00	—

KM# 76.2 15.6200 g. Nickel 32 mm.
Obv: Smaller young bust right **Obv.
Designer:** Arnold Machin **Rev:**
Voyageur **Rev. Designer:** Emanuel
Hahn

Date	Mintage	MS-63	P/L	Proof
1975	3,256,000	1.50	—	—
1975	322,325	—	2.50	—
1976	2,498,204	1.50	—	—
1976	274,106	—	2.50	—

KM# 97 23.3276 g. 0.5000 Silver
0.3750 oz. ASW 36 mm. **Subject:**
Calgary **Obv:** Youmg bust right **Rev:**
Figure on bucking horse, dates divided

below, denomination above **Rev.**
Designer: Donald D. Paterson

Date	Mintage	MS-63	P/L	Proof
1875-1975 Specimen	930,956	—	14.00	—

KM# 76.3 Nickel 32 mm. **Obv:**
Young bust right **Obv. Designer:**
Arnold Machin **Rev:** Voyageur **Rev.**
Designer: Emanuel Hahn **Note:** Only
known in prooflike sets with 1976
obverse slightly modified.

Date	Mintage	MS-63	P/L	Proof
1975	Inc. above	—	3.00	—

Note: mule with 1976 obv.

KM# 106 23.3276 g. 0.5000 Silver
0.3750 oz. ASW 36 mm. **Subject:**
Parliament Library **Obv:** Young bust
right **Rev:** Library building, dates
below, denomination above **Rev.**
Designer: Walter Ott and Patrick
Brindley

Date	Mintage	MS-63	P/L	Proof
1876-1976 Specimen	578,708	—	14.00	—
1876-1976 Proof	Inc. above	—	—	25.00

Note: Blue case VIP

KM#117 Nickel 32 mm. **Obv:** Young
bust right **Obv. Designer:** Arnold

Machin **Rev:** Voyageur modified **Rev.**
Designer: Emanuel Hahn

Date	Mintage	MS-63	P/L	Proof
1977	1,393,745	3.50	—	—
1977	—	—	4.00	—

KM# 118 23.3276 g. 0.5000 Silver
0.3750 oz. ASW 36 mm. **Subject:**
Silver Jubilee **Obv:** Young bust right,
dates below **Rev:** Throne,
denomination below **Rev. Designer:**
Raymond Lee

Date	Mintage	MS-63	P/L	Proof
1952-1977 Specimen	744,848	—	14.00	—
1952-1977 Specimen	Inc. above	—	45.00	—

Note: red case VIP

KM# 120.1 15.5000 g. Nickel
32.1 mm. **Obv:** Young bust right
Obv. Designer: Arnold Machin **Rev:**

Voyageur, date and denomination below **Rev. Designer:** Emanuel Hahn **Note:** Modified design.

Date	Mintage	MS-63	Proof
1978	2,948,488	1.50	—
1979	2,954,842	1.50	—
1980	3,291,221	1.50	—
1981	2,778,900	1.50	—
1981 Proof	—	—	5.25
1982	1,098,500	1.50	—
1982 Proof	180,908	—	5.25
1983	2,267,525	1.50	—
1983 Proof	166,779	—	5.25
1984	1,223,486	1.50	—
1984 Proof	161,602	—	6.00
1985	3,104,092	1.50	—
1985 Proof	153,950	—	7.00
1986	3,089,225	2.00	—
1986 Proof	176,224	—	7.50
1987	287,330	3.50	—
1987 Proof	175,686	—	7.50

KM# 124 23.3276 g. 0.5000 Silver 0.3750 oz. ASW 36 mm.   **Subject:** Griffon **Obv:** Young bust right **Rev:** Ship, dates below, denomination above **Rev. Designer:** Walter Schluep

Date	Mintage	MS-63	P/L	Proof
1979 Specimen	826,695	—	14.00	—

KM# 121 23.3276 g. 0.5000 Silver 0.3750 oz. ASW 36 mm.   **Subject:** XI Commonwealth Games **Obv:** Young bust right **Rev:** Commonwealth games, logo at center **Rev. Designer:** Raymond Taylor

Date	Mintage	MS-63	P/L	Proof
1978 Specimen	709,602	—	14.00	—

KM# 128 23.3276 g. 0.5000 Silver 0.3750 oz. ASW 36 mm.   **Subject:** Arctic Territories **Obv:** Young bust right **Rev:** Bear right, date below, denomination above **Rev. Designer:** Donald D. Paterson

Date	Mintage	MS-63	P/L	Proof
1980 Specimen	539,617	—	22.00	—

KM# 130 23.3276 g. 0.5000 Silver 0.3750 oz. ASW 36 mm.   **Subject:**

Transcontinental Railroad **Obv:** Young bust right **Rev:** Train engine and map, date below, denomination above **Rev. Designer:** Christopher Gorey

Date	Mintage	MS-63	P/L	Proof
1981	699,494	14.00	—	—
1981 Proof	—	—	—	14.00

KM# 133 23.3276 g. 0.5000 Silver 0.3750 oz. ASW 36 mm.   **Subject:** Regina **Obv:** Young bust right **Rev:** Cattle skull divides dates and denomination below **Rev. Designer:** Huntley Brown

Date	Mintage	MS-63	Proof
1882-1982	144,930	14.00	—
1882-1982 Proof	758,958	—	14.00

KM# 134 15.4200 g. Nickel 32 mm. **Subject:** Constitution **Obv:** Young bust right **Rev:** Meeting of Government **Rev. Designer:** Ago Aarand

Date	Mintage	MS-63	P/L	Proof
1867-1982	9,709,422	3.00	6.00	—

KM# 138 23.3276 g. 0.5000 Silver 0.3750 oz. ASW 36 mm.   **Subject:** Edmonton University Games **Obv:** Young bust right **Rev:** Athlete within game logo, date and denomination below **Rev. Designer:** Carola Tietz

Date	Mintage	MS-63	Proof
1983	159,450	14.00	—
1983 Proof	506,847	—	14.00

KM# 140 23.3276 g. 0.5000 Silver 0.3750 oz. ASW 36 mm.   **Subject:** Toronto Sesquicentennial **Obv:** Young bust right **Rev. Designer:** D. J. Craig

Date	Mintage	MS-63	Proof
1984	133,610	14.00	—
1984 Proof	732,542	—	14.00

KM# 141 15.5000 g. Nickel 32 mm. **Subject:** Jacques Cartier **Obv:** Young bust right **Rev:** Cross with shield above figures **Rev. Designer:** Hector Greville

Date	Mintage	MS-63	Proof
1534-1984	7,009,323	3.50	—
1534-1984 Proof	87,760	—	6.00

KM# 143 23.3276 g. 0.5000 Silver 0.3750 oz. ASW 36 mm.   **Subject:** National Parks **Obv:** Young bust right **Rev:** Moose right, dates above, denomination below **Rev. Designer:** Karel Rohlicek

Date	Mintage	MS-63	Proof
1885-1985	163,314	14.00	—
1885-1985 Proof	733,354	—	14.00

KM# 120.2 Nickel 32.13 mm.   **Obv:** Young bust right **Rev:** Voyageur **Note:** Mule with New Zealand 50 cent, KM-37 obverse.

Date	Mintage	MS-63	Proof
1985	—	3,000	—

KM# 157 7.0000 g. Aureate-Bronze Plated Nickel 26.5 mm.   **Obv:** Young bust right **Obv. Designer:** Arnold Machin **Rev:** Loon right, date and denomination below **Rev. Designer:** Robert R. Carmichael **Shape:** 11-sided

Date	Mintage	MS-63	Proof
1987	205,405,000	2.25	—
1987 Proof	178,120	—	8.00
1988	138,893,539	2.25	—
1988 Proof	175,259	—	6.75
1989	184,773,902	3.00	—
1989 Proof	170,928	—	6.75

KM# 149 23.3276 g. 0.5000 Silver 0.3750 oz. ASW 36 mm.   **Subject:** Vancouver **Obv:** Young bust right **Rev:** Train left, dates divided below, denomination above **Rev. Designer:** Elliot John Morrison

Date	Mintage	MS-63	Proof
1886-1986	125,949	14.00	—
1886-1986 Proof	680,004	—	14.00

KM# 154 23.3276 g. 0.5000 Silver 0.3750 oz. ASW 36 mm.   **Subject:** John Davis **Obv:** Young bust right **Rev:** Ship "John Davis" with masts, rock in background, dates below, denomination at bottom **Rev. Designer:** Christopher Gorey

Date	Mintage	MS-63	Proof
1587-1987	118,722	14.00	—
1587-1987 Proof	602,374	—	14.00

KM# 161 23.3276 g. 0.5000 Silver 0.3750 oz. ASW 36 mm.   **Subject:** Ironworks **Obv:** Young bust right **Rev:** Ironworkers, date and denomination below **Rev. Designer:** Robert R. Carmichael

Date	Mintage	MS-63	Proof
1988	106,872	14.00	—
1988 Proof	255,013	—	17.50

KM# 168 23.3276 g. 0.5000 Silver 0.3750 oz. ASW 36 mm.   **Subject:** MacKenzie River **Obv:** Young bust right **Rev:** People in canoe, date above, denomination below **Rev. Designer:** John Mardon

Date	Mintage	MS-63	Proof
1989	99,774	14.00	—
1989 Proof	244,062	—	17.50

KM# 186 7.0000 g. Aureate-Bronze Plated Nickel 26.5 mm.   **Obv:** Crowned head right **Obv. Designer:**

Dora dePedery-Hunt **Rev:** Loon right, date and denomination **Rev. Designer:** Robert R. Carmichael **Shape:** 11-sided

Date	Mintage	MS-63	Proof
1990	68,402,000	1.75	—
1990 Proof	140,649	—	7.00
1991	23,156,000	1.75	—
1991 Proof	131,888	—	13.00
1993	33,662,000	2.00	—
1993 Proof	143,065	—	6.00
1994	16,232,530	2.00	—
1994 Proof	104,485	—	7.00
1995	27,492,630	2.25	—
1995 Proof	101,560	—	7.00
1996	17,101,000	2.00	—
1996 Proof	112,835	—	7.50
1997	—	5.00	—
1997 Proof	113,647	—	8.00
1998	—	2.50	—
1998W Prooflike	—	—	—
1998 Proof	93,632	—	10.00
1999	—	2.00	—
1999 Proof	95,113	—	8.00
2000	—	2.00	—
2000W Prooflike	—	—	—
2000 Proof	90,921	—	8.00
2001	—	2.50	—
2001 Proof	74,194	—	8.00
2002	—	4.50	—
2002 Proof	65,315	—	7.50
2003	—	5.50	—

Note: Mintage of 5,101,000 includes both KM186 and KM495 examples.

2003 Proof	—	—	12.00

KM# 170 23.3276 g. 0.5000 Silver

0.3750 oz. ASW 36 mm. **Subject:** Henry Kelsey **Obv:** Crowned head right **Rev:** Kelsey with natives, dates below, denomination above **Rev. Designer:** D. J. Craig

Date	Mintage	MS-63	Proof
1690-1990	99,455	14.00	—
1690-1990 Proof	254,959	—	20.00

KM# 179 23.3276 g. 0.5000 Silver 0.3750 oz. ASW 36 mm. **Subject:** S.S. Frontenac **Obv:** Crowned head right **Rev:** Ship,"Frontenac," date and denomination below, **Rev. Designer:** D. J. Craig

Date	Mintage	MS-63	Proof
1991	73,843	14.00	—
1991 Proof	195,424	—	25.00

KM# 210 25.1750 g. 0.9250 Silver 0.7487 oz. ASW 36 mm. **Subject:** Stagecoach service **Obv:** Crowned head right **Rev:** Stagecoach, date and denomination below **Rev. Designer:** Karsten Smith

Date	Mintage	MS-63	Proof
1992	78,160	25.00	—
1992 Proof	187,612	—	25.00

KM# 209 Aureate 26.5 mm. **Subject:** Loon right, dates and denomination **Obv:** Crowned head right **Rev. Designer:** Robert R. Carmichael

Date	Mintage	MS-63	Proof
1867-1992	4,242,085	2.00	—
1867-1992 Proof	147,061	—	8.00

KM# 218 Aureate 26 mm. **Subject:** Parliament **Obv:** Crowned head right, dates below **Rev:** Backs of three seated figures in front of building, denomination below **Rev. Designer:** Rita Swanson

Date	Mintage	MS-63	Proof
1867-1992	23,915,000	2.25	—
1867-1992 Proof	24,227	—	9.00

KM# 235 25.1750 g. 0.9250 Silver 0.7487 oz. ASW 36 mm. **Subject:** Stanley Cup hockey **Obv:** Crowned head right **Rev:** Hockey players between cups, dates below, denomination above **Rev. Designer:** Stewart Sherwood

Date	Mintage	MS-63	Proof
1993	88,150	25.00	—
1993 Proof	294,314	—	25.00

KM# 248 7.0000 g. Aureate Bronze 26 mm. **Subject:** War Memorial **Obv:** Crowned head right, date below **Rev:** Memorial, denomination at right **Rev. Designer:** R. C. M. Staff

Date	Mintage	MS-63	Proof
1994	20,004,830	2.25	—
1994 Proof	54,524	—	7.50

KM# 251 25.1750 g. 0.9250 Silver 0.7487 oz. ASW 36 mm. **Subject:** Last RCMP sled-dog patrol **Obv:** Crowned head right **Rev:** Dogsled, denomination divides dates below **Rev. Designer:** Ian Sparks

Date	Mintage	MS-63	Proof
1969-1994	61,561	25.00	—
1969-1994 Proof	170,374	—	25.00

KM# 258 7.0000 g. Aureate 26 mm. **Subject:** Peacekeeping Monument in Ottawa **Obv:** Crowned head right, date below **Rev:** Monument, denomination above right **Rev. Designer:** J. K. Harmon, R. G. Henriquez and C. H.

Oberlander **Note:** Mintage included with KM#186.

Date	Mintage	MS-63	Proof
1995	18,502,750	2.25	—
1995 Proof	43,293	—	7.50

KM# 259 25.1750 g. 0.9250 Silver 0.7487 oz. ASW 36 mm. **Subject:** Hudson Bay Company **Obv:** Crowned head right **Rev:** Explorers and ship, date and denomination below **Rev. Designer:** Vincent McIndoe

Date	Mintage	MS-63	Proof
1995	61,819	25.00	—
1995 Proof	166,259	—	30.00

KM# 274 25.1750 g. 0.9250 Silver 0.7487 oz. ASW 36 mm. **Subject:** McIntosh Apple **Obv:** Crowned head right **Rev:** Apple, dates and denomination below **Rev. Designer:** Roger Hill

Date	Mintage	MS-63	Proof
1796-1996	58,834	25.00	—
1796-1996 Proof	133,779	—	25.00

KM# 282 25.1750 g. 0.9250 Silver 0.7487 oz. ASW 36 mm. **Subject:** 25th Anniversary Hockey Victory **Obv:** Crowned head right **Rev:** The winning goal by Paul Aenderson. Based on a painting by Andre l'Archeveque, dates at right, denomination at bottom **Rev. Designer:** Walter Burden

Date	Mintage	MS-63	Proof
1972-1997	155,252	25.00	—
1972-1997 Proof	184,965	—	30.00

KM# 291 7.0000 g. Aureate Bronze 26 mm. **Subject:** Loon Dollar 10th Anniversary **Obv:** Crowned head right **Rev:** Loon in flight left, dates above, denomination below **Rev. Designer:** Jean-Luc Grondin

Date	Mintage	MS-63	P/L	Proof
1987-1997	—	—	22.00	—

KM# 296 25.1750 g. 0.9250 Silver 0.7487 oz. ASW 36 mm. **Subject:**

Loon Dollar 10th Anniversary **Obv:** Crowned head right **Rev:** Loon in flight left, dates above, denomination below **Rev. Designer:** Jean-Luc Grondin

Date	Mintage	MS-63	Proof
1987-1997 Proof	24,995	—	95.00

KM# 306 25.1750 g. 0.9250 Silver 0.7487 oz. ASW 36 mm. **Subject:** 120th Anniversary Royal Canadian Mounted Police **Obv:** Crowned head right **Rev:** Mountie on horseback, dates at left, denomination above **Rev. Designer:** Adeline Halvorson **Note:** Individually cased prooflikes, proofs or specimens are from broken-up prooflike or specimen sets.

Date	Mintage	MS-63	P/L	Proof
1873-1998	79,777	—	25.00	—
1873-1998 Proof	120,172	—	—	35.00

KM# 355 25.1750 g. 0.9250 Silver 0.7487 oz. ASW 36 mm. **Subject:** International Year of Old Persons **Obv:** Crowned head right **Rev:** Figures amid trees, date and denomination below **Rev. Designer:** S. Armstrong-Hodgson

Date	Mintage	MS-63	Proof
1999 Proof	24,976	—	40.00

KM# 356 25.1750 g. 0.9250 Silver 0.7487 oz. ASW 36 mm.   **Subject:** Discovery of Queen Charlotte Isle **Obv:** Crowned head right **Rev:** Ship and three boats, dates at right, denomination below **Rev. Designer:** D. J. Craig

Date	Mintage	MS-63	P/L	Proof
1999	67,655	—	25.00	—
1999 Proof	126,435	—	—	35.00

KM# 414 25.1750 g. 0.9250 Silver 0.7487 oz. ASW 36 mm.   **Subject:** National Ballet **Obv:** Crowned head right **Rev:** Ballet dancers **Rev. Designer:** Scott McKowen **Edge:** Reeded

Date	Mintage	MS-63	Proof
2001	65,000	27.50	—
2001 Proof	225,000	—	35.00

KM# 401 25.1750 g. 0.9250 Silver 0.7487 oz. ASW 36 mm.   **Subject:** Voyage of Discovery **Obv:** Crowned head right **Rev:** Human and space shuttle, date above, denomination below **Rev. Designer:** D. F. Warkentine

Date	Mintage	MS-63	P/L	Proof
2000	60,100	—	25.00	—
2000 Proof	114,130	—	—	30.00

KM# 434 25.1750 g. 0.9250 Silver 0.7487 oz. ASW 36 mm.   **Obv:** Crowned head right **Rev:** Recycled 1911 pattern dollar design: denomination, country name and dates in crowned wreath **Edge:** Reeded

Date	Mintage	MS-63	Proof
1911-2001 Proof	24,996	—	55.00

KM#186a Gilt Aureate-Bronze Plated Nickel 26.5 mm.   **Subject:** Olympic Win

Date	Mintage	MS-63	Proof
2002 Proof	—	—	40.00

KM# 443 25.1750 g. 0.9250 Silver 0.7487 oz. ASW 36 mm.   **Subject:** Queen's Golden Jubilee **Obv:** Crowned head right, with anniversary date at left **Obv. Designer:** Dora dePédery-Hunt **Rev:** Queen in her coach and a view of the coach, denomination below **Edge:** Reeded

Date	Mintage	MS-63	Proof
1952-2002	65,140	28.50	—
1952-2002 Proof	29,688	—	40.00

KM# 443a 25.1800 g. 0.9250 Silver Gilt 0.7488 oz. ASW 36 mm.   **Subject:** Queen's Golden Jubilee **Obv:** Crowned head right with anniversary date **Rev:** Queen in her coach and a view of the coach **Edge:** Reeded **Note:** Special 24 karat gold plated issue of KM#443.

Date	Mintage	MS-63	Proof
2002 Proof	32,642	—	45.00

KM# 462 7.0000 g. Aureate-Bronze Plated Nickel   **Obv:** Commemorative dates 1952-2002 **Obv. Designer:** Dora dePédery-Hunt **Rev:** Family of Loons

Date	Mintage	MS-63	Proof
2002 Specimen	67,672	—	35.00

KM# 467 7.0000 g. Aureate-Bronze Plated Nickel   **Subject:** Elizabeth II Golden Jubilee **Obv:** Crowned head right, Jubilee commemorative dates 1952-2002 **Obv. Designer:** Dora dePédery-Hunt

Date	Mintage	MS-63	Proof
2002	2,302,000	2.50	—
2002 Proof	—	—	8.00

KM# 467a Gold **Subject:** 50th Anniversary, Accession to the Throne **Obv:** Crowned head right **Note:** Sold on the internet.

Date	Mintage	MS-63	Proof
2002	1	—	55,500

KM# 503 25.1750 g. 0.9250 Silver 0.7487 oz. ASW 36 mm.   **Subject:** Queen Mother **Obv:** Crowned head right **Obv. Designer:** Dora de Pedery-Hunt **Rev:** Queen Mother facing

Date	Mintage	MS-63	Proof
2002 Proof	9,994	—	250

KM# 450 25.1750 g. 0.9999 Silver 0.8093 oz. ASW 36 mm.   **Subject:** Cobalt Mining Centennial **Obv:** Queens portrait right **Obv. Designer:** Dora dePédery-Hunt **Rev:** Mine tower and fox **Edge:** Reeded

Date	Mintage	MS-63	Proof
2003	51,130	30.00	—
2003 Proof	88,536	—	45.00

KM# 495 7.0000 g. Aureate-Bronze Plated Nickel 26.5 mm.   **Obv:** Bare head right **Obv. Designer:** Susanna Blunt **Rev:** Loon right **Rev. Designer:** Robert R. Carmichael **Shape:** 11-sided

Date	Mintage	MS-63	Proof
2003	5,102,000	5.50	—

Note: Mintage of 5,101,000 includes both KM 186 and 495 examples.

Date	Mintage	MS-63	Proof
2003W Prooflike	—	—	—
2003 Proof	62,507	—	7.50
2004	10,894,000	1.75	—
2004 Proof	—	—	12.00
2005	44,375,000	3.00	—
2005 Proof	—	—	7.50
2006	49,111,000	3.00	—
2006 Proof	—	—	7.50
2006(ml)	49,111,000	3.00	—

Date	Mintage	MS-63	Proof
2006(ml) Proof	—	—	7.50
2007(ml)	38,045,000	3.00	—
2007(ml) Proof	—	—	7.50
2008(ml)	29,561,000	3.00	—
2008(ml) Proof	—	—	7.50
2009(ml)	39,601,000	3.00	—
2009(ml) Proof	—	—	7.50
2010(ml)	—	3.00	—
2010(ml) Proof	—	—	7.50
2011(ml)	—	3.00	—
2011(ml) Proof	—	—	7.50
2012(ml)	—	3.00	—
2012(ml) Proof	—	—	7.50

KM# 473 25.1750 g. 0.9999 Silver 0.8093 oz. ASW **Subject:** 50th Anniversary of the Coronation of Elizabeth II **Obv:** 1953 effigy of the Queen, Jubilee dates 1953-2003 **Obv. Designer:** Mary Gillick **Rev:** Voyageur, date and denomination below

Date	Mintage	MS-63	Proof
1953-2003 Proof	21,537	—	45.00

KM# 480 25.1750 g. 0.9999 Silver 0.8093 oz. ASW **Subject:** Coronation of Queen Elizabeth II **Obv:** Head right **Rev:** Voyaguers **Rev. Designer:** Emanuel Hahn

Date	Mintage	MS-63	Proof
1953-2003 Proof	29,586	—	50.00

KM# 480a Gold **Subject:** 50th Anniversary of Coronation **Obv. Designer:** Mary Gilick **Rev:** Voyageur **Note:** Sold on the internet.

Date	Mintage	MS-63	Proof
1953-2003	1	—	62,750

KM# 507 7.0000 g. Aureate-Bronze Plated Nickel 26.5 mm. **Obv:** Bare head right, date below **Obv. Designer:** Susanna Blunt **Rev:** Loon **Edge:** Plain **Shape:** 11-sided

Date	Mintage	MS-63	Proof
2004 Proof	25,105	—	75.00

KM# 512 25.1750 g. 0.9999 Silver 0.8093 oz. ASW 36 mm. **Subject:** First French Settlement in America **Obv:** Crowned head right **Rev:** Sailing ship **Edge:** Reeded

Date	Mintage	MS-63	Proof
2004	42,582	30.00	—
2004 Fleur-dis-lis privy mark	8,315	60.00	—
2004 Proof	106,974	—	50.00

KM# 513 7.0000 g. Aureate-Bronze Plated Nickel 26.5 mm. **Subject:** Olympics **Obv:** Bare head right **Rev:** Maple leaf, Olympic flame and rings above loon **Edge:** Plain **Shape:** 11-sided

Date	Mintage	MS-63	Proof
2004	6,526,000	8.00	—

KM# 513a 9.3100 g. 0.9250 Silver 0.2769 oz. ASW 26.5 mm. **Subject:** Olympics **Obv:** Bare head right **Rev:** Multicolor maple leaf, Olympic flame and rings above loon **Edge:** Plain **Shape:** 11-sided

Date	Mintage	MS-63	Proof
2004 Proof	19,994	—	50.00

KM# 549 25.1750 g. 0.9250 Silver 0.7487 oz. ASW 36.07 mm. **Subject:** 40th Anniversary of National Flag **Obv:** Head right **Obv. Designer:** Susanna Blunt **Rev. Designer:** William Woodruff

Date	Mintage	MS-63	Proof
2005	50,948	27.50	—
2005 Proof	95,431	—	40.00

KM# 549a 25.1750 g. 0.9250 Silver 0.7487 oz. ASW partially gilt 36.07 mm.   **Subject:** 40th Anniversary of National Flag **Obv:** Head right

Date	Mintage	MS-63	Proof
2005	62,562	75.00	—

KM# 549b 25.1800 g. 0.9250 Silver 0.7488 oz. ASW 36.07 mm.   **Subject:** 40th Anniversary National Flag **Rev:** National flag, colorized

Date	Mintage	MS-63	Proof
2005 Proof	4,898	—	350

KM# 552 7.0000 g. Aureate-Bronze Plated Nickel 26.5 mm.   **Subject:** Terry Fox **Obv:** Head right

Date	Mintage	MS-63	Proof
2005	1,290,900	3.50	—

KM# 553 7.0000 g. Aureate-Bronze Plated Nickel   **Subject:** Tuffed Puffin **Obv:** Head right **Obv. Designer:** Susanna Blunt

Date	Mintage	MS-63	Proof
2005	39,818	—	30.00

KM# 581 9.3100 g. 0.9250 Silver 0.2769 oz. ASW   **Subject:** Lullabies Loonie **Obv:** Head right **Obv. Designer:** Susanna Blunt **Rev:** Loon and moon, teddy bear in stars

Date	Mintage	MS-63	Proof
2006	18,103	4.50	—

KM# 582 7.0000 g. Aureate-Bronze Plated Nickel 26.5 mm.   **Subject:** Snowy owl **Obv:** Head right **Obv. Designer:** Susanna Blunt **Rev:** Snowy owl with year above

Date	Mintage	MS-63	Proof
2006 Specimen	39,935	—	30.00

KM# 583 25.1750 g. 0.9250 Silver 0.7487 oz. ASW 36 mm.   **Obv:** Head right **Rev:** Victoria Cross

Date	Mintage	MS-63	Proof
2006	27,254	25.00	—
2006 Proof	53,822	—	45.00

KM# 583a 25.1750 g. 0.9250 Silver 0.7487 oz. ASW partially gilt 36 mm. **Obv:** Head right **Rev:** Victoria Cross gilt

Date	Mintage	MS-63	Proof
2006 Proof	53,822	—	75.00

KM# 630 9.3100 g. 0.9250 Silver 0.2769 oz. ASW with enamel **Subject:** Olympic Games **Obv:** Crowned head right **Rev:** Loon in flight, colored olympic logo above

Date	Mintage	MS-63	Proof
2006	19,956	30.00	—

KM# 654 7.0000 g. 0.9250 Silver 0.2082 oz. ASW   **Obv:** Head right

Rev: Snowflake, colorized **Note:** Sold in a CD package.

Date	Mintage	MS-63	Proof
2006(ml)	34,014	35.00	—

KM# 655 7.0000 g. 0.9250 Silver 0.2082 oz. ASW **Subject:** Baby Rattle **Obv:** Head right **Rev:** Baby rattle

Date	Mintage	MS-63	Proof
2006	3,207	20.00	—

KM# 655a 7.0000 g. 0.9250 Silver 0.2082 oz. ASW **Obv:** Bust right **Rev:** Baby Rattle, partially gilt

Date	Mintage	MS-63	Proof
2006	1,911	15.00	—

KM# 688 7.0000 g. Aureate Bronze 26.5 mm. **Obv:** Head right **Rev:** Trumpeter Swan

Date	Mintage	MS-63	Proof
2007(ml)	40,000	20.00	—

KM# 656 28.1750 g. 0.9250 Silver 0.8379 oz. ASW **Subject:** Medal of Bravery **Obv:** Head right

Date	Mintage	MS-63	Proof
2006 Proof	8,343	—	50.00

KM# 653 25.1750 g. 0.9250 Silver 0.7487 oz. ASW 36.07 mm. **Subject:** Thayendanegea **Obv:** Head right **Rev:** Bust 3/4 facing right

Date	Mintage	MS-63	Proof
2007	16,378	30.00	—
2007 Proof	—	—	40.00

KM# 700 7.0000 g. 0.9250 Silver 0.2082 oz. ASW **Rev:** Alphabet Letter Blocks

Date	Mintage	MS-63	Proof
2007	3,207	—	25.00

KM# 656a 28.1750 g. 0.9250 Silver 0.8379 oz. ASW with multicolor enamel **Subject:** Medal of Bravery **Obv:** Head right **Rev:** Maple leaf within wreath. Colorized.

Date	Mintage	MS-63	Proof
2006 Proof	4,999	—	150

KM# 719 25.1800 g. 0.9250 Silver 0.7488 oz. ASW 36.07 mm. **Subject:** Celebration of the Arts **Rev:** Book, TV set, musical instruments, film montage

Rev. Designer: Friedrich Peter **Edge:** Reeded

Date	Mintage	MS-63	Proof
2007	6,466	—	55.00

KM# A727 7.0000 g. Aureate Bronze 26.5 mm. **Subject:** Vancouver Olympic Games **Rev:** Loon splashing in water, Olympics logo at right

Date	Mintage	MS-63	Proof
2007(ml)	19,973	3.00	—

KM# 767 25.1800 g. 0.9250 Silver 0.7488 oz. ASW 36.07 mm. **Rev:** Poppy at center of large maple leaf

Date	Mintage	MS-63	Proof
2008 Proof	—	—	50.00

KM# 781 25.1800 g. 0.9250 Silver 0.7488 oz. ASW partially gilt 36.07 mm. **Subject:** Ottawa Mint Centennial 1908-2008 **Rev:** Maple leaf transforming into a common loon, gilt rim and 100 **Rev. Designer:** Jason Bowman

Date	Mintage	MS-63	Proof
2008 Proof	15,000	—	65.00

KM# 784 7.0000 g. Nickel-Bronze 26.5 mm. **Rev:** Common elder

Date	Mintage	MS-63	Proof
2008 Specimen	21,227	—	50.00

KM# 785 25.1800 g. 0.9250 Silver 0.7488 oz. ASW 36.07 mm. **Subject:** Founding of Quebec 400th Anniversary **Rev:** Samuel de Champlain, ship and town view **Rev. Designer:** Susanne Duranceau

Date	Mintage	MS-63	Proof
2008	35,000	25.00	—
2008 Proof	65,000	—	40.00

KM# 785a 25.1800 g. 0.9250 Silver 0.7488 oz. ASW partially gilt. 36.07 mm. **Subject:** Founding of Quebec 400th Anniversary **Rev:** Samuel de Champlain selectively gold plated, ship, town view **Rev. Designer:** Susanne Duranceau

Date	Mintage	MS-63	Proof
2008 Proof	38,630	—	75.00

KM# 787 7.0000 g. Nickel-Bronze 26.5 mm. **Subject:** Lucky Loonie **Rev:** Loon splashing and Olympic logo at right **Rev. Designer:** Steve Hepurn

Date	Mintage	MS-63	Proof
2008	—	20.00	—

KM# 787a 9.3100 g. 0.9250 Silver 0.2769 oz. ASW 26.5 mm. **Rev:** Loon splashing with Olympic logo and maple leaf in color above **Rev. Designer:** Steve Hepurn

Date	Mintage	MS-63	Proof
2008 Proof	52,987	—	25.00

KM# 791 6.5000 g. Nickel 26.5 mm. **Rev:** Edmonton Oilers

Date	Mintage	MS-63	Proof
2008	—	25.00	—

KM# 792 6.5000 g. Nickel 26.5 mm. **Rev:** Montreal Canadiens

Date	Mintage	MS-63	Proof
2008	—	25.00	—

KM# 793 6.5000 g. Nickel 26.5 mm. **Rev:** Ottawa Senators

Date	Mintage	MS-63	Proof
2008	—	25.00	—

KM# 794 6.5000 g. Nickel 26.5 mm. **Rev:** Toronto Maple Leafs

Date	Mintage	MS-63	Proof
2008	—	25.00	—

KM# 795 6.5000 g. Nickel 26.5 mm. **Rev:** Vancouver Canucks

Date	Mintage	MS-63	Proof
2008	—	25.00	—

KM#851 33.6500 g. Nickel 26.5 mm. **Rev:** Calgary Flames Road Jersey

Date	Mintage	MS-63	Proof
2009	382	25.00	—

Date	Mintage	MS-63	Proof
2009	794	25.00	—

KM# 852 33.6500 g. 0.9990 Nickel 1.0807 oz. 26.5 mm. **Rev:** Edmonton Oilers Road Jersey

Date	Mintage	MS-63	Proof
2009	472	25.00	—

KM#853 33.6500 g. Nickel 26.5 mm. **Rev:** Montreal Canadians Road Jersey

Date	Mintage	MS-63	Proof
2009	4,857	25.00	—

KM# 864 7.0000 g. Aureate Bronze 26.5 mm. **Subject:** Montreal Canadiens, 100th Anniversary **Obv:** Bust right **Rev:** Montreal Canadiens logo and large 100 **Shape:** 11-sided

Date	Mintage	MS-63	Proof
2009	—	25.00	—

KM#854 33.6500 g. Nickel 26.5 mm. **Rev:** Ottawa Senators Road Jersey

Date	Mintage	MS-63	Proof
2009	387	25.00	—

KM# 855 33.6500 g. Nickel 26.5 mm. **Rev:** Toronto Maple Leafs Road Jersey

Date	Mintage	MS-63	Proof
2009	1,328	25.00	—

KM# 865 25.1700 g. 0.9250 Silver 0.7485 oz. ASW 36.07 mm. **Subject:** Montreal Canadiens 100th Anniversary **Obv:** Bust right **Obv. Designer:** Susanna Blunt **Rev:** Montreal Canadiens logo partially gilt

Date	Mintage	MS-63	Proof
2009 Proof in black case	15,000	—	75.00
2009 Proof in acrillic stand	5,000	—	150

KM#856 33.6500 g. Nickel 26.5 mm. **Rev:** Vancouver Canucks Road Jersey

KM# 889 25.1800 g. 0.9250 Silver 0.7488 oz. ASW 36.07 mm. **Subject:** 100th Anniversary of flight in Canada

Obv: Bust right **Obv. Legend:** Elizabeth II DG Regina **Obv. Designer:** Susanna Blunt **Rev:** Silhouette with arms spread, 3 planes, plane cutout **Rev. Legend:** Canada Dollar 1909-2009 **Rev. Designer:** Jason Bouwman

Date	Mintage	MS-63	Proof
2009	13,074	35.00	—
2009 Proof	52,549	—	55.00

KM# 889a 25.1800 g. 0.9250 Silver 0.7488 oz. ASW partially gilt. 36.07 mm. **Obv:** Bust right **Rev:** Silouette with arms spread, 3 planes, plane shadow partially gilt

Date	Mintage	MS-63	Proof
2009(ml) Proof	27,549	—	50.00

KM# 914 7.0000 g. Aureate-Bronze Plated Nickel 26.5 mm. **Obv:** Bust right **Obv. Designer:** Susanna Blunt **Rev:** Blue heron in flight

Date	Mintage	MS-63	Proof
2009 Specimen	21,677	50.00	—

KM# 883 7.0000 g. Aureate-Bronze Plated Nickel 26.5 mm. **Subject:** Lucky Loonie **Obv:** Bust right **Obv. Legend:** Elizabeth II DG Regina **Rev:** Canadian Olympic logo **Rev. Legend:** Canada Dollar

Date	Mintage	MS-63	Proof
2010	12,000	20.00	—

KM# 883a 9.3100 g. 0.9250 Silver 0.2769 oz. ASW 26.5 mm. **Subject:** Lucky Loonie **Obv:** Bust right **Obv. Legend:** Elizabeth II DG Regina **Rev:** Canadian Olympic logo in color **Rev. Legend:** Vancouver 2010 Canada Dollar **Shape:** 11-sided

Date	Mintage	MS-63	Proof
2010 Proof	40,000	—	55.00

KM#1046 Aureate Bronze 26.5 mm. **Subject:** Roughriders **Rev:** S logo **Shape:** 11-sided

Date	Mintage	MS-63	Proof
2010(ml)	—	7.50	—

KM# 975 0.9250 Silver 36 mm. **Rev:** Sun mask **Rev. Designer:** Xwa Iack Tun

Date	Mintage	MS-63	Proof
2010 Proof	1,278	—	200

Date	Mintage	MS-63	Proof
2010	35,000	30.00	—
2010(ml)	—	—	50.00

KM# 1017 7.0000 g. Aureate Bronze 26.5 mm. **Rev:** Male and female sailors saluting, HMCS Halifax and anchor above

Date	Mintage	MS-63	Proof
2010	—	5.00	—

KM# 1017a 7.0000 g. Aureate Bronze gilt 26.5 mm. **Rev:** Male and female sailors saluting, HMCS Halifax in background and anchor above

Date	Mintage	MS-63	Proof
2010 Proof	—	—	50.00

KM# 995 25.1700 g. 0.9250 Silver 0.7485 oz. ASW 36.07 mm. **Rev:** HMCS Sackville **Rev. Designer:** Yves Berube

Date	Mintage	MS-63	Proof
2010 Proof	Est. 50,000	—	50.00

KM# 995a 25.1700 g. 0.9250 Silver 0.7485 oz. ASW partially gilt 36.07 mm. **Subject:** Navy Centennial **Rev:** HMCS Sackville, sea waves in gilt

Date	Mintage	MS-63	Proof
2010	—	—	110

KM# 996 7.0000 g. Aureate Bronze 26.5 mm. **Rev:** Northern Harrier Hawk

KM# 1027 25.1800 g. 0.9250 Silver 0.7488 oz. ASW 36.07 mm. **Obv:**

George V bust left **Rev:** Voyaguers, dual dates below

Date	Mintage	MS-63	Proof
2010 Proof	7,500	—	70.00

KM# 1050 25.1800 g. 0.9250 Silver 0.7488 oz. ASW 36.07 mm. **Rev:** Red poppy in large field of poppies **Edge:** Reeded

Date	Mintage	MS-63	Proof
2010 Proof	5,000	—	55.00

KM# 1086 7.0000 g. Aureate-Bronze Plated Nickel 26.5 mm. **Rev:** Great Grey Owl **Rev. Designer:** Arnold Nagy

Date	Mintage	MS-63	Proof
2011	35,000	13.50	—

KM# 1087 25.1800 g. 0.9250 Silver 0.7488 oz. ASW 36.07 mm. **Subject:**

Parks Canada, 100th Anniversary **Rev:** Female head looking downward into hands holding nature scene **Rev. Designer:** Luc Normandin

Date	Mintage	MS-63	Proof
2011	25,000	50.00	—
2011 Proof	—	—	60.00

KM# 1087a 25.1800 g. 0.9250 Silver 0.7488 oz. ASW partially gilt 36.07 mm. **Subject:** Parks Canada, 100th Anniversary **Rev:** Female head looking downward to hands holding nature scene, partially gilt **Rev. Designer:** Luc Normandin

Date	Mintage	MS-63	Proof
2011 Proof	45,000	—	75.00

KM# 1112 25.1700 g. 0.9250 Silver 0.7485 oz. ASW 36.07 mm. **Obv:** Crowned bust left of George V **Obv. Designer:** E. B. MacKennal **Rev:** Value and date within maple wreath **Rev. Designer:** W.H.J. Blakemore

Date	Mintage	MS-63	Proof
2011 Proof	Est. 15,000	—	115

KM# 1166 7.0000 g. Aureate-Bronze Plated Nickel 26.5 mm. **Subject:** Canada Parks **Obv:** Bust right **Rev:** Stylized animals

Date	Mintage	MS-63	Proof
2011	—	5.00	—

KM# 1216 9.3100 g. 0.9250 Silver 0.2769 oz. ASW 26.5 mm. **Obv:** Bust right, SP/PA below **Rev:** Loon, 1987-2012 below

Date	Mintage	MS-63	Proof
2012 Specimen	—	—	55.00

KM# 1222 7.0000 g. Aureate-Bronze Plated Nickel 26.5 mm. **Obv:** Bust right **Rev:** Loon and two young, 1987-2012 dates

Date	Mintage	MS-63	Proof
2012 Specimen	—	—	40.00

KM# 1225 25.1800 g. 0.9250 Silver 0.7488 oz. ASW 36.07 mm. **Subject:** War of 1812, 200th Anniversary **Obv:** Bust right **Rev:** Two soldiers and guide on patrol

Date	Mintage	MS-63	Proof
2012	—	50.00	—
2012 Proof	—	—	60.00

KM# 1225a 25.1800 g. 0.9250 Silver 0.7488 oz. ASW partially gilt 36.07 mm. **Subject:** War of 1812, 200th Anniversary **Obv:** Bust right, gilt rim **Rev:** Two solders and guide, partially gilt

Date	Mintage	MS-63	Proof
2012 Proof	—	—	65.00

DOLLAR (LOUIS)

KM# 652 1.5000 g. 0.9990 Gold 0.0482 oz. AGW 14.1 mm. **Subject:** Gold Louis **Obv:** Bust right **Obv. Designer:** Susanna Blunt **Rev:** Crowned double L monogram within wreath

Date	Mintage	MS-63	Proof
2006 Proof	5,648	—	110

KM# 756 1.5550 g. 0.9990 Gold 0.0499 oz. AGW 14.1 mm. **Obv:** Bust right **Obv. Designer:** Susanna Blunt **Rev:** Crown above two oval shields

Date	Mintage	MS-63	Proof
2007 Proof	4,023	—	110

KM# 834 1.5550 g. 0.9990 Gold 0.0499 oz. AGW 14.1 mm. **Obv:** Bust right **Obv. Designer:** Susanna Blunt **Rev:** Crowned double L monogram, three lis around

Date	Mintage	MS-63	Proof
2008 Proof	3,793	—	110

2 DOLLARS

KM# 270 7.3000 g. Bi-Metallic Aluminum-Bronze center in Nickel ring 28 mm. **Obv:** Crowned head right within circle, date below **Obv. Designer:** Dora dePedery-Hunt **Rev:** Polar bear right within circle, denomination below **Rev. Designer:** Brent Townsend **Edge:** Segmented reeding

Date	Mintage	MS-63	P/L	Proof
1996	375,483,000	3.25	5.00	—
1996 Proof	—	—	—	10.00

Date	Mintage	MS-63	P/L	Proof
1997	16,942,000	3.25	—	—
1998	4,926,000	3.25	—	—
1998W	Inc. above	3.25	—	—
1999	25,130,000	3.25	—	—
2000	29,847,000	3.25	—	—
2000W	Inc. above	3.25	—	—
2001	27,008,000	5.00	—	—
2001 Proof	74,944	—	—	12.50
2002	11,910,000	5.00	—	—
2002 Proof	65,315	—	—	12.50
2003	7,123,697	5.00	—	—
2003 Proof	62,007	—	—	12.50

KM# 270b 25.0000 g. 0.9250 Bi-Metallic 0.7435 oz. Gold plated silver center on Silver planchet 28 mm. **Obv:** Crowned head right within circle, date below **Rev:** Polar bear right within circle, denomination below **Edge:** 4.5mm thick

Date	Mintage	MS-63	Proof
1996 Proof	10,000	—	55.00
1998 Proof	—	—	—

KM# 270c 8.8300 g. 0.9250 Silver 0.2626 oz. ASW gold plated center 28 mm. **Obv:** Crowned head right within circle, date below **Rev:** Polar bear right within circle, denomination below **Note:** 1.9mm thick.

Date	Mintage	MS-63	Proof
1996 Proof	10,000	—	12.00
1997 Proof	—	—	10.00
1998O Proof	—	—	12.00
1999 Proof	—	—	12.00
2000 Proof	—	—	12.00
2001 Proof	—	—	12.00

KM# 270a 10.8414 g. Bi-Metallic .999 Gold 5.7456g center in .999 Silver 5.0958g ring 28 mm. **Obv:** Crowned head right within circle, date below **Rev:** Polar bear right within circle, denomination below

Date	Mintage	MS-63	Proof
1996 Proof	5,000	—	375

KM# 357 7.3000 g. Bi-Metallic Aluminumn-Bronze center in Nickel ring 28 mm. **Subject:** Nunavut **Obv:** Crowned head right **Rev:** Inuit person with drum, denomination below **Rev. Designer:** G. Arnaktavyok **Edge:** Segmented reeding

Date	Mintage	MS-63	Proof
1999	—	4.00	—

KM# 357a 8.5200 g. 0.9250 Silver 0.2534 oz. ASW gold plated center. 28 mm. **Subject:** Nunavut **Obv:** Crowned head right **Rev:** Drum dancer **Edge:** Interrupted reeding

Date	Mintage	MS-63	Proof
1999 Proof	39,873	—	15.00

KM# 357b Gold Yellow gold center in White Gold ring **Subject:** Nunavut **Obv:** Crowned head right **Rev:** Drum dancer

Date	Mintage	MS-63	Proof
1999 Proof	4,298	—	375

KM# 399 7.3000 g. Bi-Metallic Aluminum-Bronze center in Nickel ring 28 mm. **Subject:** Knowledge **Obv:** Crowned head right within circle, denomination below **Rev:** Polar bear and 2 cubs right within circle, date above **Rev. Designer:** Tony Bianco **Edge:** Segmented reeding

Date	Mintage	MS-63	Proof
2000 Specimen	1,500	5.00	—

KM# 399a 8.5200 g. 0.9250 Silver 0.2534 oz. ASW gold plated center. **Subject:** Knowledge **Obv:** Crowned head right within circle, denomination below **Rev:** Polar bear and 2 cubs within circle, date above

Date	Mintage	MS-63	Proof
2000 Proof	39,768	—	15.00

KM# 399b 6.3100 g. 0.9160 Gold 0.1858 oz. AGW Yellow gold center in White Gold ring **Subject:** Knowledge **Obv:** Crowned head right within circle, denomination below **Rev:** Polar bear and two cubs right within circle, date above

Date	Mintage	MS-63	Proof
2000 Proof	5,881	—	350

KM# 449 7.3000 g. Bi-Metallic Aluminum-Bronze center in Nickel ring 28 mm.   **Subject:** Elizabeth II Golden Jubilee **Obv:** Crowned head right, jubilee commemorative dates 1952-2002 **Edge:** Segmented reeding

Date	Mintage	MS-63	Proof
2002	27,020,000	4.00	—

KM# 449a 8.8300 g. 0.9250 Silver 0.2626 oz. ASW gold plated center **Subject:** Elizabeth II Golden Jubilee **Obv:** Crowned head right, jubilee commemorative dates 1952-2002

Date	Mintage	MS-63	Proof
2002 Proof	100,000	—	14.00

KM# 496 7.3000 g. Bi-Metallic Aluminum-Bronze center in Nickel ring 28 mm.   **Obv:** Head right **Obv. Designer:** Susanna Blunt **Rev:** Polar bear advancing right **Rev. Designer:** Brent Townsend **Edge:** Segmented reeding

Date	Mintage	MS-63	Proof
2003	11,244,000	5.00	—
2003W	71,142	25.00	—
2004	12,908,000	5.00	—
2004 Proof	—	—	12.50
2005	38,317,000	5.00	—
2005 Proof	—	—	12.50
2006(ml)	35,319,000	5.00	—
2006(ml) Proof	—	—	12.50
2007(ml)	38,957,000	5.00	—
2007(ml) Proof	—	—	12.50
2008(ml)	18,400,000	5.00	—
2008(ml) Proof	—	—	12.50

Date	Mintage	MS-63	Proof
2009(ml)	38,430,000	5.00	—
2009(ml) Proof	—	—	12.50
2010(ml)	—	5.00	—
2010(ml) Proof	—	—	12.50
2011(ml)	—	5.00	—
2011(ml) Proof	—	—	12.50

KM# 270d 8.8300 g. 0.9250 Silver 0.2626 oz. ASW gold plated center **Subject:** 100th Anniversary of the Cobalt Silver Strike **Obv:** Crowned head right, within circle, date below **Rev:** Polar bear right, within circle, denomination below

Date	Mintage	MS-63	Proof
2003 Proof	100,000	—	25.00

KM# 496a 10.8414 g. 0.9250 Bi-Metallic 0.3224 oz. Gold plated Silver center in Silver ring 28 mm.   **Obv:** Head right **Obv. Designer:** Susanna Blunt **Rev:** Polar Bear **Edge:** Segmented reeding

Date	Mintage	MS-63	Proof
2004 Proof	—	—	25.00

KM# 835 8.8000 g. 0.9250 Silver 0.2617 oz. ASW 27.95 mm.   **Rev:** Proud Polar Bear advancing right

Date	Mintage	MS-63	Proof
2004 Proof	12,607	—	40.00

KM# 837 7.3000 g. Bi-Metallic Aluminum-Bronze center in Nickel ring   **Obv:** Bust left, date at top **Rev:** Polar Bear advancing right

Date	Mintage	MS-63	Proof
2006(ml)	—	7.50	—
2007(ml)	38,957,000	7.50	—

KM# 631 7.3000 g. Bi-Metallic Aluminum-Bronze center in Nickel ring 28 mm.   **Subject:** 10th Anniversary of $2 coin **Obv:** Crowned head right **Edge:** Segmented reeding

Date	Mintage	MS-63	Proof
2006(ml)	5,005,000	25.00	—
2006(ml) Proof	—	—	40.00

KM# 631a Bi-Metallic 22 Kt Gold ring around 4.1 Kt. Gold core   **Subject:** 10th Anniversary of $2 coin **Obv:** Crowned head right **Rev:** Polar bear

Date	Mintage	MS-63	Proof
2006 Proof	2,068	—	400

KM# 836 7.3000 g. Bi-Metallic Aluminum-Bronze center in Nickel ring 28 mm.   **Subject:** $2 coin, 10th Anniversary **Rev:** "Churchill" Polar Bear, northern lights **Edge:** Segmented reeding

Date	Mintage	MS-63	Proof
2006(ml)	31,636	7.50	—

KM# 796 8.8300 g. 0.9250 Silver 0.2626 oz. ASW 28.07 mm.   **Rev:** Bear, gold plated center

Date	Mintage	MS-63	Proof
2008	—	25.00	—

KM# 1040 7.3000 g. Bi-Metallic Aluminumn-Bronze center in Nickel ring 27.95 mm.   **Subject:** Quebec

400th Anniversary **Rev:** Lis and small sailing ship

Date	Mintage	MS-63	Proof
2008	—	7.50	—

KM# 1020 7.3000 g. Bi-Metallic Aluminum-Bronze center in Nickel ring 28 mm.   **Rev:** Two lynx cubs **Rev. Designer:** Christie Paquet **Edge:** Segmented reeding

Date	Mintage	MS-63	Proof
2010 Specimen	15,000	—	40.00

KM# 1088 7.3000 g. Bi-Metallic Copper-Nickel center in Nickel ring 28.03 mm.   **Rev:** Elk Calf **Rev. Designer:** Christine Paquet

Date	Mintage	MS-63	Proof
2011	—	7.50	—

KM# 1167 7.3000 g. Bi-Metallic Aluminumn-Bronze center in Nickel ring. 28 mm.   **Subject:** Canada Parks **Obv:** Bust right **Rev:** Stylized trees

Date	Mintage	MS-63	Proof
2011	—	7.50	—

3 DOLLARS

KM# 657 11.7200 g. 0.9250 Silver 0.3485 oz. ASW gilt 27x27 mm.   **Rev:** Beaver within wreath **Shape:** Square

Date	Mintage	MS-63	Proof
2006 Proof	19,963	—	225

KM# 1051 11.6000 g. 0.9250 Silver 0.3450 oz. ASW gilt 27x27 mm. **Subject:** Wildlife conservation **Rev:** Stylized polar bear and northern lights **Shape:** square

Date	Mintage	MS-63	Proof
2010 Specimen	15,000	55.00	—

KM# 1089 11.6000 g. 0.9250 Silver 0.3450 oz. ASW gilt 27x27 mm.   **Rev:** Orca Whale **Rev. Designer:** Jason Bouwman **Shape:** Square

Date	Mintage	MS-63	Proof
2011 Proof	15,000	—	65.00

KM# 978 7.9600 g. Silver Partially Gilt 27 mm.   **Rev:** Return of the Tyee (giant salmon)

Date	Mintage	MS-63	Proof
2010 Proof	15,000	—	50.00

KM# 1090 7.9600 g. 0.9990 Silver 0.2557 oz. ASW with red and yellow partial gilding 27 mm.   **Obv:** Bust right **Rev:** Eskimo mother kneeling, child on back, partially gilt **Rev. Designer:** Andrew Oappik

Date	Mintage	MS-63	Proof
2011 Proof	10,000	—	65.00

KM# 1011 11.6000 g. 0.9250 Silver 0.3450 oz. ASW gilt 27x27 mm.   **Rev:** Barn Owl **Rev. Designer:** Jason Bouwman **Shape:** Square

Date	Mintage	MS-63	Proof
2010 Proof	15,000	—	65.00

KM# 1117 7.9600 g. 0.9999 Silver 0.2559 oz. ASW 27 mm.   **Subject:** January birthstone, Garnet **Obv:** Bust left **Rev:** Birthstone at cener of artistic sunburst **Edge:** Reeded

Date	Mintage	MS-63	Proof
2011 Proof	—	—	65.00

KM# 1118 7.9600 g. 0.9999 Silver 0.2559 oz. ASW 27 mm. **Subject:** February birthstone, Amythest **Obv:** Bust right **Rev:** Birthstone at cener of artistic sunburst **Edge:** Reeded

Date	Mintage	MS-63	Proof
2011 Proof	—	—	65.00

KM# 1122 7.9600 g. 0.9999 Silver 0.2559 oz. ASW 27 mm. **Subject:** June birthstone, Alexandrite **Obv:** Bust right **Rev:** Birthstone at cener of artistic sunburst

Date	Mintage	MS-63	Proof
2011 Proof	—	—	65.00

KM# 1119 7.9600 g. 0.9999 Silver 0.2559 oz. ASW 27 mm. **Subject:** March birthstone, Aquamarine **Obv:** Bust right **Rev:** Birthstone at cener of artistic sunburst **Edge:** Reeded

Date	Mintage	MS-63	Proof
2011 Proof	—	—	65.00

KM# 1123 7.9600 g. 0.9999 Silver 0.2559 oz. ASW 27 mm. **Subject:** July birthstone, Ruby **Obv:** Bust right **Rev:** Birthstone at cener of artistic sunburst

Date	Mintage	MS-63	Proof
2011 Proof	—	—	65.00

KM# 1120 7.9600 g. 0.9999 Silver 0.2559 oz. ASW 27 mm. **Subject:** April birthstone, diamond **Obv:** Bust right **Rev:** Birthstone at cener of artistic sunburst **Edge:** Reeded

Date	Mintage	MS-63	Proof
2011 Proof	—	—	65.00

KM# 1121 7.9600 g. 0.9999 Silver 0.2559 oz. ASW 27 mm. **Subject:** May birthstone **Obv:** Bust right **Rev:** Birthstone at cener of artistic sunburst **Edge:** Reeded

Date	Mintage	MS-63	Proof
2011 Proof	—	—	65.00

KM# 1124 7.9600 g. 0.9999 Silver 0.2559 oz. ASW 27 mm. **Subject:** August birthstone, Priedot **Obv:** Bust right **Rev:** Birthstone at cener of artistic sunburst

Date	Mintage	MS-63	Proof
2011 Proof	—	—	65.00

KM# 1126 7.9600 g. 0.9999 Silver 0.2559 oz. ASW 27 mm. **Subject:** October birthstone **Obv:** Bust right **Rev:** Birthstone at cener of artistic sunburst

Date	Mintage	MS-63	Proof
2011 Proof	—	—	65.00

KM# 1127 7.9600 g. 0.9999 Silver 0.2559 oz. ASW 27 mm. **Subject:** November birthstone **Obv:** Bust right **Rev:** Birthstone at cener of artistic sunburst

Date	Mintage	MS-63	Proof
2011 Proof	—	—	65.00

KM# 1128 7.9600 g. 0.9999 Silver 0.2559 oz. ASW 27 mm. **Subject:** December birhtstone **Obv:** Bust right **Rev:** Birthstone at cener of artistic sunburst

Date	Mintage	MS-63	Proof
2011 Proof	—	—	65.00

KM# 1151 11.8000 g. 0.9250 Silver 0.3509 oz. ASW gold plated 27x27 mm. **Obv:** Bust right **Rev:** Black footed ferret

Date	Mintage	MS-63	Proof
2011 Proof	Est. 15,000	—	65.00

4 DOLLARS

KM# 728 15.8700 g. 0.9250 Silver 0.4719 oz. ASW 34 mm. **Subject:** Dinosaur fossil **Obv:** Bust right **Rev:** Parasaurolophus, selective enameling

Date	Mintage	MS-63	Proof
2007 Proof	14,946	—	125

KM# 797 15.8700 g. 0.9990 Silver 0.5097 oz. ASW 34 mm. **Subject:** Dinosaur fossil **Obv:** Bust right **Rev:** Triceratops, enameled **Rev. Designer:** Kerri Burnett

Date	Mintage	MS-63	Proof
2008 Proof	13,046	—	75.00

KM# 890 15.8700 g. 0.9990 Silver 0.5097 oz. ASW 34 mm. **Subject:** Tyrannosaurus Rex **Obv:** Bust right **Obv. Legend:** Elizabeth II DG Regina **Obv. Designer:** Susanna Blunt **Rev:** T-Rex skeleton in selective aging **Rev. Legend:** Canada 4 Dollars **Rev. Designer:** Kerri Burnette

Date	Mintage	MS-63	Proof
2009 Proof	13,572	—	55.00

KM# 1014 15.8700 g. 0.9990 Silver 0.5097 oz. ASW selectively plated 34 mm. **Rev:** Euoplocephalus **Rev. Designer:** Kerri Burnett

Date	Mintage	MS-63	Proof
2010 Proof	Est. 13,000	—	55.00

KM# 1022 Silver selective plating **Rev:** Dromaeosaurus

Date	Mintage	MS-63	Proof
2010 Proof	8,982	—	55.00

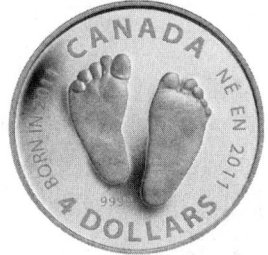

KM# 942 15.8700 g. Silver 34 mm. **Rev:** Kids hanging stocking on fireplace, Christmas tree on right

Date	Mintage	MS-63	Proof
2009 Proof	6,011	—	45.00

KM# 1129 15.8700 g. 0.9999 Silver 0.5102 oz. ASW 34 mm. **Obv:** Bust right **Rev:** Baby's footprint **Edge:** Reeded

Date	Mintage	MS-63	Proof
2011 Proof	Est. 10,000	—	60.00

SOVEREIGN

KM# 14 7.9881 g. 0.9170 Gold 0.2355 oz. AGW **Rev:** St. George slaying dragon, mint mark below horse's rear hooves

Date	Mintage	F-12	VF-20	XF-40	AU-50	MS-60	MS-63
1908C	636	1,800	2,500	3,500	4,000	4,500	5,500
1909C	16,273	—	—	BV	450	650	2,000
1910C	28,012	—	—	BV	450	650	2,900

KM# 20 7.9881 g. 0.9170 Gold 0.2355 oz. AGW   **Rev:** St. George slaying dragon, mint mark below horse's rear hooves

Date	Mintage	F-12	VF-20	XF-40	AU-50	MS-60	MS-63
1911C Specimen	—	—	—	—	—	—	—
1911C	256,946	—	—	—	BV	450	650
1913C	3,715	650	800	1,050	1,300	1,800	3,500
1914C	14,871	—	BV	450	500	650	1,150
1916C About 20 known	—	16,000	17,000	18,000	20,000	24,000	40,000
Note: *Stacks' A.G. Carter Jr. Sale 12-89 Gem BU realized $82,500*							
1917C	58,845	—	—	—	BV	450	700
1918C	106,514	—	—	—	BV	450	1,000
1919C	135,889	—	—	—	BV	450	800

5 DOLLARS

KM# 26 8.3592 g. 0.9000 Gold 0.2419 oz. AGW   **Obv:** Crowned bust left **Obv. Designer:** E. B. MacKennal **Rev:** Arms within wreath, date and denomination below **Rev. Designer:** W. H. J. Blakemore

Date	Mintage	F-12	VF-20	XF-40	AU-50	MS-60	MS-63
1912	165,680	—	—	—	BV	450	650
1913	98,832	—	—	—	BV	450	800
1914	31,122	—	BV	450	600	900	3,000

KM# 84 24.3000 g. 0.9250 Silver 0.7226 oz. ASW 38 mm.   **Subject:** 1976 Montreal Olympics **Obv:** Young bust right, small maple below, date at right **Rev:** Sailboat "Kingston", date at left, denomination below **Rev. Designer:** Georges Huel **Note:** Series I.

Date	Mintage	MS-63	Proof
1973	—	24.00	—
1973 Proof	165,203	—	24.00

KM# 90   24.3000 g. 0.9250 Silver 0.7226 oz. ASW 38 mm.   **Subject:** 1976 Montreal Olympics **Obv:** Young bust right, small maple leaf below, date at right **Rev:** Athlete with torch, denomination below **Rev. Designer:** Anthony Mann **Note:** Series II.

Date	Mintage	MS-63	Proof
1974	—	24.00	—
1974 Proof	97,431	—	24.00

KM# 85   24.3000 g. 0.9250 Silver 0.7226 oz. ASW 38 mm.   **Subject:** 1976 Montreal Olympics **Obv:** Young bust right, small maple leaf below, date at right **Rev:** North American map, denominaton below **Rev. Designer:** Georges Huel **Note:** Series I.

Date	Mintage	MS-63	Proof
1973	—	24.00	—
1973 Proof	165,203	—	24.00

KM# 89   24.3000 g. 0.9250 Silver 0.7226 oz. ASW 38 mm.   **Subject:** 1976 Montreal Olympics **Obv:** Young bust right, small maple leaf below, date at right **Rev:** Olympic rings, denomination below **Rev. Designer:** Anthony Mann **Note:** Series II.

Date	Mintage	MS-63	Proof
1974	—	24.00	—
1974 Proof	97,431	—	24.00

KM# 91   24.3000 g. 0.9250 Silver 0.7226 oz. ASW 38 mm.   **Subject:** 1976 Montreal Olympics **Obv:** Young bust right, small maple leaf below, date at right **Rev:** Rower, denomination below **Rev. Designer:** Ken Danby **Note:** Series III.

Date	Mintage	MS-63	Proof
1974	—	24.00	—
1974 Proof	104,684	—	24.00

KM# 92 24.3000 g. 0.9250 Silver 0.7226 oz. ASW 38 mm. **Subject:** 1976 Montreal Olympics **Obv:** Young bust right, small maple leaf below, date at right **Rev:** Canoeing, denomination below **Rev. Designer:** Ken Danby **Note:** Series III.

Date	Mintage	MS-63	Proof
1974	—	24.00	—
1974 Proof	104,684	—	24.00

KM# 99 24.3000 g. 0.9250 Silver 0.7226 oz. ASW 38 mm. **Subject:** Montreal 1976 - 21st Summer Olympic Games **Obv:** Young bust right, small maple leaf below, date at right **Rev:** Women's javelin event, denomination below **Rev. Designer:** Leo Yerxa **Note:** Series IV.

Date	Mintage	MS-63	Proof
1975	—	24.00	—
1975 Proof	89,155	—	24.00

KM# 98 24.3000 g. 0.9250 Silver 0.7226 oz. ASW 38 mm. **Subject:** 1976 Montreal Olympics **Obv:** Young bust right, small maple leaf below, date at right **Rev:** Marathon, denomination below **Rev. Designer:** Leo Yerxa **Note:** Series IV.

Date	Mintage	MS-63	Proof
1975	—	24.00	—
1975 Proof	89,155	—	24.00

KM# 100 24.3000 g. 0.9250 Silver 0.7226 oz. ASW 38 mm. **Subject:** 1976 Montreal Olympics **Obv:** Young bust right, small maple leaf below, date at right **Rev:** Swimmer, denomination below **Rev. Designer:** Lynda Cooper **Note:** Series V.

Date	Mintage	MS-63	Proof
1975	—	24.00	—
1975 Proof	89,155	—	24.00

KM# 101 24.3000 g. 0.9250 Silver 0.7226 oz. ASW 38 mm. **Subject:** Montreal 1976 - 21st Summer Olympic Games **Obv:** Young bust right, small maple leaf below, date at right **Rev:** Platform Diver, denomination below **Rev. Designer:** Lynda Cooper **Note:** Series V.

Date	Mintage	MS-63	Proof
1975	—	24.00	—
1975 Proof	89,155	—	24.00

KM# 108 24.3000 g. 0.9250 Silver 0.7226 oz. ASW 38 mm. **Subject:** 1976 Montreal Olympics **Obv:** Young bust right, small maple leaf below, date at right **Obv. Legend:** Boxing **Rev:** Boxers, denomination below **Rev. Designer:** Shigeo Fukada **Note:** Series VI.

Date	Mintage	MS-63	Proof
1976	—	24.00	—
1976 Proof	82,302	—	24.00

KM# 107 24.3000 g. 0.9250 Silver 0.7226 oz. ASW 38 mm. **Subject:** 1976 Montreal Olympics **Obv:** Young bust right, small maple leaf below, date at right **Rev:** Fencing, denomination below **Rev. Designer:** Shigeo Fukada **Note:** Series VI.

Date	Mintage	MS-63	Proof
1976	—	24.00	—
1976 Proof	82,302	—	24.00

KM# 109 24.3000 g. 0.9250 Silver 0.7226 oz. ASW 38 mm. **Subject:** 1976 Montreal Olympics **Obv:** Young bust right, small maple leaf below, date at right **Rev:** Olympic village, denomination below **Rev. Designer:** Elliot John Morrison **Note:** Series VII.

Date	Mintage	MS-63	Proof
1976	—	24.00	—
1976 Proof	76,908	—	24.00

KM# 110 24.3000 g. 0.9250 Silver
0.7226 oz. ASW 38 mm.   **Subject:**
1976 Montreal Olympics **Obv:** Young
bust right, maple leaf below, date at
right **Rev:** Olympic flame,
denomination below **Rev. Designer:**
Elliot John Morrison **Note:** Series VII.

Date	Mintage	MS-63	Proof
1976	—	24.00	—
1976 Proof	79,102	—	24.00

KM# 316 31.3900 g. 0.9999 Silver
1.0091 oz. ASW   **Subject:** Dr. Norman
Bethune **Obv:** Young bust right **Rev:**
Bethune and party, date at upper right
Rev. Designer: Harvey Chan

Date	Mintage	MS-63	Proof
1998 Proof	61,000	—	40.00

KM#398 Copper-Nickel-Zinc   **Obv:**
Young bust right **Rev:** Viking ship

under sail **Rev. Designer:** Donald
Curley **Note:** Sold in sets with Norway
20 kroner, KM#465.

Date	Mintage	MS-63	Proof
1999 Proof	28,450	—	18.50

KM# 435 16.8600 g. 0.9250 Silver
0.5014 oz. ASW 28.4 mm.   **Subject:**
Guglielmo Marconi **Obv:** Crowned
head right **Rev:** Gold-plated cameo
portrait of Marconi **Rev. Designer:**
Cosme Saffioti **Edge:** Reeded **Note:**
Only issued in two coin set with British
2 pounds KM#1014a.

Date	Mintage	MS-63	Proof
2001 Proof	15,011	—	30.00

KM# 519 8.3600 g. 0.9000 Gold
0.2419 oz. AGW 21.6 mm.   **Obv:**
Crowned head right **Rev:** National
arms **Edge:** Reeded

Date	Mintage	MS-63	Proof
1912-2002 Proof	2,002	—	450

KM# 603 31.1050 g. 0.9999 Silver
0.9999 oz. ASW   **Obv:** Head right
Rev: Loon splashing in the water,
hologram

Date	Mintage	MS-63	Proof
2002 Satin Proof	30,000	—	45.00

KM# 518 31.1200 g. 0.9999 Silver
1.0004 oz. ASW 38 mm.   **Subject:**
F.I.F.A. World Cup Soccer , Germany
2006 **Obv:** Crowned head right,
denomination **Rev:** Goalie on knees
Edge: Reeded

Date	Mintage	MS-63	Proof
2003 Proof	21,542	—	40.00

KM# 514 31.1200 g. 0.9999 Silver
1.0004 oz. ASW 38 mm.   **Obv:**
Crowned head right **Rev:** Moose **Edge:**
Reeded

Date	Mintage	MS-63	Proof
2004 Proof	12,822	—	175

KM# 527 31.1200 g. 0.9999 Silver
1.0004 oz. ASW   **Subject:** Golf,
Championship of Canada, Centennial
Obv: Head right

Date	Mintage	MS-63	Proof
2004 Proof	18,750	—	30.00

KM# 554 31.1200 g. 0.9999 Silver
1.0004 oz. ASW   **Subject:** Alberta
Obv. Designer: Head right **Rev.
Designer:** Michelle Grant

Date	Mintage	MS-63	Proof
2005 Proof	20,000	—	35.00

KM# 555 31.1200 g. 0.9999 Silver
1.0004 oz. ASW   **Subject:**
Saskatchewan **Obv:** Head right **Obv.
Designer:** Susanna Blunt **Rev.
Designer:** Paulett Sapergia

Date	Mintage	MS-63	Proof
2005 Proof	20,000	—	35.00

KM# 556.1 31.1200 g. 0.9990 Silver
0.9995 oz. ASW 38.02 mm.   **Subject:**
60th Anniversay Victory WWII -

Veterans **Obv:** Bust right **Rev:** Large V
and heads of sailor, soldier and aviator
on large maple leaf **Edge:** Reeded

Date	Mintage	MS-63	Proof
2005	25,000	32.00	—

KM# 556.2 31.1200 g. 0.9999 Silver
1.0004 oz. ASW 38.02 mm.   **Subject:**
60th Anniversary Victory WW II -
Veterans **Obv:** Bust right **Rev:** Large V
and heads of sailor, soldier and aviator
on maple leaf with small maple leaf
added at left and right **Edge:** Reeded

Date	Mintage	MS-63	Proof
2005	10,000	125	—

KM# 557 31.1200 g. 0.9999 Silver
1.0004 oz. ASW 36 mm.   **Subject:**
Walrus and calf **Obv:** Head right **Obv.
Designer:** Susanna Blunt **Rev:** Two
walrusus and calf **Rev. Designer:** Pierre
Leduc

Date	Mintage	MS-63	Proof
2005 Proof	5,519	—	40.00

KM# 558 31.1200 g. 0.9999 Silver 1.0004 oz. ASW 36 mm. **Subject:** White tailed deer **Obv:** Head right **Obv. Designer:** Susanna Blunt **Rev:** Two deer standing **Rev. Designer:** Xerxes Irani

Date	Mintage	MS-63	Proof
2005 Proof	6,439	—	40.00

KM# 585 31.1200 g. 0.9999 Silver 1.0004 oz. ASW 36 mm. **Obv:** Head right **Obv. Designer:** Susanna Blunt **Rev:** Peregrine Falcon feeding young ones **Rev. Designer:** Dwayne Harty

Date	Mintage	MS-63	Proof
2006 Proof	7,226	—	45.00

KM# 586 31.1200 g. 0.9999 Silver 1.0004 oz. ASW 36 mm. **Subject:** Sable Island horses **Obv:** Head right **Obv. Designer:** Susanna Blunt **Rev:** Horse and foal standing **Rev. Designer:** Christie Paquet

Date	Mintage	MS-63	Proof
2006 Proof	10,108	—	45.00

KM# 659 31.1200 g. 0.9999 Silver 1.0004 oz. ASW **Subject:** C.A.F. Snowbirds Acrobatic Jet Flying Team **Rev:** Image of fighter jets and pilot

Date	Mintage	MS-63	Proof
2006 Proof	10,034	—	50.00

KM# 1036 31.1200 g. 0.9990 Silver 0.9995 oz. ASW **Subject:** 80th Anniversary **Rev:** Two deer standing, one eating branch

Date	Mintage	MS-63	Proof
2009 Proof	27,872	—	70.00

KM# 658 31.1200 g. 0.9999 Silver 1.0004 oz. ASW 36.07 mm. **Subject:** Breast Cancer Awareness **Rev:** Colorized pink ribbon

Date	Mintage	MS-63	Proof
2006 Proof	11,048	—	50.00

KM# 1130 8.5000 g. Bi-Metallic Niobium center in .925 Silver ring 28 mm. **Subject:** Summer - Buck Moon **Obv:** Bust right **Rev:** Buck against summer moon

Date	Mintage	MS-63	Proof
2011 Proof	7,500	—	125

KM# 1131 8.5000 g. Bi-Metallic Niobium center in .925 Silver ring 28 mm. **Subject:** Fall Moon **Obv:** Bust right **Rev:** Native American hunter seated tracking prey before Harvest Moon

Date	Mintage	MS-63	Proof
2011 Proof	7,500	—	125

KM# 1132 8.5000 g. Bi-Metallic Niobium center in .925 Silver ring 28 mm. **Subject:** Winter Moon **Obv:** Bust right **Rev:** Wolf howling before Winter Moon

Date	Mintage	MS-63	Proof
2011 Proof	7,500	—	125

KM# 1133 8.5000 g. Bi-Metallic Niobium center in .925 Silver ring 28 mm. **Subject:** Spring Moon **Obv:** Bust right **Rev:** Phlox blossoming agains a Spring Moon

Date	Mintage	MS-63	Proof
2011 Proof	7,500	—	125

KM# 1149 3.1300 g. 0.9999 Gold 0.1006 oz. AGW 16 mm. **Subject:** Norman Bethune **Obv:** Bust right **Rev:** Half-length figure at right, looking left

Date	Mintage	MS-63	Proof
2011 Proof	Est. 5,000	—	300

KM# 1194 Gold **Obv:** Bust right **Rev:** Royal Cypher, wreath below

Date	Mintage	MS-63	Proof
2012 Proof	—	—	200

KM# 1220 3.1300 g. 0.9999 Gold 0.1006 oz. AGW 16 mm. **Subject:** Year of the Dragon **Obv:** Bust right **Rev:** Dragon forpart right

Date	Mintage	MS-63	Proof
2012 Specimen	Est. 38,888	—	225

8 DOLLARS

KM# 515 28.8000 g. 0.9250 Silver 0.8565 oz. ASW 39 mm. **Obv:** Head right **Obv. Designer:** Susanna Blunt **Rev:** Grizzly bear walking left **Edge:** Reeded

Date	Mintage	MS-63	Proof
2004 Proof	12,942	—	85.00

KM# 597 32.1500 g. 0.9999 Silver 1.0335 oz. ASW partially gilt **Subject:** Canadian Pacific Railway, 120th Anniversary **Obv:** Head right **Obv. Designer:** Susanna Blunt **Rev:** Railway bridge, center is gilt

Date	Mintage	MS-63	Proof
2005 Proof	9,892	—	65.00

KM# 598 32.1500 g. 0.9999 Silver 1.0335 oz. ASW partially gilt **Subject:** Canadian Pacific Railway, 120th Anniversary **Obv:** Head right **Rev:** Railway memorial to the Chinese workers, center gilt

Date	Mintage	MS-63	Proof
2005 Proof	9,892	—	65.00

KM# 730 25.1800 g. 0.9999 Silver 0.8094 oz. ASW 36.07 mm. **Obv:** Queens's head at top in circle, three Chinese characters **Rev:** Dragon and other creatures

Date	Mintage	MS-63	Proof
2007 Proof	19,996	—	55.00

KM# 943 25.1800 g. Silver 36.1 mm. **Rev:** Hologram maple of wisdom at top left, crystal in center, dragons around

Date	Mintage	MS-63	Proof
2009 Proof	7,273	—	90.00

KM# 731 0.9990 Silver **Rev:** Maple leaf, long life hologram

Date	Mintage	MS-63	Proof
2007	15,000	—	60.00

KM# 1012 25.3000 g. 0.9250 Silver 0.7524 oz. ASW 36.07 mm. **Rev:** Horses around central maple leaf hologram **Rev. Designer:** Simon Ng

Date	Mintage	MS-63	Proof
2010 Proof	8,888	—	100

10 DOLLARS

KM# 27 16.7185 g. 0.9000 Gold 0.4837 oz. AGW 26.92 mm. **Obv:** Crowned bust left **Obv. Designer:** E. B. MacKennal **Rev:** Arms within wreath, date and denomination below **Rev. Designer:** W. H. J. Blakemore

Date	Mintage	F-12	VF-20	XF-40	AU-50	MS-60	MS-63
1912	74,759	—	—	—	BV	900	2,700
1913	149,232	—	—	—	BV	900	3,000
1914	140,068	—	—	—	BV	1,150	3,000

Date	Mintage	MS-63	Proof
1973	—	47.50	—
1973 Proof	165,203	—	47.50

KM# 86.2 48.6000 g. 0.9250 Silver 1.4453 oz. ASW 45 mm. **Subject:** 1976 Montreal Olympics **Obv:** Young bust right, small maple leaf below, date at right **Rev:** World map **Rev. Designer:** Georges Huel **Note:** Series I.

Date	Mintage	MS-63	Proof
1974	320	325	—

Note: *Error: mule*

KM# 93 48.6000 g. 0.9250 Silver 1.4453 oz. ASW 45 mm. **Subject:** 1976 Montreal Olympics **Obv:** Young bust right, small maple leaf below, date at right **Rev:** Head of Zeus, denomination below **Rev. Designer:** Anthony Mann **Note:** Series II.

Date	Mintage	MS-63	Proof
1974	—	47.50	—
1974 Proof	104,684	—	47.50

KM# 86.1 48.6000 g. 0.9250 Silver 1.4453 oz. ASW 45 mm. **Subject:** 1976 Montreal Olympics **Obv:** Young bust right, maple leaf below, date at right **Rev:** World map, denomination below **Rev. Designer:** Georges Huel **Note:** Series I.

Date	Mintage	MS-63	Proof
1973	103,426	47.50	—
1973 Proof	165,203	—	47.50

KM# 87 48.6000 g. 0.9250 Silver 1.4453 oz. ASW 45 mm. **Subject:** 1976 Montreal Olympics **Obv:** Young bust right, small maple leaf below, date at right **Rev:** Montreal skyline, denomination below **Rev. Designer:** Georges Huel **Note:** Series I.

KM# 94 48.6000 g. 0.9250 Silver 1.4453 oz. ASW 45 mm. **Subject:** 1976 Montreal Olympics **Obv:** Young bust right, small maple leaf below, date at

right **Rev:** Temple of Zeus, denomination below **Rev. Designer:** Anthony Mann **Note:** Series II.

Date	Mintage	MS-63	Proof
1974	—	47.50	—
1974 Proof	104,684	—	47.50

KM# 95 48.6000 g. 0.9250 Silver 1.4453 oz. ASW 45 mm.   **Subject:** 1976 Montreal Olympics **Obv:** Young bust right, small maple leaf below, date at right **Rev:** Cycling, denomination below **Rev. Designer:** Ken Danby **Note:** Series III.

Date	Mintage	MS-63	Proof
1974	—	47.50	—
1974 Proof	97,431	—	47.50

KM# 96 48.6000 g. 0.9250 Silver 1.4453 oz. ASW 45 mm.   **Subject:** 1976 Montreal Olympics **Obv:** Young bust right, small maple leaf below, date at right **Rev:** Lacrosse, denomination below **Rev. Designer:** Ken Danby **Note:** Series III.

Date	Mintage	MS-63	Proof
1974	—	47.50	—
1974 Proof	97,431	—	47.50

KM# 102 48.6000 g. 0.9250 Silver 1.4453 oz. ASW 45 mm.   **Subject:** 1976 Montreal Olympics **Obv:** Young bust right, small maple leaf below, date at right **Rev:** Men's hurdles, denomination below **Rev. Designer:** Leo Yerxa **Note:** Series IV.

Date	Mintage	MS-63	Proof
1975	—	47.50	—
1975 Proof	82,302	—	47.50

KM# 103 48.6000 g. 0.9250 Silver 1.4453 oz. ASW 45 mm.   **Subject:** Montreal 1976 - 21st Summer Olympic Games **Obv:** Young bust right, small maple leaf below, date at right **Rev:** Women's shot put, denomination below **Rev. Designer:** Leo Yerxa **Note:** Series IV.

Date	Mintage	MS-63	Proof
1975	—	47.50	—
1975 Proof	82,302	—	47.50

KM# 104 48.6000 g. 0.9250 Silver 1.4453 oz. ASW 45 mm. **Subject:** 1976 Montreal Olympics **Obv:** Young bust right, small maple leaf below, date at right **Rev:** Sailing, denomination below **Rev. Designer:** Lynda Cooper **Note:** Series V.

Date	Mintage	MS-63	Proof
1975	—	47.50	—
1975 Proof	89,155	—	47.50

KM# 105 48.6000 g. 0.9250 Silver 1.4453 oz. ASW 45 mm. **Subject:** 1976 Montreal Olympics **Obv:** Young bust right, small maple leaf below, date at

right **Rev:** Canoeing, denomination below **Rev. Designer:** Lynda Cooper **Note:** Series V.

Date	Mintage	MS-63	Proof
1975	—	47.50	—
1975 Proof	89,155	—	47.50

KM# 111 48.6000 g. 0.9250 Silver 1.4453 oz. ASW 45 mm. **Subject:** 1976 Montreal Olympics **Obv:** Young bust right, small maple leaf below, date at right **Rev:** Football, denomination below **Rev. Designer:** Shigeo Fukada **Note:** Series VI.

Date	Mintage	MS-63	Proof
1976	—	47.50	—
1976 Proof	76,908	—	47.50

KM# 112 48.6000 g. 0.9250 Silver 1.4453 oz. ASW 45 mm. **Subject:** 1976 Montreal Olympics **Obv:** Young bust right, small maple leaf below, date at right **Rev:** Field hockey **Rev. Designer:** Shigeo Fukada **Note:** Series VI.

Date	Mintage	MS-63	Proof
1976	—	47.50	—
1976 Proof	76,908	—	47.50

KM# 113 48.6000 g. 0.9250 Silver
1.4453 oz. ASW 45 mm. **Subject:**
1976 Montreal Olympics **Obv:** Young
bust right, small maple leaf below, date
at right **Rev:** Olympic Stadium,
denomination below **Rev. Designer:**
Elliot John Morrison **Note:** Series VII.

Date	Mintage	MS-63	Proof
1976	—	47.50	—
1976 Proof	79,102	—	47.50

KM# 114 48.6000 g. 0.9250 Silver
1.4453 oz. ASW 45 mm. **Subject:**
1976 Montreal Olympics **Obv:** Young

bust right, small maple leaf below, date
at right **Rev:** Olympic Velodrome,
denomination below **Rev. Designer:**
Elliot John Morrison **Note:** Series VII.

Date	Mintage	MS-63	Proof
1976	—	47.50	—
1976 Proof	79,102	—	47.50

KM# 520 16.7200 g. 0.9000 Gold
0.4838 oz. AGW 26.92 mm. **Obv:**
Crowned head right **Rev:** National
arms **Edge:** Reeded

Date	Mintage	MS-63	Proof
1912-2002 Proof	2,002	—	850

KM# 559 25.1750 g. 0.9999 Silver
0.8093 oz. ASW 36 mm. **Subject:**
Pope John Paul II **Obv:** Head right

Date	Mintage	MS-63	Proof
2005 Proof	24,716	—	45.00

KM# 757 25.1750 g. 0.9999 Silver
0.8093 oz. ASW **Subject:** Year of the
Veteran **Rev:** Profile left of young and
old veteran

Date	Mintage	MS-63	Proof
2005 Proof	6,549	—	225

KM# 661 25.1750 g. 0.9999 Silver
0.8093 oz. ASW   **Subject:** National
Historic Sites **Obv:** Head right **Rev:**
Fortress of Louisbourg

Date	Mintage	MS-63	Proof
2006 Proof	5,544	—	40.00

KM# 1010 0.9990 Silver   **Subject:**
75th Anniversary Canadian Bank
Notes **Rev:** Female seated

Date	Mintage	MS-63	Proof
2010 Proof	7,500	—	80.00

KM# 1096 27.7800 g. 0.9250 Silver
0.8261 oz. ASW 40 mm.   **Obv:** Bust
right **Rev:** Blue whale diving in sea

Date	Mintage	MS-63	Proof
2010 Proof	10,000	—	85.00

KM# 1199 15.8700 g. 0.9999 Silver
0.5102 oz. ASW 34 mm.   **Subject:**
Winter Scene - Skating **Rev:** Three kids
skating on pond, colored holly at left

Date	Mintage	MS-63	Proof
2011 Proof	Est. 8,000	—	40.00

KM# 1198 15.8700 g. 0.9990 Silver
0.5097 oz. ASW 34 mm.   **Subject:**
Highway of Heroes **Obv:** Bust right
Obv. Designer: Susanna Blunt **Rev:**
Citizens on Highway 401 overpass with
signs and flags, large maple leaf in
background, Memorial Cross medal at
top left. **Rev. Designer:** Stan Witten and
Major Carl Gauthier **Edge:** Reeded

Date	Mintage	MS-63	Proof
2011	25,000	—	70.00

KM# 1200 15.8700 g. 0.9999 Silver
0.5102 oz. ASW 34 mm.   **Subject:**
Winter scene - Two houses **Rev:** Two
houses in snowy lane, colored holly
flanking

Date	Mintage	MS-63	Proof
2011 Proof	Est. 8,000	—	40.00

KM# 1201 15.8700 g. 0.9999 Silver
0.5102 oz. ASW 34 mm.   **Obv:** Bust
right **Rev:** Wood Bison **Rev. Designer:**
Corrine Hunt

Date	Mintage	MS-63	Proof
2011 Proof	Est. 10,000	—	50.00

KM# 1203 15.8700 g. 0.9999 Silver 0.5102 oz. ASW 34 mm.   **Subject:** Boreal Forest **Rev:** Bird and tree **Rev. Designer:** Corrine Hunt

Date	Mintage	MS-63	Proof
2011 Proof	Est. 10,000	—	50.00

KM# 1205 15.8700 g. 0.9999 Silver 0.5102 oz. ASW 34 mm.   **Obv:** Bust right **Rev:** Peregrine Falcon perched on branch **Rev. Designer:** Corrine Hunt

Date	Mintage	MS-63	Proof
2011 Proof	Est. 10,000	—	50.00

KM# 1207 15.8700 g. 0.9999 Silver 0.5102 oz. ASW 34 mm.   **Obv:** Bust right **Rev:** Orca Whale **Rev. Designer:** Corrine Hunt

Date	Mintage	MS-63	Proof
2011 Proof	Est. 10,000	—	50.00

KM# 1221 15.8700 g. 0.9990 Silver 0.5097 oz. ASW 34 mm.   **Subject:** Year of the Dragon **Obv:** Bust right **Rev:** Dragon forepart right

Date	Mintage	MS-63	Proof
2012 Specimen	58,888	—	40.00

15 DOLLARS

KM# 216 33.6300 g. 0.9250 Silver 1.0000 oz. ASW   **Subject:** 1992 Olympics **Obv:** Crowned head right, date at left, denomination below **Rev:** High jump, rings, speed skating **Rev. Designer:** David Craig

Date	Mintage	MS-63	Proof
1992 Proof	275,000	—	35.00

KM# 215 33.6300 g. 0.9250 Silver 1.0000 oz. ASW 39 mm.   **Subject:** 1992 Olympics **Obv:** Crowned head right, date at left, denomination below **Rev:** Coaching track **Rev. Designer:** Stewart Sherwood

Date	Mintage	MS-63	Proof
1992 Proof	275,000	—	35.00

KM# 304 Bi-Metallic 0.999 gold center in 0.925 silver ring 40 mm.   **Subject:** Year of the Tiger **Obv:** Crowned head right **Rev:** Tiger within octagon at

center, animal figures surround **Rev. Designer:** Harvey Chan

Date	Mintage	MS-63	Proof
1998 Proof	68,888	—	375

KM #331 Bi-Metallic 0.999 Gold center in 0.925 Silver ring   **Subject:** Year of the Rabbitt **Obv:** Crowned head right **Rev:** Rabbit within octagon at center, animal figures surround **Rev. Designer:** Harvey Chan

Date	Mintage	MS-63	Proof
1999 Proof	77,791	—	100

KM #387 Bi-Metallic 0.999 Gold center in 0.925 Silver ring   **Subject:** Year of the Dragon **Obv:** Crowned head right **Rev. Designer:** Harvey Chan

Date	Mintage	MS-63	Proof
2000 Proof	88,634	—	150

KM# 415 33.6300 g. 0.9250 Silver 1.0000 oz. ASW with gold insert

40 mm.   **Subject:** Year of the Snake **Obv:** Crowned head right **Rev:** Snake within circle of lunar calendar signs **Rev. Designer:** Harvey Chain **Edge:** Reeded

Date	Mintage	MS-63	Proof
2001 Proof	60,754	—	85.00

KM# 463 33.6300 g. 0.9250 Silver 1.0000 oz. ASW with gold insert **Subject:** Year of the Horse **Obv:** Crowned head right **Obv. Designer:** Dora dePédery-Hunt **Rev:** Horse in center with Chinese Lunar calendar around **Rev. Designer:** Harvey Chain

Date	Mintage	MS-63	Proof
2002 Proof	59,395	—	85.00

KM# 481 33.6300 g. 0.9250 Silver 1.0000 oz. ASW with gold insert 40 mm.   **Subject:** Year of the Sheep **Obv:** Crowned head right **Rev:** Sheep in center with Chinese Lunar calendar around **Rev. Designer:** Harvey Chain

Date	Mintage	MS-63	Proof
2003 Proof	53,714	—	85.00

KM# 610 33.6300 g. 0.9250 Silver 1.0000 oz. ASW Gold octagon applique in center   **Subject:** Year of the Monkey **Obv:** Crowned head right **Rev:** Monkey in center with Chinese Lunar calendar around

Date	Mintage	MS-63	Proof
2004 Proof	46,175	—	150

KM# 560 33.6300 g. 0.9250 Silver 1.0000 oz. ASW with gold insert **Subject:** Year of the Rooster **Obv:** Crowned head right **Rev:** Rooster in center with Chinese Lunar calendar around

Date	Mintage	MS-63	Proof
2005 Proof	44,690	—	125

KM# 587 33.6300 g. 0.9250 Silver 1.0000 oz. ASW with gold insert **Subject:** Year of the Dog **Obv:** Crowned head left **Rev:** Dog in center with Chinese Lunar calendar around

Date	Mintage	MS-63	Proof
2006 Proof	41,617	—	100

KM# 732 33.6300 g. 0.9250 Silver 1.0000 oz. ASW with gold insert 40 mm.   **Subject:** Year of the Pig **Rev:** Pig at center of lunar characters

Date	Mintage	MS-63	Proof
2007 Proof	48,888	—	100

KM# 801 33.6300 g. 0.9250 Silver 1.0000 oz. ASW with gold insert 40 mm.   **Subject:** Year of the Rat **Rev:** Rat, gold octagonal insert at center

Date	Mintage	MS-63	Proof
2008 Proof	48,888	—	90.00

KM# 803 30.0000 g. 0.9250 Silver 0.8921 oz. ASW 36.15 mm.   **Rev:** Queen Victoria's coinage portrait

Date	Mintage	MS-63	Proof
2008	3,442	100.00	—

KM# 804 30.0000 g. 0.9250 Silver 0.8921 oz. ASW 36.15 mm.   **Rev:** Edward VII coinage portrait **Rev. Designer:** G. W. DeSaulles

Date	Mintage	MS-63	Proof
2008	6,261	100.00	—

KM# 805 20.0000 g. 0.9250 Silver 0.5948 oz. ASW 36.15 mm.   **Rev:** George V coinage portrait

Date	Mintage	MS-63	Proof
2008	—	100.00	—

KM# 806 31.5600 g. 0.9250 Silver 0.9385 oz. ASW 49.8 x 28.6 mm.   **Rev:** Queen of Spades, multicolor playing card

Date	Mintage	MS-63	Proof
2008 Proof	8,714	—	90.00

KM# 807 31.5600 g. 0.9250 Silver 0.9385 oz. ASW 28.6x49.8 mm.   **Rev:** Jack of Hearts, multicolor playing card

Date	Mintage	MS-63	Proof
2008 Proof	11,362	—	90.00

KM# 919 31.5600 g. 0.9250 Silver
0.9385 oz. ASW 49.8 x 28.6 mm.   **Obv:**
Bust right **Obv. Designer:** Susanna
Blunt **Rev:** Ten of spades, multicolor
Shape: rectangle

Date	Mintage	MS-63	Proof
2009 Proof	5,921	—	90.00

KM# 866 33.6300 g. 0.9250 Silver
1.0000 oz. ASW with gold insert
40 mm.   **Subject:** Year of the Ox **Rev:**
Ox, octagon gold insert

Date	Mintage	MS-63	Proof
2009 Proof	48,888	—	90.00

KM# 920 31.5600 g. 0.9250 Silver
0.9385 oz. ASW 49.8 x 28.6 mm.   **Obv:**
Bust right **Obv. Designer:** Susanna
Blunt **Rev:** King of hearts, multicolor
Shape: Rectangle

Date	Mintage	MS-63	Proof
2009 Proof	5,798	—	90.00

KM# 922 30.0000 g. 0.9250 Silver
0.8921 oz. ASW 36.15 mm.   **Obv:** Bust
right **Obv. Designer:** Susanna Blunt
Rev: Paget portrait of George VI

Date	Mintage	MS-63	Proof
2009(ml) Prooflike	—	100.00	—

KM# 923 30.0000 g. 0.9250 Silver 0.8921 oz. ASW 36.15 mm.   **Obv:** Bust right **Obv. Designer:** Susanna Blunt **Rev:** Gillick portrait of Queen Elizabeth II

Date	Mintage	MS-63	Proof
2009(ml) Prooflike	2,643	100.00	—

KM# 1032 0.9990 Silver   **Subject:** Year of the tiger **Rev:** Tiger walking tiger

Date	Mintage	MS-63	Proof
2010 Proof	9,999	—	85.00

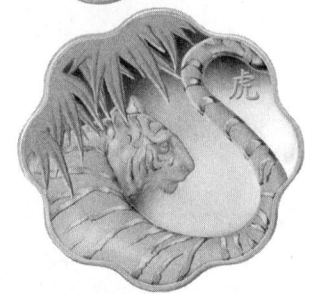

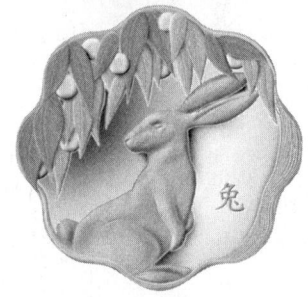

KM# 1038 Silver 38 mm.   **Subject:** Year of the tiger **Rev:** Tiger in forest **Shape:** scalloped

Date	Mintage	MS-63	Proof
2009 Proof	10,268	—	85.00

KM# 980 34.0000 g. 0.9250 Silver 1.0111 oz. ASW 40 mm.   **Rev:** Tiger in gold insert

Date	Mintage	MS-63	Proof
2010 Proof	48,888	—	100

KM# 1055 31.1050 g. 0.9990 Silver 0.9990 oz. ASW 38 mm.   **Rev:** Rabbit sitting, head turned left **Shape:** scalloped

Date	Mintage	MS-63	Proof
2011 Proof	19,888	—	85.00

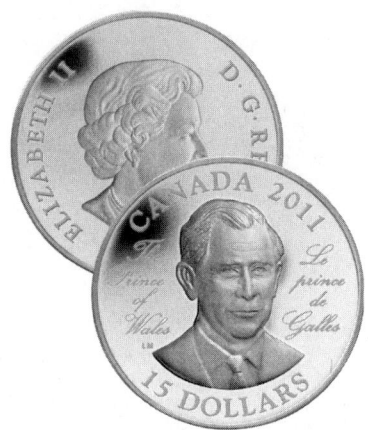

KM# 1091 25.1100 g. 0.9250 Silver 0.7467 oz. ASW 36.15 mm.   **Rev:** Prince Charles bust **Rev. Designer:** Laurie McGaw

Date	Mintage	MS-63	Proof
2011 Prooflike	10,000	100.00	—

KM# 1092 25.1100 g. 0.9250 Silver 0.7467 oz. ASW 36.15 mm.   **Rev:** Prince William **Rev. Designer:** Laurie McGaw

Date	Mintage	MS-63	Proof
2011 Prooflike	10,000	100.00	—

KM# 1093 25.1800 g. 0.9250 Silver 0.7488 oz. ASW 36.15 mm.   **Rev:**

Prince Harry bust 1/4 right **Rev. Designer:** Laurie McGaw

Date	Mintage	MS-63	Proof
2011 Prooflike	10,000	100.00	—

KM# 1094 31.3900 g. 0.9990 Silver 1.0082 oz. ASW 38 mm.   **Rev:** Rabbit bounding left **Rev. Designer:** Aries Cheung

Date	Mintage	MS-63	Proof
2011 Proof	9,999	—	100

KM# 1152 31.3900 g. 0.9999 Silver 1.0091 oz. ASW 38 mm.   **Obv:** Bust right **Rev:** Magpie, bird of happyness in flight at top, lotus flowers at bottom, maple leaf hologram at center

Date	Mintage	MS-63	Proof
2011 Proof	Est. 8,888	—	100

KM# 1183 31.1050 g. 0.9990 Silver 0.9990 oz. ASW 36.5 mm.   **Subject:** Year of the Dragon **Obv:** Bust right **Rev:** Dragon right

Date	Mintage	MS-63	Proof
2012 Proof	—	—	75.00

KM# 1186 31.1050 g. 0.9990 Silver 0.9990 oz. ASW 36.5 mm.   **Subject:** Year of the Dragon **Obv:** Bust right **Rev:** Dragon left **Shape:** Scalloped

Date	Mintage	MS-63	Proof
2012 Proof	—	—	75.00

20 DOLLARS

KM# 71 18.2733 g. 0.9000 Gold 0.5287 oz. AGW 27.05 mm. **Subject:** Centennial **Obv:** Crowned head right **Rev:** Crowned and supported arms **Edge:** Reeded

Date	Mintage	MS-63	Proof
1967 Proof	337,688	—	1,000

KM# 146 33.6300 g. 0.9250 Silver 1.0000 oz. ASW 40 mm. **Subject:** 1988 Calgary Olympics **Obv:** Young bust right, small maple leaf below, date at right **Rev:** Speed skater, denomination below **Rev. Designer:** Friedrich Peter **Edge:** Lettered

Date	Mintage	MS-63	Proof
1985 Proof	354,222	—	35.00
1985 Proof	Inc. above	—	200

Note: Plain edge

KM# 145 33.6300 g. 0.9250 Silver 1.0000 oz. ASW 40 mm. **Subject:** 1988 Calgary Olympics **Obv:** Young bust right, maple leaf below, date at right **Rev:** Downhill skier, denomination below **Rev. Designer:** Ian Stewart **Edge:** Lettered

Date	Mintage	MS-63	Proof
1985 Proof	406,360	—	35.00
1985 Proof	Inc. above	—	200

Note: Plain edge

KM# 150 33.6300 g. 0.9250 Silver 1.0000 oz. ASW 40 mm. **Subject:** Calgary 1988 - 15th Winter Olympic Games **Obv:** Young bust right, small

maple leaf below, date at right **Rev:**
Cross-country skier, denomination
below **Rev. Designer:** Ian Stewart
Edge: Lettered

Date	Mintage	MS-63	Proof
1986 Proof	303,199	—	35.00

KM# 147 33.6300 g. 0.9250 Silver
1.0000 oz. ASW 40 mm.   **Subject:** 1988
Calgary Olympics **Obv:** Young bust
right, small maple leaf below, date at
right **Rev:** Biathlon, denomination
below **Rev. Designer:** John Mardon
Edge: Lettered

Date	Mintage	MS-63	Proof
1986 Proof	308,086	—	35.00
1986 Proof	Inc. above	—	200

Note: Plain edge

KM# 148 33.6300 g. 0.9250 Silver
1.0000 oz. ASW 40 mm.   **Subject:** 1988
Calgary Olympics **Obv:** Young bust
right, small maple leaf below, date at
right **Rev:** Hockey, denomination
below **Rev. Designer:** Ian Stewart
Edge: Lettered

Date	Mintage	MS-63	Proof
1986 Proof	396,602	—	35.00
1986 Proof	Inc. above	—	200

Note: Plain edge

KM# 151 33.6300 g. 0.9250 Silver
1.0000 oz. ASW 40 mm.   **Subject:** 1988
Calgary Olympics **Obv:** Young bust
right, small maple leaf below, date at
right **Rev:** Free-style skier,
denomination below **Rev. Designer:**
Walter Ott **Edge:** Lettered

Date	Mintage	MS-63	Proof
1986 Proof	294,322	—	35.00
1986 Proof	Inc. above	—	200

Note: Plain edge

KM# 155 34.1070 g. 0.9250 Silver
1.0143 oz. ASW 40 mm.   **Subject:**
Calgary 1988 - 15th Winter Olympic
Games **Obv:** Young bust right, small

maple leaf below, date at right **Rev:**
Figure skating pairs event,
denomination below **Rev. Designer:**
Raymond Taylor **Edge:** Lettered

Date	Mintage	MS-63	Proof
1987 Proof	334,875	—	35.00

KM# 156 34.1070 g. 0.9250 Silver
1.0143 oz. ASW 40 mm. **Subject:**
1988 Calgary Olympics **Obv:** Young
bust right, small maple leaf below, date
at right **Rev:** Curling, denomination
below **Rev. Designer:** Ian Stewart
Edge: Lettered

Date	Mintage	MS-63	Proof
1987 Proof	286,457	—	35.00

KM# 159 34.1070 g. 0.9250 Silver
1.0143 oz. ASW 40 mm. **Subject:**
1988 Calgary Olympics **Obv:** Young
bust right, small maple leaf below, date
at right **Rev:** Ski jumper, denomination
below **Rev. Designer:** Raymond Taylor
Edge: Lettered

Date	Mintage	MS-63	Proof
1987 Proof	290,954	—	35.00

KM# 160 34.1070 g. 0.9250 Silver
1.0143 oz. ASW 40 mm. **Subject:**
1988 Calgary Olympics **Obv:** Young
bust right, maple leaf below, date at
right **Rev:** Bobsled, denomination
below **Rev. Designer:** John Mardon
Edge: Lettered

Date	Mintage	MS-63	Proof
1987 Proof	274,326	—	35.00

KM# 172 31.1030 g. 0.9250 Silver
0.9249 oz. ASW gold cameo insert
38 mm. **Subject:** Aviation **Obv:**
Crowned head right, date below **Rev:**
Lancaster, Fauquier in cameo,
denomination below **Rev. Designer:**
Robert R. Carmichael

Date	Mintage	MS-63	Proof
1990 Proof	43,596	—	125

KM# 197 31.1030 g. 0.9250 Silver 0.9249 oz. ASW gold cameo insert 38 mm. **Subject:** Aviation **Obv:** Crowned head right, date below **Rev:** de Haviland Beaver, Philip C. Garratt in cameo, denomination below **Rev. Designer:** Peter Massman

Date	Mintage	MS-63	Proof
1991 Proof	29,399	—	45.00

KM# 173 31.1030 g. 0.9250 Silver 0.9249 oz. ASW with Gold cameo insert. 38 mm. **Subject:** Aviation **Obv:** Crowned head right, date below **Rev:** Anson and Harvard, Air Marshal Robert Leckie in cameo, denomination below **Rev. Designer:** Geoff Bennett

Date	Mintage	MS-63	Proof
1990 Proof	41,844	—	45.00

KM# 196 31.1030 g. 0.9250 Silver 0.9249 oz. ASW gold cameo insert 38 mm. **Subject:** Aviation **Obv:** Crowned head right, date below **Rev:** Silver Dart, John A. D. McCurdy and F. W. "Casey" Baldwin in cameo, denomination below **Rev. Designer:** George Velinger

Date	Mintage	MS-63	Proof
1991 Proof	28,791	—	45.00

KM# 224 31.1030 g. 0.9250 Silver 0.9249 oz. ASW gold cameo insert 38 mm. **Subject:** Aviation **Obv:** Crowned head right, date below **Rev:** Curtiss JN-4 Canick ("Jenny"), Sir Frank W. Baillie in cameo, denomination below **Rev. Designer:** George Velinger

Date	Mintage	MS-63	Proof
1992 Proof	33,105	—	45.00

KM# 237 31.1030 g. 0.9250 Silver
0.9249 oz. ASW with Gold cameo
insert. 38 mm.   **Subject:** Aviation
Obv: Crowned head right, date below
Rev: Lockheed 14, Zebulon Lewis
Leigh in cameo, denomination below
Rev. Designer: Robert R. Carmichael

Date	Mintage	MS-63	Proof
1993 Proof	32,550	—	45.00

KM# 225 31.1030 g. 0.9250 Silver
0.9249 oz. ASW with Gold cameo
insert. 38 mm.   **Subject:** Aviation
Obv: Crowned head right, date below
Rev: de Haviland Gypsy Moth, Murton
A. Seymour in cameo, denomination
below **Rev. Designer:** John Mardon

Date	Mintage	MS-63	Proof
1992 Proof	32,537	—	45.00

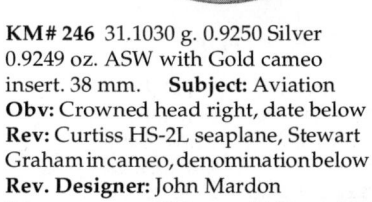

KM# 236 31.1030 g. 0.9250 Silver
0.9249 oz. ASW with Gold cameo
insert. 38 mm.   **Subject:** Aviation
Obv: Crowned head right, date below
Rev: Fairchild 71C float plane, James A.
Richardson, Sr. in cameo,
denomination below **Rev. Designer:**
Robert R. Carmichael

Date	Mintage	MS-63	Proof
1993 Proof	32,199	—	45.00

KM# 246 31.1030 g. 0.9250 Silver
0.9249 oz. ASW with Gold cameo
insert. 38 mm.   **Subject:** Aviation
Obv: Crowned head right, date below
Rev: Curtiss HS-2L seaplane, Stewart
Graham in cameo, denomination below
Rev. Designer: John Mardon

Date	Mintage	MS-63	Proof
1994 Proof	31,242	—	45.00

KM# 247 31.1030 g. 0.9250 Silver 0.9249 oz. ASW with Gold cameo insert. 38 mm.   **Subject:** Aviation **Obv:** Crowned head right, date below **Rev:** Vickers Vedette, Wilfred T. Reid in cameo, denomination below **Rev. Designer:** Robert R. Carmichael

Date	Mintage	MS-63	Proof
1994 Proof	30,880	—	45.00

KM# 271 31.1030 g. 0.9250 Silver 0.9249 oz. ASW gold cameo insert 38 mm.   **Subject:** Aviation **Obv:** Crowned head right, date below **Rev:** C-FEA1 Fleet Cannuck, denomination below **Rev. Designer:** Robert Bradford

Date	Mintage	MS-63	Proof
1995 Proof	17,438	—	45.00

KM# 272 31.1030 g. 0.9250 Silver 0.9249 oz. ASW gold cameo insert 38 mm.   **Subject:** Aviation **Obv:** Crowned head right, date below **Rev:** DHC-1 Chipmunk, denomination below **Rev. Designer:** Robert Bradford

Date	Mintage	MS-63	Proof
1995 Proof	17,722	—	45.00

KM# 276 31.1030 g. 0.9250 Silver 0.9249 oz. ASW gold cameo insert 38 mm.   **Subject:** Aviation **Obv:** Crowned head right, date below **Rev:** CF-100 Cannuck, denomination below **Rev. Designer:** Jim Bruce

Date	Mintage	MS-63	Proof
1996 Proof	18,508	—	45.00

0.9249 oz. ASW with Gold cameo insert. 38 mm.   **Subject:** Aviation **Obv:** Crowned head right, date below **Rev:** Canadair CT-114 Tutor, denomination below **Rev. Designer:** Ross Buckland

Date	Mintage	MS-63	Proof
1997 Proof	15,669	—	45.00

KM# 329 31.1030 g. 0.9250 Silver 0.9249 oz. ASW gold cameo insert 38 mm.   **Subject:** Aviation **Obv:** Crowned head, right, date below **Rev:** CP-107 Argus, denomination below

Date	Mintage	MS-63	Proof
1998 Proof	Est. 50,000	—	50.00

KM# 330 31.1030 g. 0.9250 Silver 0.9249 oz. ASW gold cameo insert 38 mm.   **Subject:** Aviation **Obv:** Crowned head right, date below **Rev:** CP-215 Waterbomber, denomination below **Rev. Designer:** Peter Mossman

Date	Mintage	MS-63	Proof
1998 Proof	Est. 50,000	—	75.00

KM# 277 31.1030 g. 0.9250 Silver 0.9249 oz. ASW gold cameo insert 38 mm.   **Subject:** Aviation **Obv:** Crowned head right, date below **Obv. Legend:** CF-105 Arrow, denomination below **Rev. Designer:** Jim Bruce

Date	Mintage	MS-63	Proof
1996 Proof	27,163	—	100

KM# 297 31.1030 g. 0.9250 Silver 0.9249 oz. ASW gold cameo insert 38 mm.   **Subject:** Aviation **Obv:** Crowned head right, date below **Rev:** Canadair F-86 Sabre, denomination below **Rev. Designer:** Ross Buckland

Date	Mintage	MS-63	Proof
1997 Proof	14,389	—	45.00

KM# 298 31.1030 g. 0.9250 Silver

KM# 339 31.1030 g. 0.9250 Silver 0.9249 oz. ASW gold cameo insert 38 mm.   **Subject:** Aviation **Obv:** Crowned head right, date below **Rev:** DHC-6 Twin Otter, denomination below **Rev. Designer:** Neil Aird

Date	Mintage	MS-63	Proof
1999 Proof	Est. 50,000	—	95.00

KM# 340 31.1030 g. 0.9250 Silver 0.9249 oz. ASW gold cameo insert 38 mm.   **Subject:** Aviation **Obv:** Crowned head right, date below **Rev:** DHC-8 Dash 8, denomination below

Date	Mintage	MS-63	Proof
1999 Proof	50,000	—	100

KM# 395 0.9250 Silver 38 mm.
Subject: First Canadian locomotive

Obv: Crowned head right, date below
Rev: Locomotive below multicolored cameo, denomination below

Date	Mintage	MS-63	Proof
2000 Proof	—	—	50.00

KM# 396 0.9250 Silver 38 mm.
Subject: First Canadian self-propelled car **Obv:** Crowned head right, date below **Rev:** Car below multicolored cameo, denomination below

Date	Mintage	MS-63	Proof
2000 Proof	—	—	50.00

KM# 397 0.9250 Silver 38 mm.
Subject: Bluenose sailboat **Obv:** Crowned head right, date below **Rev:** Bluenose sailing left below multicolored cameo, denomination below

Date	Mintage	MS-63	Proof
2000 Proof	—	—	150

KM# 428 31.1030 g. 0.9250 Silver 0.9249 oz. ASW 38 mm.   **Series:** Transportation - Russell Touring Car **Obv:** Crowned head right **Rev:** Russell touring car with hologram cameo **Rev. Designer:** John Mardon **Edge:** Segmented reeding

Date	Mintage	MS-63	Proof
2001 Proof	15,000	—	45.00

KM# 464 31.1030 g. 0.9250 Silver 0.9249 oz. ASW   **Obv:** Crowned head right **Obv. Designer:** Dora dePédery-Hunt **Rev:** Gray-Dort Model 25-SM with cameo hologram **Rev. Designer:** John Mardon

Date	Mintage	MS-63	Proof
2002 Proof	15,000	—	45.00

KM# 465 31.1030 g. 0.9250 Silver 0.9249 oz. ASW   **Obv:** Crowned head right **Obv. Designer:** Dora dePédery-Hunt **Rev:** Sailing ship William D. Lawrence **Rev. Designer:** Bonnie Ross

Date	Mintage	MS-63	Proof
2002 Proof	15,000	—	45.00

KM# 411 31.1035 g. 0.9250 Silver 0.9250 oz. ASW 38 mm.   **Subject:** Transportation - Steam Locomotive **Obv:** Crowned head right **Obv. Designer:** Dora dePédery-Hunt **Rev:** First Canadian Steel Steam Locomotive and cameo hologram **Rev. Designer:** Don Curely **Edge:** Segmented reeding

Date	Mintage	MS-63	Proof
2001 Proof	15,000	—	45.00

KM# 427 31.1030 g. 0.9250 Silver 0.9249 oz. ASW 38 mm.   **Series:** Transportation - The Marco Polo **Obv:** Crowned head right **Rev:** Sailship with hologram cameo **Rev. Designer:** J. Franklin Wright **Edge:** Segmented reeding

Date	Mintage	MS-63	Proof
2001 Proof	15,000	—	45.00

KM# 482 31.3900 g. 0.9999 Silver 1.0091 oz. ASW 38 mm.   **Obv:** Crowned head right **Obv. Designer:** Dora dePédery-Hunt **Rev:** Niagara Falls hologram **Rev. Designer:** Gary Corcoran

Date	Mintage	MS-63	Proof
2003 Proof	29,967	—	75.00

KM# 483 31.1030 g. 0.9250 Silver 0.9249 oz. ASW with selective gold plating **Subject:** The HMCS Bras d'or (FHE-400) **Obv:** Crowned head right **Obv. Designer:** Dora dePédery-Hunt **Rev:** Ship in water **Rev. Designer:** Donald Curley, Stan Witten

Date	Mintage	MS-63	Proof
2003 Proof	15,000	—	45.00

KM# 611 31.3900 g. 0.9999 Silver 1.0091 oz. ASW 38 mm. **Obv:** Head right **Obv. Designer:** Susanna Blunt **Rev:** Iceberg, hologram

Date	Mintage	MS-63	Proof
2004 Proof	24,879	—	45.00

KM# 523 31.3900 g. 0.9990 Silver 1.0082 oz. ASW 38 mm. **Obv:** Crowned head right **Obv. Designer:** Dora dePédery-Hunt **Rev:** Canadian Rockies, multicolor

Date	Mintage	MS-63	Proof
2003 Proof	29,967	—	50.00

KM# 484 31.1030 g. 0.9250 Silver 0.9249 oz. ASW with selective gold plating **Subject:** Canadian National FA-1 diesel-electric locomotive **Obv:** Crowned head right **Obv. Designer:** Dora dePédery-Hunt **Rev. Designer:** John Mardon, William Woodruff

Date	Mintage	MS-63	Proof
2003 Proof	15,000	—	45.00

KM# 485 31.1030 g. 0.9250 Silver 0.9249 oz. ASW with selective gold plating **Obv:** Crowned head right **Obv. Designer:** Dora dePédery-Hunt **Rev:** The Bricklin SV-1 **Rev. Designer:** Brian Hughes, José Oslo

Date	Mintage	MS-63	Proof
2003 Proof	15,000	—	45.00

KM# 838 31.3900 g. 0.9999 Silver 1.0091 oz. ASW partially gilt 38 mm. **Rev:** Hopewell Rocks, gilt

Date	Mintage	MS-63	Proof
2004 Proof	16,918	—	45.00

KM# 561 31.3900 g. 0.9999 Silver 1.0091 oz. ASW 38 mm. **Obv:** Head right **Obv. Designer:** Susanna Blunt **Rev:** Three-masted sailing ship, hologram of the sea **Rev. Designer:** Bonnie Ross

Date	Mintage	MS-63	Proof
2005 Proof	18,276	—	55.00

KM# 565 31.3900 g. 0.9999 Silver 1.0091 oz. ASW 38 mm. **Subject:** Toronto Island National Park **Obv:** Head right **Rev:** Toronto Island Lighthouse, Toronto skyline in background

Date	Mintage	MS-63	Proof
2005 Proof	—	—	45.00

KM# 588 31.3900 g. 0.9999 Silver 1.0091 oz. ASW **Subject:** Georgian Bay National Park **Obv:** Head right **Rev:** Canoe and small trees on island

Date	Mintage	MS-63	Proof
2006 Proof	—	—	60.00

KM# 562 31.3900 g. 0.9999 Silver 1.0091 oz. ASW 38 mm. **Subject:** Northwest Territories Diamonds **Obv:** Head right **Obv. Designer:** Susanna Blunt **Rev:** Multicolor diamond hologram on landscape **Rev. Designer:** José Oslo **Edge:** Reeded

Date	Mintage	MS-63	Proof
2005 Proof	35,000	—	45.00

KM# 563 31.3900 g. 0.9999 Silver 1.0091 oz. ASW **Subject:** Mingan Archepelago **Obv:** Head right **Obv. Designer:** Susanna Blunt **Rev:** Cliffs with whale tail out of water **Rev. Designer:** Pierre Leduc

Date	Mintage	MS-63	Proof
2005 Proof	—	—	45.00

KM# 564 31.3900 g. 0.9999 Silver 1.0091 oz. ASW **Subject:** Rainforests of the Pacific Northwest **Obv:** Head right **Rev:** Open winged bird

Date	Mintage	MS-63	Proof
2005 Proof	—	—	45.00

KM# 589 31.1000 g. 0.9999 Silver 0.9997 oz. ASW 38 mm. **Obv:** Head right **Rev:** Notre Dame Basilica, Montreal, as a hologram

Date	Mintage	MS-63	Proof
2006 Proof	15,000	—	50.00

KM# 663 31.3900 g. 0.9999 Silver 1.0091 oz. ASW 38 mm. **Subject:** Nahanni National Park **Obv:** Head right **Rev:** Bear walking along sream, cliff in background

Date	Mintage	MS-63	Proof
2006 Proof	—	—	60.00

KM# 664 31.3900 g. 0.9999 Silver 1.0091 oz. ASW 38 mm. **Subject:** Jasper National Park **Obv:** Head right **Rev:** Cowboy on horseback in majestic scene

Date	Mintage	MS-63	Proof
2006 Proof	—	—	60.00

KM# 665 31.1000 g. 0.9999 Silver 0.9997 oz. ASW 38 mm. **Obv:** Head

right **Rev:** Holographic rendering of CN Tower

Date	Mintage	MS-63	Proof
2006 Proof	15,000	—	60.00

KM# 666 31.1000 g. 0.9999 Silver 0.9997 oz. ASW **Obv:** Head right **Rev:** Holographic view of Pengrowth Saddledome in Calgary

Date	Mintage	MS-63	Proof
2006 Proof	15,000	—	55.00

KM# 667 31.3900 g. 0.9999 Silver 1.0091 oz. ASW **Subject:** Tall Ship **Obv:** Head right **Rev:** Ketch and holographic image of thunderstorm in sky

Date	Mintage	MS-63	Proof
2006 Proof	10,299	—	60.00

KM# 734 31.1000 g. 0.9990 Silver
0.9988 oz. ASW 38 mm.   **Rev:** Holiday
sleigh ride

Date	Mintage	MS-63	Proof
2007 Proof	6,804	—	70.00

KM# 737a 31.1000 g. 0.9990 Silver
0.9988 oz. ASW 38 mm.   **Subject:**
International Polar Year **Rev:** Blue
plasma coating

Date	Mintage	MS-63	Proof
2007 Proof	3,005	—	250

KM# 735 31.1000 g. 0.9990 Silver
0.9988 oz. ASW 38 mm.   **Rev:**
Snowflake, aquamarine crystal

Date	Mintage	MS-63	Proof
2007 Proof	4,989	—	175

KM# 737 31.1000 g. 0.9990 Silver
0.9988 oz. ASW 38 mm.   **Subject:**
International Polar Year

Date	Mintage	MS-63	Proof
2007 Proof	9,164	—	65.00

KM# 738 31.3900 g. 0.9999 Silver
1.0091 oz. ASW 38 mm.   **Subject:** Tall
ships **Rev:** Brigantine in harbor,
hologram

Date	Mintage	MS-63	Proof
2007 Proof	16,000	—	60.00

KM# 839 31.3900 g. 0.9999 Silver
1.0091 oz. ASW   **Rev:** Northern lights
in hologram

Date	Mintage	MS-63	Proof
2007	—	35.00	—

KM# 808 31.5000 g. 0.9250 Silver
0.9368 oz. ASW 38 mm.   **Subject:**
Agriculture trade **Rev:** Team of horses
plowing

Date	Mintage	MS-63	Proof
2008 Proof	5,802	—	70.00

KM# 811 31.1050 g. 0.9990 Silver
0.9990 oz. ASW   **Rev:** Snowflake,
amethyst crystal

Date	Mintage	MS-63	Proof
2008 Proof	7,172	—	90.00

KM# 809 31.1050 g. 0.9990 Silver
0.9990 oz. ASW 38 mm.   **Rev:** Royal
Hudson Steam locomotive

Date	Mintage	MS-63	Proof
2008 Proof	8,345	—	70.00

KM# 813 31.1050 g. 0.9990 Silver
0.9990 oz. ASW 38 mm.   **Rev:**
Carolers around tree

Date	Mintage	MS-63	Proof
2008 Proof	10,000	—	70.00

KM# 810 31.3900 g. 0.9990 Silver
1.0082 oz. ASW 38 mm.   **Rev:** Green
leaf and crystal raindrop **Rev.
Designer:** Stanley Witten

Date	Mintage	MS-63	Proof
2008 Proof	15,000	—	110

KM# 872 31.1050 g. 0.9990 Silver
0.9990 oz. ASW 38 mm.   **Rev:**
Snowflake, sapphire crystal

Date	Mintage	MS-63	Proof
2008 Proof	7,765	—	85.00

KM# 893 31.3900 g. 0.9990 Silver 1.0082 oz. ASW 38 mm. **Subject:** Coal mining trade **Obv:** Bust right **Obv. Legend:** Elizabeth II DG Regina **Obv. Designer:** Susanna Blunt **Rev:** Miner pushing cart with coal **Rev. Legend:** Canada 20 Dollars **Rev. Designer:** John Marder

Date	Mintage	MS-63	Proof
2009 Proof	10,000	—	75.00

KM# 870 27.7800 g. 0.9250 Silver 0.8261 oz. ASW 40 mm. **Rev:** Calgary Flames goalie mask multicolor on goal net

Date	Mintage	MS-63	Proof
2009 Proof	10,000	—	70.00

KM# 891 31.3900 g. 0.9990 Silver 1.0082 oz. ASW 38 mm. **Subject:** Great Canadian Locomotives - Jubilee **Obv:** Bust right **Obv. Legend:** Elizabeth II DG Regina **Obv. Designer:** Susanna Blunt **Rev:** Jubilee locomotive side view **Rev. Legend:** Canada 20 Dollars **Edge Lettering:** Jubilee

Date	Mintage	MS-63	Proof
2009 Proof	6,036	—	70.00

KM# 871 27.7800 g. 0.9250 Silver 0.8261 oz. ASW 40 mm. **Rev:** Edmonton Oilers goalie mask, multicolor on goal net

Date	Mintage	MS-63	Proof
2009 Proof	10,000	—	70.00

KM# 872A 27.7800 g. 0.9250 Silver
0.8261 oz. ASW 40 mm.   **Rev:**
Montreal Canadians goalie mask
multicolor

Date	Mintage	MS-63	Proof
2009 Proof	10,000	—	70.00

KM# 873 27.7800 g. 0.9250 Silver
0.8261 oz. ASW 40 mm.   **Rev:** Ottawa
Senators goalie mask on goal net

Date	Mintage	MS-63	Proof
2009 Proof	10,000	—	70.00

KM# 874 27.7800 g. 0.9250 Silver
0.8261 oz. ASW 40 mm.   **Rev:** Toronto
Maple Leafs goalie mask, multicolor on
goal net

Date	Mintage	MS-63	Proof
2009 Proof	10,000	—	70.00

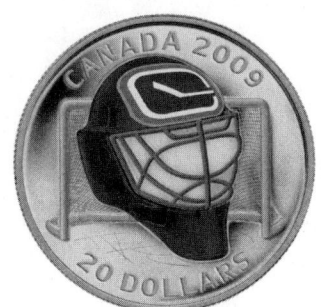

KM# 875 27.7800 g. 0.9250 Silver
0.8261 oz. ASW 40 mm.   **Rev:**
Vancouver Canucks goalie mask,
multicolor on goal net

Date	Mintage	MS-63	Proof
2009 Proof	10,000	—	70.00

KM# 876 31.5000 g. 0.9250 Silver
0.9368 oz. ASW 40 mm.   **Rev:**
Summer moon mask

Date	Mintage	MS-63	Proof
2009 Proof	2,834	—	75.00

KM# 944 31.1050 g. 0.9990 Silver
0.9990 oz. ASW 38 mm.   **Rev:**
Snowflake - light blue crystal

Date	Mintage	MS-63	Proof
2009 Proof	7,477	—	95.00

KM# 945 31.1050 g. 0.9990 Silver 0.9990 oz. ASW 38 mm. **Rev:** Snowflake - light red crystal

Date	Mintage	MS-63	Proof
2009 Proof	7,004	—	95.00

KM# 892 31.3900 g. 0.9990 Silver 1.0082 oz. ASW 38 mm. **Subject:** Crystal raindrop **Obv:** Bust right **Rev:** Maple leaf and rain drop - fall colors **Rev. Designer:** Celia Godkin

Date	Mintage	MS-63	Proof
2009 Proof	9,998	—	75.00

KM# 987 31.3900 g. 0.9999 Silver 1.0091 oz. ASW 38 mm. **Rev:** Lotus

Water Lilly in multicolor and crystal
Rev. Designer: Cladio D'Angelo

Date	Mintage	MS-63	Proof
2010 Proof	10,000	—	100

KM# 1009 31.3900 g. 0.9990 Silver 1.0082 oz. ASW **Subject:** 75th Anniversary of Canadian Bank Notes **Rev:** Female and farmer seated

Date	Mintage	MS-63	Proof
2010 Proof	7,500	—	70.00

KM# 1013 31.3900 g. 0.9990 Silver 1.0082 oz. ASW 38 mm. **Rev:** Maple leaf and crystal **Rev. Designer:** Celia Godkin

Date	Mintage	MS-63	Proof
2010 Proof	10,000	—	95.00

KM# 1018 31.3900 g. 0.9990 Silver 1.0082 oz. ASW 38 mm.   **Rev:** Steam Locomotive Selkirk

Date	Mintage	MS-63	Proof
2010 Proof	10,000	—	80.00

KM# 1066 31.9900 g. 0.9990 Silver 1.0274 oz. ASW 38 mm.   **Rev:** Pinecone with ruby crystals **Rev. Designer:** Susan Taylor

Date	Mintage	MS-63	Proof
2010 Proof	5,000	—	120

KM# 1048 31.1050 g. 0.9999 Silver 0.9999 oz. ASW 38 mm.   **Rev:** Snowflake, blue crystals

Date	Mintage	MS-63	Proof
2010 Proof	7,500	—	85.00

KM# 1067 31.9900 g. 0.9990 Silver 1.0274 oz. ASW 38 mm.   **Rev:** Pinecone with moonlight blue crystals **Rev. Designer:** Susan Taylor

Date	Mintage	MS-63	Proof
2010 Proof	5,000	—	120

KM# 1049 31.1050 g. 0.9999 Silver 0.9999 oz. ASW 38 mm.   **Rev:** Snowflake, tanzanite crystals

Date	Mintage	MS-63	Proof
2010 Proof	7,500	—	85.00

KM# 1075 27.7800 g. 0.9250 Silver 0.8261 oz. ASW 40 mm.   **Subject:** Winter Scene **Rev:** Horse pulling cut Christmas Tree **Rev. Designer:** Rene Clark

Date	Mintage	MS-63	Proof
2011 Proof	8,000	—	70.00

KM# 1134 31.3900 g. 0.9999 Silver 1.0091 oz. ASW 38 mm.   **Subject:** Canadian Pacific's D-10 Steam Locomotive **Obv:** Bust right **Rev:** Steam locomotive right **Edge:** Lettered

Date	Mintage	MS-63	Proof
2011 Proof	10,000	—	80.00

KM# 1111 31.3900 g. 0.9990 Silver 1.0082 oz. ASW 40 mm.   **Subject:** Royal Wedding **Rev:** Portraits of Katherine and William facing each other, crystal insert

Date	Mintage	MS-63	Proof
2011 Proof	—	—	85.00

KM# 1135 31.3900 g. 0.9999 Silver 1.0091 oz. ASW 38 mm.   **Obv:** Bust right **Rev:** Tulip in color and Vienitian glass lady bug

Date	Mintage	MS-63	Proof
2011 Proof	—	—	140

KM# 1145 31.3900 g. 0.9999 Silver 1.0091 oz. ASW 38 mm.   **Obv:** Bust right **Rev:** Wild rose in color, swarovski crystrals

Date	Mintage	MS-63	Proof
2011 Proof	Est. 10,000	—	110

KM# 1147 31.3900 g. 0.9999 Silver 1.0091 oz. ASW 38 mm.   **Obv:** Bust right **Rev:** Maple leaves, seeds in color, swarovski crystal drop

Date	Mintage	MS-63	Proof
2011 Proof	—	—	110

KM# 1181 31.3900 g. 0.9990 Silver 1.0082 oz. ASW 38 mm. **Obv:** Bust right **Rev:** Winnipeg Jets Logo, jet over maple leaf

Date	Mintage	MS-63	Proof
2011 Proof	15,000	—	95.00

KM# 1182 31.9900 g. 0.9999 Silver 1.0284 oz. ASW 38 mm. **Obv:** Bust right **Rev:** Christmas tree with six crystals

Date	Mintage	MS-63	Proof
2011 Proof	—	—	75.00

KM# 1187 31.3900 g. 0.9990 Silver 1.0082 oz. ASW 38 mm. **Obv:** Bust right **Rev:** Snowflake with emerald crystals

Date	Mintage	MS-63	Proof
2011 Proof	15,000	—	85.00

KM# 1188 31.8900 g. 0.9990 Silver 1.0242 oz. ASW 38 mm. **Obv:** Bust right **Rev:** Snowflake with topaz crystals

Date	Mintage	MS-63	Proof
2011 Proof	15,000	—	95.00

KM# 1189 31.8900 g. 0.9990 Silver 1.0242 oz. ASW 38 mm. **Obv:** Bust right **Rev:** Three snowflakes with three Hyacinth red crystals

Date	Mintage	MS-63	Proof
2011 Proof	15,000	—	115

KM# 1190 31.8900 g. 0.9990 Silver 1.0242 oz. ASW 38 mm. **Obv:** Bust right **Rev:** Three snowflakes with three Montana blue crystals

Date	Mintage	MS-63	Proof
2011 Proof	15,000	—	115

KM# 1137 31.3900 g. 0.9990 Silver 1.0082 oz. ASW 38 mm. **Subject:** Elizabeth II, 60th Anniversary of reign **Obv:** Bust right **Rev:** Crowned bust right with swarovski crystal insert **Edge:** Reeded

Date	Mintage	MS-63	Proof
2012 Proof	15,000	—	105

KM# 1177 27.7800 g. 0.9250 Silver 0.8261 oz. ASW 38 mm. **Obv:** Bust right **Rev:** Youthful busts right of Elizabeth II and Prince Philip

Date	Mintage	MS-63	Proof
2012 Proof	—	—	85.00

KM# 1178 27.7800 g. 0.9250 Silver 0.8261 oz. ASW 38 mm. **Obv:** Bust right **Rev:** Royal cypher, wreath below

Date	Mintage	MS-63	Proof
2012 Proof	—	—	85.00

25 DOLLARS

KM# 742 27.7800 g. 0.9250 Silver 0.8261 oz. ASW 40 mm. **Subject:** Vancouver Olympics **Rev:** Alpine skiing, hologram

Date	Mintage	MS-63	Proof
2007 Proof	45,000	—	65.00

KM# 743 27.7800 g. 0.9250 Silver 0.8261 oz. ASW 40 mm. **Subject:** Vancouver Olympics **Rev:** Athletics pride hologram

Date	Mintage	MS-63	Proof
2007 Proof	45,000	—	65.00

KM# 744 27.7500 g. 0.9250 Silver 0.8252 oz. ASW 40 mm. **Subject:**

Vancouver Olympics **Rev:** Biathleon hologram

Date	Mintage	MS-63	Proof
2007 Proof	54,000	—	65.00

KM# 745 27.7800 g. 0.9250 Silver 0.8261 oz. ASW 40 mm. **Subject:** Vancouver Olympics **Rev:** Curling hologram

Date	Mintage	MS-63	Proof
2007 Proof	—	—	65.00

KM# 746 27.7800 g. 0.9250 Silver 0.8261 oz. ASW 40 mm. **Subject:** Vancouver Olympics **Rev:** Hockey, hologram

Date	Mintage	MS-63	Proof
2007 Proof	45,000	—	65.00

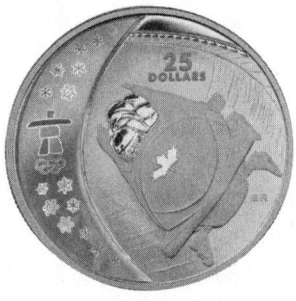

KM# 814 27.7800 g. 0.9250 Silver 0.8261 oz. ASW 40 mm. **Subject:** Vancouver Olympics **Rev:** Bobsleigh, hologram

Date	Mintage	MS-63	Proof
2008 Proof	45,000	—	65.00

KM# 815 27.7800 g. 0.9250 Silver 0.8261 oz. ASW 40 mm. **Subject:**

Vancouver Olympics **Rev:** Figure skating, hologram

Date	Mintage	MS-63	Proof
2008 Proof	45,000	—	65.00

KM# 816 27.7800 g. 0.9250 Silver 0.8261 oz. ASW 40 mm. **Subject:** Vancouver Olympics **Rev:** Freestyle skating, hologram

Date	Mintage	MS-63	Proof
2008 Proof	45,000	—	65.00

KM# 817 27.7800 g. 0.9250 Silver 0.8261 oz. ASW 40 mm. **Subject:** Vancouver Olympics **Rev:** Snowboarding, hologram

Date	Mintage	MS-63	Proof
2008 Proof	45,000	—	65.00

KM# 818 27.7800 g. 0.9250 Silver
0.8261 oz. ASW 40 mm.   **Subject:**
Vancouver Olympics **Rev:** Home of the
2010 Olympics

Date	Mintage	MS-63	Proof
2008 Proof	45,000	—	65.00

KM# 903 27.7800 g. 0.9250 Silver
0.8261 oz. ASW 40 mm.   **Subject:**
2010 Vancouver Olympics **Obv:** Bust
right **Obv. Designer:** Susanna Blunt
Rev: Cross Country Skiing and
hologram at left

Date	Mintage	MS-63	Proof
2009 Proof	45,000	—	65.00

KM# 904 27.7800 g. 0.9250 Silver
0.8261 oz. ASW 40 mm.   **Subject:**

2010 Vancouver Olympics **Obv:** Bust
right **Obv. Designer:** Susanna Blunt
Rev: Olympians holding torch,
hologram at left

Date	Mintage	MS-63	Proof
2009 Proof	45,000	—	65.00

KM# 905 27.7800 g. 0.9250 Silver
0.8261 oz. ASW 40 mm.   **Subject:**
2010 Vancouver Olympics **Obv:** Bust
right **Obv. Designer:** Susanna Blunt
Rev: Sled, hologram at left

Date	Mintage	MS-63	Proof
2009 Proof	45,000	—	65.00

KM# 906 27.7800 g. 0.9250 Silver
0.8261 oz. ASW 40 mm.   **Subject:**
2010 Vancouver Olympics **Obv:** Bust

right **Obv. Designer:** Susanna Blunt
Rev: Ski Jumper, hologram at left

Date	Mintage	MS-63	Proof
2009 Proof	45,000	—	65.00

KM# 907 27.7800 g. 0.9250 Silver
0.8261 oz. ASW 40 mm.   **Subject:** 2010
Vancouver Olympics **Obv:** Bust right
Obv. Designer: Susanna Blunt **Rev:**
Speed Skaters, hologram at left

Date	Mintage	MS-63	Proof
2009 Proof	45,000	—	65.00

KM# 1146 62.4100 g. 0.9999 Silver
2.0062 oz. ASW selectively gilt
60 mm.   **Obv:** Bust right **Rev:** Toronto
map and skyline, partilly gilt **Edge:**
Reeded

Date	Mintage	MS-63	Proof
2011 Proof	Est. 7,500	—	180

KM# 1173 31.3900 g. 0.9999 Silver
1.0091 oz. ASW 38 mm.   **Obv:** Bust
right **Rev:** Wayne Greskey skating
right, father's portrait in circle at right,
99 in hologram at lower right

Date	Mintage	MS-63	Proof
2011 Proof	—	—	85.00

30 DOLLARS

KM# 590 31.5000 g. 0.9250 Silver
0.9368 oz. ASW   **Subject:** Pacific
Northwest Wood Carvings **Obv:** Head
right **Rev:** Welcome figure totem pole

Date	Mintage	MS-63	Proof
2006 Proof	9,904	—	75.00

KM# 668 31.5000 g. 0.9250 Silver
0.9368 oz. ASW   **Subject:** Canadarm
and Col. C. Hadfield **Obv:** Head right
Rev: Hologram of Canadarm

Date	Mintage	MS-63	Proof
2006 Proof	9,357	—	90.00

KM# 669 31.5000 g. 0.9250 Silver
0.9368 oz. ASW   **Subject:** National
War Memorial **Obv:** Head right **Rev:**
Statue of three soldiers

Date	Mintage	MS-63	Proof
2006 Proof	8,876	—	85.00

KM# 670 31.5000 g. 0.9250 Silver 0.9368 oz. ASW **Subject:** Beaumont Hamel Newfoundland **Obv:** Head right **Rev:** Caribou statue on rock outcrop

Date	Mintage	MS-63	Proof
2006 Proof	15,325	—	95.00

KM# 671 31.5000 g. 0.9250 Silver 0.9368 oz. ASW **Obv:** Head right **Rev:** Dog Sled Team in color

Date	Mintage	MS-63	Proof
2006 Proof	7,384	—	85.00

KM# 819 31.5000 g. 0.9250 Silver 0.9368 oz. ASW 40 mm. **Subject:** IMAX **Rev:** Youth reaching out to shark on large screen

Date	Mintage	MS-63	Proof
2008 Proof	3,861	—	75.00

KM# 739 31.5000 g. 0.9250 Silver 0.9368 oz. ASW 40 mm. **Rev:** Niagra Falls panoramic hologram

Date	Mintage	MS-63	Proof
2007 Proof	7,384	—	85.00

KM# 741 31.5000 g. 0.9250 Silver 0.9368 oz. ASW 40 mm. **Rev:** War Memorial, Vimy Ridge

Date	Mintage	MS-63	Proof
2007 Proof	5,335	—	85.00

KM# 895 33.7500 g. 0.9250 Silver 1.0037 oz. ASW 40 mm. **Subject:** International year of astronomy **Obv:** Bust right **Obv. Legend:** Elizabeth II 30 Dollars DG Regina **Obv. Designer:** Susanna Blunt **Rev:** Observatory with planets and colored sky **Rev. Legend:** Canada **Rev. Designer:** Colin Mayne

Date	Mintage	MS-63	Proof
2009 Proof	7,174	—	90.00

50 DOLLARS

KM# 566 12.0000 g. 0.5833 Gold
0.2250 oz. AGW 27 mm. **Subject:**
End of World War II, 60th Anniversary
Obv: Head right **Rev:** Large V and three
portraits

Date	Mintage	MS-63	Proof
2005 Specimen	4,000	—	375

KM# 672 31.1600 g. 0.9995 Palladium
1.0013 oz. **Subject:** Constellation in
Spring sky position **Rev:** Large Bear at top

Date	Mintage	MS-63	Proof
2006 Proof	297	—	1,200

KM# 673 31.1600 g. 0.9995 Palladium
1.0013 oz. **Subject:** Constellation in
Summer sky position **Rev:** Large Bear
at left

Date	Mintage	MS-63	Proof
2006 Proof	296	—	1,200

KM# 674 31.1600 g. 0.9995 Palladium
1.0013 oz. **Subject:** Constellation in
Autumn sky position **Rev:** Large Bear
towards bottom

Date	Mintage	MS-63	Proof
2006 Proof	296	—	1,200

KM# 675 31.1600 g. 0.9995 Palladium
1.0013 oz. **Subject:** Constellation in
Winter sky position **Rev:** Large Bear
towards right

Date	Mintage	MS-63	Proof
2006 Proof	293	—	1,200

KM# 709   155.5000 g. 0.9999 Silver 4.9987 oz. ASW   **Subject:** Queen's 60th Wedding Anniversary **Rev:** Coat of Arms and Mascots of Elizabeth and Philip

Date	Mintage	MS-63	Proof
2007 Proof	1,957	—	350

KM#783   156.7700 g. 0.9990 Silver 5.0350 oz. ASW 65 mm.   **Subject:** Ottawa Mint Centennial 1908-2008 **Rev:** Mint building facade **Note:** Photo reduced.

Date	Mintage	MS-63	Proof
2008 Proof	2,078	—	400

KM# 896 156.7700 g. 0.9990 Silver 5.0350 oz. ASW 65.25 mm.   **Subject:** 150 Anniversary of the start of construction of the parliament buildings **Obv:** Bust right **Obv. Legend:** Elizabeth II Canada DG Regina **Obv. Designer:** Susanna Blunt **Rev:** Incomplete west block, original architecture **Rev. Legend:** 50 Dollars 1859-2009

Date	Mintage	MS-63	Proof
2009 Proof	910	—	450

KM# 1008 157.6000 g. 0.9990 Silver 5.0617 oz. ASW 65.25 mm.   **Subject:** 75th Anniverary of Canadian Bank Notes **Rev:** Female seated speaking into microphone **Note:** Photo reduced.

Date	Mintage	MS-63	Proof
2010 Proof	2,000	—	450

75 DOLLARS

KM# 567 31.4400 g. 0.4166 Gold
0.4211 oz. AGW 36.07 mm. **Subject:**
Pope John Paul II **Obv:** Head right **Rev:**
Pope giving blessing

Date	Mintage	MS-63	Proof
2005 Proof	1,870	—	825

KM# 749 12.0000 g. 0.5830 Gold
0.2249 oz. AGW 27 mm. **Rev:**
Mountie, multicolor

Date	Mintage	MS-63	Proof
2007 Proof	6,687	—	440

KM# 747 12.0000 g. 0.5830 Gold
0.2249 oz. AGW 27 mm. **Subject:**
Vancouver Olympics - Athletics Pride
Rev: Athletics celebrating, holding flag
aloft

Date	Mintage	MS-63	Proof
2007 Proof	4,524	—	440

KM# 821 12.0000 g. 0.5830 Gold
0.2249 oz. AGW 27 mm. **Rev:** Four
Host Nations mask emblems, colored
Rev. Designer: Jody Broomfield

Date	Mintage	MS-63	Proof
2008 Proof	8,000	—	440

KM# 748 12.0000 g. 0.5830 Gold
0.2249 oz. AGW 27 mm. **Obv:** Bust
right **Obv. Designer:** Susanna Blunt
Rev: Canada geese in flight left,
multicolor

Date	Mintage	MS-63	Proof
2007 Proof	4,418	—	440

KM# 947 12.0000 g. 0.5830 Gold
0.2249 oz. AGW 27 mm. **Subject:**
Vancouver Olympics **Rev:** Tent
building at Olympic site, color

Date	Mintage	MS-63	Proof
2008 Proof	8,000	—	440

KM# 908 12.0000 g. 0.5830 Gold 0.2249 oz. AGW 27 mm. **Subject:** 2010 Vancouver Olympics **Obv:** Bust right **Obv. Designer:** Susana Blunt **Rev:** Multicolor moose

Date	Mintage	MS-63	Proof
2009 Proof	4,075	—	440

KM# 1002 12.0000 g. 0.5830 Gold 0.2249 oz. AGW 27 mm. **Rev:** Spring color maple leaves

Date	Mintage	MS-63	Proof
2010 Proof	1,000	—	500

KM# 909 12.0000 g. 0.5830 Gold 0.2249 oz. AGW 27 mm. **Subject:** 2010 Vancouver Olympics **Obv:** Bust right **Obv. Designer:** Susanna Blunt **Rev:** Multicolor athletics and torch

Date	Mintage	MS-63	Proof
2009 Proof	4,479	—	440

KM# 1003 12.0000 g. 0.5830 Gold 0.2249 oz. AGW 27 mm. **Rev:** Summer color maple leaves

Date	Mintage	MS-63	Proof
2010 Proof	1,000	—	500

KM# 910 12.0000 g. 0.5830 Gold 0.2249 oz. AGW 27 mm. **Subject:** 2010 Vancouver Olympics **Obv:** Bust right **Obv. Designer:** Susanna Blunt **Rev:** Wolf, multicolor

Date	Mintage	MS-63	Proof
2009 Proof	4,161	—	440

KM# 1004 12.0000 g. 0.5830 Gold 0.2249 oz. AGW 27 mm. **Rev:** Fall color maple leaves

Date	Mintage	MS-63	Proof
2010 Proof	1,000	—	500

KM# 1005 12.0000 g. 0.5830 Gold 0.2249 oz. AGW 27 mm.   **Rev:** Winter color maple leaves

Date	Mintage	MS-63	Proof
2010 Proof	1,000	—	500

100 DOLLARS

KM# 115 13.3375 g. 0.5830 Gold 0.2500 oz. AGW 27 mm.   **Subject:** 1976 Montreal Olympics **Obv:** Young bust right, maple leaf below, date at right, beaded borders **Rev:** Past and present Olympic figures, denomination at right **Rev. Designer:** Dora dePedery-Hunt

Date	Mintage	MS-63	Proof
1976	650,000	475	—

KM# 116 16.9655 g. 0.9170 Gold 0.5002 oz. AGW 25 mm.   **Subject:** 1976 Montreal Olympics **Obv:** Young bust right, maple leaf below, date at right, plain borders **Rev:** Past and present Olympic figures, denomination at right **Rev. Designer:** Dora dePedery-Hunt

Date	Mintage	MS-63	Proof
1976 Proof	337,342	—	950

KM# 119 16.9655 g. 0.9170 Gold 0.5002 oz. AGW   **Subject:** Queen's silver jubilee **Obv:** Young bust right **Rev:** Bouquet of provincial flowers, denomination below **Rev. Designer:** Raymond Lee

Date	Mintage	MS-63	Proof
1952-1977 Proof	180,396	—	950

KM# 122 16.9655 g. 0.9170 Gold 0.5002 oz. AGW   **Subject:** Canadian unification **Obv:** Young bust right, denomination at left, date upper right **Rev:** Geese (representing the provinces) in flight formation **Rev. Designer:** Roger Savage

Date	Mintage	MS-63	Proof
1978 Proof	200,000	—	950

KM# 126 16.9655 g. 0.9170 Gold
0.5002 oz. AGW   **Subject:**
International Year of the Child **Obv:**
Young bust right **Rev:** Children with
hands joined divide denomination and
date **Rev. Designer:** Carola Tietz

Date	Mintage	MS-63	Proof
1979 Proof	250,000	—	950

KM# 137 16.9655 g. 0.9170 Gold
0.5002 oz. AGW   **Subject:** New
Constitution **Obv:** Young bust right,
denomination at left **Rev:** Open book,
maple leaf on right page, date below
Rev. Designer: Friedrich Peter

Date	Mintage	MS-63	Proof
1982 Proof	121,708	—	950

KM# 129 16.9655 g. 0.9170 Gold
0.5002 oz. AGW   **Subject:** Arctic
Territories **Obv:** Young bust right,
denomination at left, date above right
Rev: Kayaker **Rev. Designer:** Arnaldo
Marchetti

Date	Mintage	MS-63	Proof
1980 Proof	300,000	—	950

KM# 139 16.9655 g. 0.9170 Gold
0.5002 oz. AGW   **Subject:** 400th
Anniversary of St. John's,
Newfoundland **Obv:** Young bust right
Rev: Anchor divides building and ship,
denomination below, dates above **Rev.
Designer:** John Jaciw

Date	Mintage	MS-63	Proof
1583-1983 Proof	83,128	—	950

KM# 131 16.9655 g. 0.9170 Gold
0.5002 oz. AGW   **Subject:** National
anthem **Obv:** Young bust right,
denomination at left, date above right
Rev: Music score on map **Rev.
Designer:** Roger Savage

Date	Mintage	MS-63	Proof
1981 Proof	102,000	—	950

KM# 142 16.9655 g. 0.9170 Gold
0.5002 oz. AGW   **Subject:** Jacques
Cartier **Obv:** Young bust right **Rev:**
Cartier head on right facing left, ship on
left, date lower right, denomination
above **Rev. Designer:** Carola Tietz

Date	Mintage	MS-63	Proof
1534-1984 Proof	67,662	—	950

KM# 144 16.9655 g. 0.9170 Gold 0.5002 oz. AGW **Subject:** National Parks **Obv:** Young bust right **Rev:** Bighorn sheep, denomination divides dates below **Rev. Designer:** Hector Greville

Date	Mintage	MS-63	Proof
1885-1985 Proof	61,332	—	950

KM# 152 16.9655 g. 0.9170 Gold 0.5002 oz. AGW **Subject:** Peace **Obv:** Young bust right **Rev:** Maple leaves and letters intertwined, date at right, denomination below **Rev. Designer:** Dora dePedery-Hunt

Date	Mintage	MS-63	Proof
1986 Proof	76,409	—	950

KM# 158 13.3375 g. 0.5830 Gold 0.2500 oz. AGW **Subject:** 1988 Calgary Olympics **Obv:** Young bust right, maple leaf below, date at right **Rev:** Torch and logo, denomination below **Rev. Designer:** Friedrich Peter **Edge Lettering:** In English and French

Date	Mintage	MS-63	Proof
1987 Proof, letter edge	142,750	—	475
1987 Proof, plain edge	Inc. above	—	475

KM# 162 13.3375 g. 0.5830 Gold 0.2500 oz. AGW **Subject:** Bowhead Whales, balaera mysticetus **Rev:** Whales left, date below, within circle, denomination below **Rev. Designer:** Robert R. Carmichael

Date	Mintage	MS-63	Proof
1988 Proof	52,594	—	475

KM# 169 13.3375 g. 0.5830 Gold 0.2500 oz. AGW **Subject:** Sainte-Marie **Obv:** Young bust right **Rev:** Huron Indian, Missionary and Mission building, denomination below, dates above **Rev. Designer:** D. J. Craig

Date	Mintage	MS-63	Proof
1639-1989 Proof	59,657	—	475

KM# 171 13.3375 g. 0.5830 Gold 0.2500 oz. AGW **Subject:** International Literacy Year **Obv:** Crowned head right, date below **Rev:** Woman with children, denomination below **Rev. Designer:** John Mardon

Date	Mintage	MS-63	Proof
1990 Proof	49,940	—	475

KM# 180 13.3375 g. 0.5830 Gold
0.2500 oz. AGW   **Subject:** S.S.
Empress of India **Obv:** Crowned head
right, date below **Rev:** Ship,"SS
Empress", denomination below **Rev.
Designer:** Karsten Smith

Date	Mintage	MS-63	Proof
1991 Proof	33,966	—	475

KM# 249 13.3375 g. 0.5830 Gold
0.2500 oz. AGW   **Subject:** World War
II Home Front **Obv:** Crowned head
right, date below **Rev:** Kneeling figure
working on plane, denomination below
Rev. Designer: Paraskeva Clark

Date	Mintage	MS-63	Proof
1994 Proof	16,201	—	475

KM# 211 13.3375 g. 0.5830 Gold
0.2500 oz. AGW   **Subject:** Montreal
Obv: Crowned head right, date below
Rev: Half figure in foreground with
paper, buildings in back, denomination
below **Rev. Designer:** Stewart Sherwood

Date	Mintage	MS-63	Proof
1992 Proof	28,162	—	475

KM# 260 13.3375 g. 0.5830 Gold
0.2500 oz. AGW   **Subject:** Louisbourg
Obv: Crowned head right, date below
Rev: Ship and buildings, dates and
denomination above **Rev. Designer:**
Lewis Parker

Date	Mintage	MS-63	Proof
1995 Proof	16,916	—	475

KM# 245 13.3375 g. 0.5830 Gold
0.2500 oz. AGW   **Subject:** Antique
Automobiles **Obv:** Crowned head right,
date below **Rev:** German Bene Victoria;
Simmonds Steam Carriage; French
Panhard-Levassor's Daimler; American
Duryea; Canadian Featherston Haugh in
center, denomination below **Rev.
Designer:** John Mardon

Date	Mintage	MS-63	Proof
1993 Proof	25,971	—	475

KM# 273 13.3375 g. 0.5830 Gold
0.2500 oz. AGW   **Subject:** Klondike
Gold Rush Centennial **Obv:** Crowned
head right, date below **Rev:** Scene of
Kate Carmack panning for gold, dates
above, denomination lower left **Rev.
Designer:** John Mantha

Date	Mintage	MS-63	Proof
1896-1996 Proof	17,973	—	450

KM# 287 13.3375 g. 0.5830 Gold 0.2500 oz. AGW **Subject:** Alexander Graham Bell **Obv:** Crowned head right, date below **Rev:** A. G. Bell head right, globe and telephone, denomination upper right **Rev. Designer:** Donald H. Carley

Date	Mintage	MS-63	Proof
1997 Proof	14,775	—	475

KM# 402 13.3375 g. 0.5830 Gold 0.2500 oz. AGW 27 mm. **Subject:** McClure's Arctic expedition **Obv:** Crowned head right, date below **Rev:** Six men pulling supply sled to an icebound ship, denomination below **Rev. Designer:** John Mardon **Edge:** Reeded

Date	Mintage	MS-63	Proof
2000 Proof	9,767	—	475

KM# 307 13.3375 g. 0.5830 Gold 0.2500 oz. AGW **Subject:** Discovery of Insulin **Obv:** Crowned head right, date below **Rev:** Nobel prize award figurine, dates at left, denomination at right **Rev. Designer:** Robert R. Carmichael

Date	Mintage	MS-63	Proof
1998 Proof	11,220	—	475

KM# 416 13.3375 g. 0.5830 Gold 0.2500 oz. AGW alloyed with 5.5579 g of .999 Silver, .1787 oz ASW 27 mm. **Subject:** Library of Parliament **Obv:** Crowned head right **Obv. Designer:** Dora dePedery-Hunt **Rev:** Statue in domed building **Rev. Designer:** Robert R. Carmichael **Edge:** Reeded

Date	Mintage	MS-63	Proof
2001 Proof	8,080	—	475

KM# 341 13.3375 g. 0.5830 Gold 0.2500 oz. AGW **Subject:** 50th Anniversary Newfoundland Unity With Canada **Obv:** Crowned head right, date below **Rev:** Two designs at front, mountains in back, denomination below **Rev. Designer:** Jackie Gale-Vaillancourt

Date	Mintage	MS-63	Proof
1999 Proof	10,242	—	475

KM# 452 13.3375 g. 0.5830 Gold 0.2500 oz. AGW 27 mm. **Subject:** Discovery of Oil in Alberta **Obv:** Crowned head right **Rev:** Oil well with black oil spill on ground **Rev. Designer:** John Marden **Edge:** Reeded

Date	Mintage	MS-63	Proof
2002 Proof	9,994	—	475

KM# 486 13.3375 g. 0.5830 Gold
0.2500 oz. AGW   **Subject:** 100th
Anniversary of the Discovery of
Marquis Wheat **Obv:** Head right

Date	Mintage	MS-63	Proof
2003 Proof	9,993	—	475

KM# 528 12.0000 g. 0.5830 Gold
0.2249 oz. AGW   **Subject:** St.
Lawrence Seaway, 50th Anniversary
Obv: Head right

Date	Mintage	MS-63	Proof
2004 Proof	7,454	—	425

KM# 593 12.0000 g. 0.5833 Gold
0.2250 oz. AGW   **Subject:** 130th
Anniversary, Supreme Court **Obv:**
Head right

Date	Mintage	MS-63	Proof
2005 Proof	5,092	—	425

KM# 591 12.0000 g. 0.5833 Gold
0.2250 oz. AGW   **Subject:** 75th
Anniversary, Hockey Classic between
Royal Military College and U.S.
Military Academy **Obv:** Head right

Date	Mintage	MS-63	Proof
2006 Proof	5,439	—	425

KM# 689 12.0000 g. 0.5833 Gold
0.2250 oz. AGW 27 mm.   **Subject:**
140th Anniversary Dominion **Obv:**
Head right

Date	Mintage	MS-63	Proof
2007 Proof	4,453	—	425

KM# 823 12.0000 g. 0.5830 Gold
0.2249 oz. AGW 27 mm.   **Rev:** Fraser
River

Date	Mintage	MS-63	Proof
2008 Proof	3,089	—	425

KM# 898 12.0000 g. 0.5830 Gold
0.2249 oz. AGW 27 mm.   **Subject:**
10th Anniversary of Nunavut **Obv:**
Bust right **Obv. Legend:** Elizabeth II
DG Regina **Obv. Designer:** Susanna
Blunt **Rev:** Inuit dancer with 3 faces
behind **Rev. Legend:** Canada 100
Dollars 1999-2009

Date	Mintage	MS-63	Proof
2009 Proof	2,309	—	425

KM# 997 12.0000 g. 0.5830 Gold
0.2249 oz. AGW 27 mm.   **Rev:** Henry
Hudson, Map of Hudson's Bay **Rev.
Designer:** John Mantha

Date	Mintage	MS-63	Proof
2010 Proof	Est. 5,000	—	425

KM# 1073 12.0000 g. 0.5830 Gold 0.2249 oz. AGW 27 mm. **Subject:** Canadian Railroads, 175th Anniversary **Rev:** Early steam locomotive

Date	Mintage	MS-63	Proof
2011	3,000	—	425

150 DOLLARS

KM# 388 13.6100 g. 0.7500 Gold 0.3282 oz. AGW **Subject:** Year of the Dragon **Obv:** Crowned head right **Rev. Designer:** Harvey Chan

Date	Mintage	MS-63	Proof
2000 Proof	8,851	—	625

KM# 417 13.6100 g. 0.7500 Gold 0.3282 oz. AGW 28 mm. **Subject:** Year of the Snake **Obv:** Crowned head right **Obv. Designer:** Dora dePedery-Hunt **Rev:** Multicolor snake hologram **Edge:** Reeded

Date	Mintage	MS-63	Proof
2001 Proof	6,571	—	625

KM# 604 13.6100 g. 0.7500 Gold 0.3282 oz. AGW **Obv:** Head right **Rev:** Stylized horse left

Date	Mintage	MS-63	Proof
2002 Proof	6,843	—	625

KM# 487 13.6100 g. 0.7500 Gold 0.3282 oz. AGW 28 mm. **Subject:**

Year of the Ram **Obv:** Crowned head right **Rev:** Stylized ram left, hologram **Rev. Designer:** Harvey Chan

Date	Mintage	MS-63	Proof
2003 Proof	3,927	—	625

KM# 614 13.6100 g. 0.7500 Gold 0.3282 oz. AGW **Obv:** Head right **Rev:** Year of the Monkey, hologram

Date	Mintage	MS-63	Proof
2004 Proof	3,392	—	625

KM# 568 13.6100 g. 0.7500 Gold 0.3282 oz. AGW **Subject:** Year of the Rooster **Obv:** Head right **Rev:** Rooster left, hologram

Date	Mintage	MS-63	Proof
2005 Proof	3,731	—	625

KM# 592 13.6100 g. 0.7500 Gold 0.3282 oz. AGW 28 mm. **Subject:** Year of the Dog, hologram **Obv:** Head right **Rev:** Stylized dog left

Date	Mintage	MS-63	Proof
2006 Proof	2,604	—	625

KM# 733 11.8400 g. 0.7500 Gold 0.2855 oz. AGW 28 mm. **Subject:** Year of the Pig **Obv:** Head right **Rev:** Pig in center with Chinese lunar calendar around, hologram

Date	Mintage	MS-63	Proof
2007 Proof	826	—	733

KM# 802 11.8400 g. 0.7500 Gold
0.2855 oz. AGW 28 mm. **Subject:**
Year of the Rat **Rev:** Rat, hologram

Date	Mintage	MS-63	Proof
2008 Proof	582	—	550

KM# 899 10.4000 g. 0.9990 Gold
0.3340 oz. AGW 22.5 mm. **Subject:**
Blessings of wealth **Obv:** Bust right
Obv. Legend: Elizabeth II, DG Regina,
Fine Gold 99999 or PUR **Obv. Designer:**
Susanna Blunt **Rev:** Three goldfish
surround peony, clouds **Rev. Legend:**
Canada 150 Dollars (Chinese symbols
of good fortune) **Rev. Designer:**
Harvey Chan **Edge:** Scalloped

Date	Mintage	MS-63	Proof
2009 Proof	1,273	—	650

KM# 867 11.8400 g. 0.7500 Gold
0.2855 oz. AGW 28 mm. **Subject:**
Year of the Ox **Rev:** Ox, hologram

Date	Mintage	MS-63	Proof
2009 Proof	486	—	550

KM# 979 11.8400 g. 0.7500 Gold
0.2855 oz. AGW 28 mm. **Subject:**
Year of the Tiger **Rev:** Tiger in hologram

Date	Mintage	MS-63	Proof
2010 Proof	1,507	—	550

KM# 1030 10.4000 g. 0.9999 Gold
0.3343 oz. AGW **Subject:** Blessing of
Wealth **Shape:** Scalloped

Date	Mintage	MS-63	Proof
2010 Proof	1,388	—	650

KM# 1031 Gold **Subject:** Year of the
Tiger **Rev:** Tiger walking

Date	Mintage	MS-63	Proof
2010 Proof	2,500	—	600

KM# 1053 13.6100 g. 0.7500 Gold
0.3282 oz. AGW 28 mm. **Subject:**
Year of the rabbit **Rev:** Rabbit hologram

Date	Mintage	MS-63	Proof
2011 Proof	Est. 4,888	—	600

KM# 1184 13.6100 g. 0.7500 Gold 0.3282 oz. AGW 28 mm. **Subject:**

Year of the Dragon **Obv:** Bust right **Rev:** Dragon left

Date	Mintage	MS-63	Proof
2012 Proof	—	—	650

175 DOLLARS

KM# 217 16.9700 g. 0.9170 Gold 0.5003 oz. AGW **Subject:** 1992 Olympics **Obv:** Crowned head right, date at left, denomination below **Rev:** Passing the torch **Rev. Designer:** Stewart Sherwood **Edge:** Lettered

Date	Mintage	MS-63	Proof
1992 Proof	22,092	—	950

200 DOLLARS

KM# 178 17.1350 g. 0.9166 Gold 0.5049 oz. AGW 29 mm. **Subject:** Canadian flag silver jubilee **Obv:** Crowned head right, date below **Rev:** People with flag, denomination above **Rev. Designer:** Stewart Sherwood

Date	Mintage	MS-63	Proof
1990 Proof	20,980	—	975

KM# 230 17.1350 g. 0.9166 Gold 0.5049 oz. AGW 29 mm. **Subject:** Niagara Falls **Obv:** Crowned head right **Rev:** Niagara Falls, denomination above **Rev. Designer:** John Mardon

Date	Mintage	MS-63	Proof
1992 Proof	9,465	—	975

KM# 202 17.1350 g. 0.9166 Gold 0.5049 oz. AGW 29 mm. **Subject:** Hockey **Obv:** Crowned head right **Rev:** Hockey players, denomination above **Rev. Designer:** Stewart Sherwood

Date	Mintage	MS-63	Proof
1991 Proof	10,215	—	975

KM# 244 17.1350 g. 0.9166 Gold 0.5049 oz. AGW 29 mm. **Subject:** Mounted police **Obv:** Crowned head right, date below **Rev:** Mountie with children, denomination above **Rev. Designer:** Stewart Sherwood

Date	Mintage	MS-63	Proof
1993 Proof	10,807	—	975

KM# 250 17.1350 g. 0.9166 Gold 0.5049 oz. AGW 29 mm. **Subject:** Interpretation of 1908 novel by Lucy Maud Montgomery, 1874-1942, Anne of Green Gables **Obv:** Crowned head right **Rev:** Figure sitting in window, denomination above **Rev. Designer:** Phoebe Gilman

Date	Mintage	MS-63	Proof
1994 Proof	10,655	—	975

KM# 265 17.1350 g. 0.9166 Gold 0.5049 oz. AGW 29 mm. **Subject:** Maple-syrup production **Obv:** Crowned head right, date below **Rev:** Maple syrup making, denomination at right **Rev. Designer:** J. D. Mantha

Date	Mintage	MS-63	Proof
1995 Proof	6,579	—	975

KM# 275 17.1350 g. 0.9166 Gold 0.5049 oz. AGW 29 mm. **Subject:** Transcontinental Canadian Railway **Obv:** Crowned head right, date below

Rev: Train going through mountains, denomination below **Rev. Designer:** Suzanne Duranceau

Date	Mintage	MS-63	Proof
1996 Proof	8,047	—	975

KM# 288 17.1350 g. 0.9166 Gold 0.5049 oz. AGW 29 mm. **Subject:** Haida mask **Obv:** Crowned head right, date below **Rev:** Haida mask **Rev. Designer:** Robert Davidson

Date	Mintage	MS-63	Proof
1997 Proof	11,610	—	975

KM# 317 17.1350 g. 0.9166 Gold 0.5049 oz. AGW 29 mm. **Subject:** Legendary white buffalo **Obv:** Crowned head right, date below **Rev:** Buffalo **Rev. Designer:** Alex Janvler

Date	Mintage	MS-63	Proof
1998 Proof	7,149	—	975

KM# 358 17.1350 g. 0.9166 Gold 0.5049 oz. AGW 29 mm. **Subject:** Mikmaq butterfly **Obv:** Crowned head right **Rev:** Butterfly within design **Rev. Designer:** Alan Syliboy

Date	Mintage	MS-63	Proof
1999 Proof	6,510	—	975

KM# 488 17.1350 g. 0.9166 Gold 0.5049 oz. AGW   **Subject:** Fitzgerald's "Houses" (1929) **Obv:** Crowned head right **Rev:** House with trees

Date	Mintage	MS-63	Proof
2003 Proof	4,118	—	975

KM# 403 17.1350 g. 0.9166 Gold 0.5049 oz. AGW 29 mm.   **Subject:** Motherhood **Obv:** Crowned head right, date above, denomination at right **Rev:** Inuit mother with infant **Rev. Designer:** Germaine Arnaktauyak **Edge:** Reeded

Date	Mintage	MS-63	Proof
2000 Proof	6,284	—	975

KM# 516 16.0000 g. 0.9166 Gold 0.4715 oz. AGW 29 mm.   **Subject:** "Fragments" **Obv:** Crowned head right **Rev:** Fragmented face **Edge:** Reeded

Date	Mintage	MS-63	Proof
2004 Proof	3,917	—	900

KM# 569 16.0000 g. 0.9166 Gold 0.4715 oz. AGW   **Subject:** Fur traders **Obv:** Head right **Rev:** Men in canoe riding wave

Date	Mintage	MS-63	Proof
2005 Proof	3,669	—	900

KM# 594 16.0000 g. 0.9166 Gold 0.4715 oz. AGW   **Subject:** Timber trade **Obv:** Head right **Rev:** Lumberjacks felling tree

Date	Mintage	MS-63	Proof
2006 Proof	3,218	—	900

KM# 418 17.1350 g. 0.9166 Gold 0.5049 oz. AGW 29 mm.   **Subject:** Cornelius D. Krieghoff's "The Habitant farm" **Obv:** Queens head right **Edge:** Reeded

Date	Mintage	MS-63	Proof
2001 Proof	5,406	—	975

KM# 691 16.0000 g. 0.9166 Gold 0.4715 oz. AGW 29 mm.   **Subject:** Fishing Trade **Obv:** Head right **Rev:** Two fishermen hauling net

Date	Mintage	MS-63	Proof
2007 Proof	2,137	—	900

KM# 466 17.1350 g. 0.9166 Gold 0.5049 oz. AGW 29 mm.   **Subject:** Thomas Thompson "The Jack Pine" (1916-17) **Obv:** Crowned head right

Date	Mintage	MS-63	Proof
2002 Proof	5,264	—	975

KM# 824 16.0000 g. 0.9170 Gold 0.4717 oz. AGW 29 mm. **Subject:** Commerce **Rev:** Horse drawn plow

Date	Mintage	MS-63	Proof
2008 Proof	1,951	—	900

KM# 894 16.0000 g. 0.9160 Gold 0.4712 oz. AGW 29 mm. **Subject:** Coal mining trade **Obv:** Bust right **Obv. Legend:** Elizabeth II DG Regina **Obv. Designer:** Susanna Blunt **Rev:** Miner pushing cart with black coal **Rev. Legend:** Canada 200 Dollars **Rev. Designer:** John Marder

Date	Mintage	MS-63	Proof
2009 Proof	2,241	—	900

KM# 1000 16.0000 g. 0.9160 Gold 0.4712 oz. AGW 29 mm. **Subject:** Petroleum and Oil Trade **Rev:** Oil railcar and well head

Date	Mintage	MS-63	Proof
2010 Proof	Est. 4,000	—	900

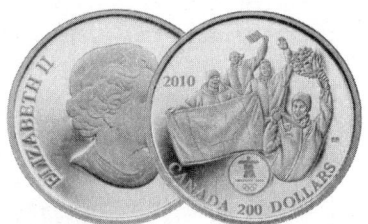

KM# 1060 16.0000 g. 0.9167 Gold 0.4715 oz. AGW 29 mm. **Rev:** Olympic athletics with medal, flag and flowers

Date	Mintage	MS-63	Proof
2010 Proof	—	—	900

KM# 1074 16.0000 g. 0.9167 Gold 0.4715 oz. AGW 29 mm. **Rev:** SS Beaver - Seam Sail ship **Rev. Designer:** John Mardon

Date	Mintage	MS-63	Proof
2011 Proof	2,800	—	900

KM# 1143 16.0000 g. 0.9167 Gold 0.4715 oz. AGW 27 mm. **Subject:** Wedding, Prince William and Katherine Middleton **Obv:** Bust right **Rev:** Half-length figures facing, swarovski crystal **Edge:** Reeded

Date	Mintage	MS-63	Proof
2011 Proof	2,000	—	900

KM# 1174 16.0000 g. 0.9160 Gold 0.4712 oz. AGW 29 mm. **Obv:** Bust right **Rev:** Wayne Greskey skating right, father's portrait in circle at right, 99 in color at lower right **Rev. Designer:** Glen Green

Date	Mintage	MS-63	Proof
2011 Proof	999	—	900

KM# 1219 16.0000 g. 0.9167 Gold
0.4715 oz. AGW 29 mm.   **Obv:** Bust
right **Rev:** Prospector panning for gold
in stream

Date	Mintage	MS-63	Proof
2012 Proof	—	—	900

KM# 1223 16.0000 g. 0.9167 Gold
0.4715 oz. AGW 29 mm.   **Obv:** Bust
right **Rev:** Vikings and ship

Date	Mintage	MS-63	Proof
2012 Proof	—	—	900

250 DOLLARS

KM# 677 45.0000 g. 0.5833 Gold 0.8439 oz. AGW 40 mm.   **Rev:** Dog Sled Team

Date	Mintage	MS-63	Proof
2006 Proof	953	—	1,625

KM# 751 1000.0000 g. 0.9999 Silver 32.146 oz. ASW 101.6 mm.   **Subject:**
Vancouver Olympics, 2010 **Rev:** Early Canada motif **Note:** Illustration reduced.

Date	Mintage	MS-63	Proof
2007 Proof	2,500	—	1,250

KM# 833 1000.0000 g. 0.9990 Silver 32.117 oz. ASW 101.6 mm.   **Subject:**
Vancouver Olympics 2010 **Rev:** Towards confederation **Note:** Illustration reduced.

Date	Mintage	MS-63	Proof
2008 Proof	2,500	—	1,350

KM# 913 1000.0000 g. 0.9999 Silver 32.146 oz. ASW 101.5 mm.   **Obv:** Bust right
Obv. Designer: Susanna Blunt **Rev:** Mask with fish - Surviving the flood **Note:**
Illustration reduced.

Date	Mintage	MS-63	Proof
2009 Proof	815	—	1,350

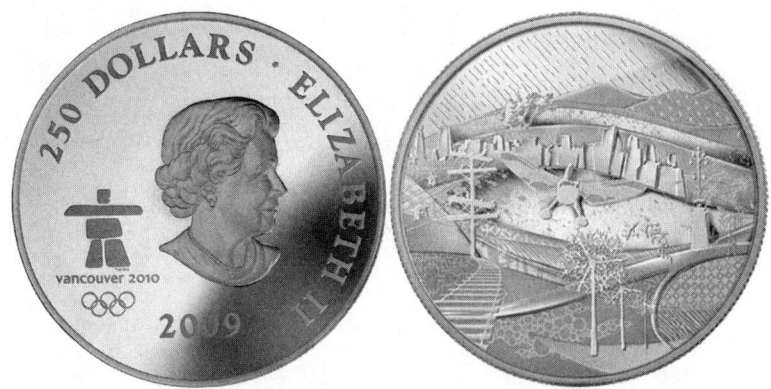

KM# 949 1000.0000 g. 0.9990 Silver 32.117 oz. ASW 101.6 mm.   **Rev:** Modern
Canada

Date	Mintage	MS-63	Proof
2009 Proof	905	—	1,350

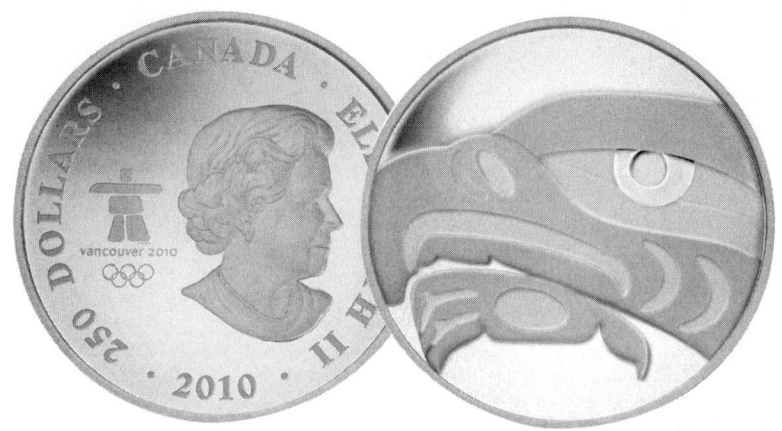

KM# 981 1000.0000 g. 0.9990 Silver 32.117 oz. ASW 101.6 mm. **Rev:** Eagle head

Date	Mintage	MS-63	Proof
2010 Antique Patina	500	1,350	—
2010 Proof	500	—	1,400

KM#981a 1000.0000 g. 0.9990 Silver 32.117 oz. ASW 101.6 mm. **Rev:** Eagle head, blue enamel

Date	Mintage	MS-63	Proof
2010 Proof	500	—	1,400

KM# 1044 1000.0000 g. 0.9990 Silver 32.117 oz. ASW 101.6 mm.   **Subject:** Baniff, 125th Anniversary of resort founding **Rev:** Features of Baniff

Date	Mintage	MS-63	Proof
2010 Proof	750	—	1,650

KM# 1150 1000.0000 g. 0.9999 Silver 32.146 oz. ASW 100 mm.   **Rev:** Lacrosse

Date	Mintage	MS-63	Proof
2011 Proof	—	—	1,350

KM# 1185 1000.0000 g. 0.9990 Silver 32.117 oz. ASW 101.6 mm.   **Subject:** Year of the Dragon **Obv:** Bust left **Rev:** Dragon left

Date	Mintage	MS-63	Proof
2012 Proof	—	—	1,350

300 DOLLARS

KM# 501 60.0000 g. 0.5833 Gold 1.1252 oz. AGW 50 mm. **Obv:** Triple cameo portraits of Queen Elizabeth II by Gillick, Machin and de Pedery-Hunt, each in 14K gold, rose in center **Rev:** Dates "1952-2002" and denomination in legend, rose in center **Note:** Housed in anodized gold-colored aluminum box with cherrywood stained siding

Date	Mintage	MS-63	Proof
1952-2002 Proof	999	—	2,150

KM# 517 60.0000 g. 0.5833 Gold 1.1252 oz. AGW 50 mm. **Obv:** Four coinage portraits of Elizabeth II **Rev:** Canadian arms above value **Edge:** Plain

Date	Mintage	MS-63	Proof
2004 Proof	998	—	2,150

KM# 600 60.0000 g. 0.5833 Gold 1.1252 oz. AGW 40 mm. **Subject:** Welcome Figure Totem Pole **Obv:** Head right **Rev:** Men with totem pole

Date	Mintage	MS-63	Proof
2005 Proof	948	—	2,150

KM# 570.1 45.0000 g. 0.5833 Gold 0.8439 oz. AGW 40 mm. **Subject:** Standard Time - 4 AM Pacific **Obv:** Head right **Rev:** Roman numeral clock with world inside

Date	Mintage	MS-63	Proof
2005 Proof	200	—	1,650

KM# 570.2 45.0000 g. 0.5830 Gold 0.8434 oz. AGW 40 mm.   **Subject:** Standard Time - Mountian 5 AM **Obv:** Head right **Rev:** Roman numeral clock with world inside.

Date	Mintage	MS-63	Proof
2005 Proof	200	—	1,650

KM# 570.3 45.0000 g. 0.5830 Gold 0.8434 oz. AGW 40 mm.   **Subject:** Standard Time - Central 6 PM **Obv:** Head right **Rev:** Roman numeral clock with world inside

Date	Mintage	MS-63	Proof
2005 Proof	200	—	1,650

KM# 570.4 45.0000 g. 0.5830 Gold 0.8434 oz. AGW 40 mm.   **Subject:** Standard Time - Eastern 7 AM **Obv:** Head right **Rev:** Roman numeral clock with world inside

Date	Mintage	MS-63	Proof
2005 Proof	200	—	1,650

KM# 570.5 45.0000 g. 0.5830 Gold 0.8434 oz. AGW 40 mm.   **Subject:** Standard Time - Atlantic 8 AM **Obv:** Head right **Rev:** Roman numeral clock with world inside

Date	Mintage	MS-63	Proof
2005 Proof	200	—	1,650

KM# 570.6 45.0000 g. 0.5830 Gold 0.8434 oz. AGW 40 mm.   **Subject:** Standard Time - Newfoundland 8:30 **Obv:** Head right **Rev:** Roman numeral clock with world inside

Date	Mintage	MS-63	Proof
2005 Proof	200	—	1,650

KM# 596 60.0000 g. 0.5833 Gold 1.1252 oz. AGW 50 mm.   **Subject:** Shinplaster **Obv:** Head right **Rev:** Britannia bust, spear over shoulder

Date	Mintage	MS-63	Proof
2005 Proof	994	—	2,150

KM# 678 45.0000 g. 0.5833 Gold 0.8439 oz. AGW 40 mm. **Rev:** Hologram of Canadarm, Col. C. Hadfield in spacewalk

Date	Mintage	MS-63	Proof
2006 Proof	581	—	1,650

KM# 679 60.0000 g. 0.5833 Gold 1.1252 oz. AGW 50 mm. **Subject:** Queen Elizabeth's 80th Birthday **Rev:** State Crown, colorized

Date	Mintage	MS-63	Proof
2006 Proof	996	—	2,150

KM# 680 60.0000 g. 0.5833 Gold 1.1252 oz. AGW 50 mm. **Subject:** Crystal Snowflake

Date	Mintage	MS-63	Proof
2006 Proof	998	—	2,150

KM# 595 60.0000 g. 0.5833 Gold 1.1252 oz. AGW 50 mm. **Subject:** Shinplaster **Obv:** Head right **Rev:** Seated Britannia with shield

Date	Mintage	MS-63	Proof
2006 Proof	940	—	2,150

KM# 692 60.0000 g. 0.5833 Gold 1.1252 oz. AGW 50 mm. **Subject:** Shinplaster **Rev:** 1923 25 cent bank note

Date	Mintage	MS-63	Proof
2007 Proof	778	—	2,150

KM#740 45.0000 g. 0.5830 Gold 0.8434 oz. AGW 40 mm. **Rev:** Canadian Rockies panoramic hologram

Date	Mintage	MS-63	Proof
2007 Proof	511	—	1,650

KM# 752 60.0000 g. 0.5830 Gold 1.1246 oz. AGW 50 mm.   **Subject:** Vancouver
Olympics **Rev:** Olympic ideals, classic figures and torch

Date	Mintage	MS-63	Proof
2007 Proof	953	—	2,150

KM# 825 45.0000 g. 0.5830 Gold 0.8434 oz. AGW 50 mm.   **Rev:** Alberta Coat of
Arms

Date	Mintage	MS-63	Proof
2008 Proof	344	—	1,650

KM# 826 60.0000 g. 0.5830 Gold 1.1246 oz. AGW 50 mm.   **Rev:** Newfoundland
and Labrador Coat of Arms

Date	Mintage	MS-63	Proof
2008 Proof	472	—	2,150

KM# 827 45.0000 g. 0.5830 Gold 0.8434 oz. AGW 40 mm.   **Subject:** Canadian achievements IMAX **Rev:** Kid in audience reaching out to shark on big screen

Date	Mintage	MS-63	Proof
2008 Proof	—	—	1,650

KM# 828 60.0000 g. 0.5830 Gold 1.1246 oz. AGW 50 mm.   **Rev:** Four seasons moon mask in color, blue design in border

Date	Mintage	MS-63	Proof
2008 Proof	544	—	2,150

KM# 830 60.0000 g. 0.5830 Gold 1.1246 oz. AGW 50 mm.   **Subject:** Vancouver Olympics **Rev:** Olympic competition, athletics and torch

Date	Mintage	MS-63	Proof
2008 Proof	334	—	2,150

KM# 900 60.0000 g. 0.5830 Gold 1.1246 oz. AGW 50 mm.   **Subject:** Yukon Coat of Arms **Obv:** Bust right **Obv. Legend:** Elizabeth II DG Regina **Obv. Designer:** Susanna Blunt **Rev:** Yukon Coat of Arms **Rev. Legend:** Canada 300 Dollars

Date	Mintage	MS-63	Proof
2009 Proof	325	—	2,150

KM# 877 60.0000 g. 0.5830 Gold 1.1246 oz. AGW 50 mm.   **Rev:** Summer moon mask, enameled

Date	Mintage	MS-63	Proof
2009 Proof	—	—	2,150

KM# 911 60.0000 g. 0.5830 Gold 1.1246 oz. AGW 50 mm.   **Subject:** 2010 Vancouver Olympics **Obv:** Bust right **Obv. Designer:** Susanna Blunt **Rev:** Athletics with torch - Olympic firendship

Date	Mintage	MS-63	Proof
2009 Proof	880	—	2,150

KM# 999 54.0000 g. 0.5830 Gold 1.0121 oz. AGW 50 mm.   **Rev:** British Columbia Arms

Date	Mintage	MS-63	Proof
2010 Proof	500	—	1,900

KM# 1047 60.0000 g. 0.5830 Gold 1.1246 oz. AGW 50 mm.   **Rev:** Snowflake, white crystals

Date	Mintage	MS-63	Proof
2010 Proof	750	—	2,150

KM# 1078 60.0000 g. 0.5830 Gold 1.1246 oz. AGW 50 mm.   **Rev:** New Brunswick Coat of arms

Date	Mintage	MS-63	Proof
2010 Proof	500	—	2,150

KM# 1095 60.0000 g. 0.9167 Gold 1.7683 oz. AGW 50 mm.   **Rev:** Manitoba Coat of arms

Date	Mintage	MS-63	Proof
2011 Proof	500	—	3,300

KM# 1215 60.0000 g. 0.9170 Gold 1.7689 oz. AGW 50 mm.   **Obv:** Bust right **Rev:** Arms of Nova Scotia

Date	Mintage	MS-63	Proof
2011 Proof	—	—	3,300

KM# 1195   Gold   **Obv:** Bust right **Rev:** Youthful Elizabeth II right, hands uplifted, crystal

Date	Mintage	MS-63	Proof
2012 Proof	—	—	1,650

KM# 1224 60.0000 g. 0.9167 Gold 1.7683 oz. AGW 50 mm.   **Obv:** Bust right **Rev:** Shield of Quebec

Date	Mintage	MS-63	Proof
2012 Proof	—	—	3,300

350 DOLLARS

KM# 308 38.0500 g. 0.9999 Gold 1.2232 oz. AGW   **Subject:** Flowers of Canada's Coat of Arms **Obv:** Crowned head right, date behind, denomination at bottom **Rev:** Flowers **Rev. Designer:** Pierre Leduc

Date	Mintage	MS-63	Proof
1998 Proof	664	—	2,350

KM# 370 38.0500 g. 0.9999 Gold 1.2232 oz. AGW   **Rev:** Lady's slipper **Rev. Designer:** Henry Purdy

Date	Mintage	MS-63	Proof
1999 Proof	1,990	—	2,350

KM# 404 38.0500 g. 0.9999 Gold 1.2232 oz. AGW 34 mm. **Obv:** Crowned head right **Rev:** Three Pacific Dogwood flowers **Rev. Designer:** Caren Heine **Edge:** Reeded

Date	Mintage	MS-63	Proof
2000 Proof	1,506	—	2,350

KM# 504 38.0500 g. 0.9999 Gold 1.2232 oz. AGW 34 mm. **Subject:** The White Trillium **Obv:** Crowned head right **Obv. Designer:** Dora de Pedery-Hunt **Rev:** White Trillium

Date	Mintage	MS-63	Proof
2003 Proof	1,865	—	2,350

KM# 601 38.0500 g. 0.9999 Gold 1.2232 oz. AGW **Subject:** Western Red Lilly **Obv:** Head right **Rev:** Western Red Lilies

Date	Mintage	MS-63	Proof
2005 Proof	1,634	—	2,350

KM# 433 38.0500 g. 0.9999 Gold 1.2232 oz. AGW 34 mm. **Subject:** The Mayflower Flower **Obv:** Crowned head right **Rev:** Two flowers **Rev. Designer:** Bonnie Ross **Edge:** Reeded

Date	Mintage	MS-63	Proof
2001 Proof	1,988	—	2,350

KM# 502 38.0500 g. 0.9999 Gold 1.2232 oz. AGW 34 mm. **Subject:** The Wild Rose **Obv:** Crowned head right **Obv. Designer:** Dora de Pedery-Hunt **Rev:** Wild rose plant **Rev. Designer:** Dr. Andreas Kare Hellum

Date	Mintage	MS-63	Proof
2002 Proof	2,001	—	2,350

KM# 626 38.0500 g. 0.9999 Gold 1.2232 oz. AGW 34 mm. **Subject:** Iris Vericolor **Obv:** Crowned head right **Rev:** Iris

Date	Mintage	MS-63	Proof
2006 Proof	1,995	—	2,350

KM# 754   35.0000 g. 0.9999 Gold 1.1251 oz. AGW 34 mm.   **Rev:** Purple violet

Date	Mintage	MS-63	Proof
2007 Proof	1,392	—	2,200

KM# 832   35.0000 g. 0.9999 Gold 1.1251 oz. AGW 34 mm.   **Rev:** Purple saxifrage

Date	Mintage	MS-63	Proof
2008 Proof	1,313	—	2,200

KM# 1019   35.0000 g. 0.9990 Gold 1.1241 oz. AGW 34 mm.   **Rev:** Praire Crocus **Rev. Designer:** Celia Godkin

Date	Mintage	MS-63	Proof
2010 Proof	Est. 1,400	—	2,200

KM# 1136   35.0000 g. 0.9999 Gold 1.1251 oz. AGW 34 mm.   **Obv:** Bust right **Rev:** Mountain Avens in bloom **Edge:** Reeded

Date	Mintage	MS-63	Proof
2011 Proof	1,300	—	2,200

KM# 901   35.0000 g. 0.9990 Gold 1.1241 oz. AGW 34 mm.   **Subject:** Pitcher plant **Obv:** Bust right **Obv. Legend:** Elizabeth II Canada DG Regina Fine Gold 350 Dollars or PUR 99999 **Obv. Designer:** Susana Blunt **Rev:** Cluster of pitcher flowers **Rev. Legend:** Julie Wilson

Date	Mintage	MS-63	Proof
2009 Proof	1,003	—	2,200

500 DOLLARS

KM# 710 156.5000 g. 0.9999 Gold 5.0309 oz. AGW 60 mm.   **Subject:** Queen's 60th Wedding **Rev:** Coat of Arms and Mascots of Elizabeth and Philip

Date	Mintage	MS-63	Proof
2007	198	9,150	—

KM# 782 155.7600 g. 0.9990 Gold 5.0026 oz. AGW 60 mm.   **Subject:** Ottawa Mint Centennial 1908-2008 **Rev:** Mint building facade **Note:** Illustration reduced.

Date	Mintage	MS-63	Proof
2008	248	9,150	—

KM# 897 156.0500 g. 0.9990 Gold 5.0119 oz. AGW 60 mm.   **Subject:** 150th Anniversary of the start of construction of the Parliament Buildings **Obv:** Bust right **Rev:** Incomplete west block, original architecture **Rev. Legend:** 500 Dollars 1859-2009

Date	Mintage	MS-63	Proof
2009 Proof	77	—	9,150

KM# 1007 156.5000 g. 0.9990 Gold 5.0263 oz. AGW 60 mm.   **Subject:** 75th Anniversary of Canadian Bank Notes **Rev:** Abundance seated under tree

Date	Mintage	MS-63	Proof
2010 Proof	200	—	9,150

KM# 1179   156.5000 g. 0.9999 Gold 5.0309 oz. AGW 60 mm.   **Obv:** Crowned bust of George V **Rev:** Arms of Canada, dual dates and denomination below **Edge:** Serially numbered

Date	Mintage	MS-63	Proof
1912-2012 Proof	200	—	9,150

2500 DOLLARS

KM# 681   1000.0000 g. 0.9999 Gold 32.146 oz. AGW 101.6 mm.   **Subject:** Kilo **Rev:** Common Characters, Early Canada **Note:** Illustration reduced.

Date	Mintage	MS-63	Proof
2007	20	57,000	—

KM# 902   1000.0000 g. 0.9990 Silver 32.117 oz. ASW 101.6 mm.   **Series:** History and Culture Collection **Subject:** Modern Canada **Obv:** Bust right **Obv. Legend:** Vancouver 2010, 2500 Dollars, Elizabeth II **Obv. Designer:** Susanna Blunt **Rev:** Canadian landscape with modern elements **Note:** Illustration reduced.

Date	Mintage	MS-63	Proof
2009 Proof	2,500	—	1,250

KM# 902a 1000.0000 g. 0.9990 Gold 32.117 oz. AGW 101.6 mm.   **Series:** History and Culture Collection **Subject:** Modern Canada **Obv:** Bust right **Obv. Legend:** Vancouver 2010, 2500 Dollars, Elizabeth II **Obv. Designer:** Susana Blunt **Rev:** Canadian landscape with modern elements

Date	Mintage	MS-63	Proof
2009 Proof	50	—	57,000

KM# 912 1000.0000 g. 0.9999 Gold 32.146 oz. AGW 101 mm.   **Obv:** Bust right **Obv. Designer:** Susanna Blunt **Rev:** Mask with fish - Surviving the flood **Note:** Illustration reduced.

Date	Mintage	MS-63	Proof
2009 Proof	40	—	57,000

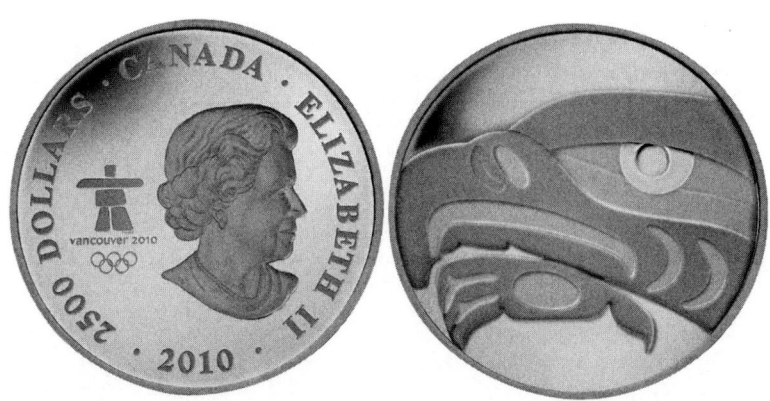

KM# 984 1000.0000 g. 0.9990 Gold 32.117 oz. AGW 101 mm.   **Note:** Illustration reduced.

Date	Mintage	MS-63	Proof
2010 Proof	20	—	57,000

KM# 1045 1000.0000 g. 0.9999 Gold 32.146 oz. AGW 101 mm.   **Subject:** Baniff, 125th Anniversary **Rev:** Highlights of Baniff **Note:** Illustration reduced.

Date	Mintage	MS-63	Proof
2010	—	—	57,000

KM# 1197 1000.0000 g. 0.9990 Gold 32.117 oz. AGW 101.6 mm.   **Subject:** LaCrosse, 350th Anniversary **Obv:** Bust right **Rev:** LaCrosse players

Date	Mintage	MS-63	Proof
2011 Proof	35	—	57,000

KM# 1217 1000.0000 g. 0.9999 Gold 32.146 oz. AGW 101 mm.   **Obv:** Bust right **Rev:** Early lacrosse game

Date	Mintage	MS-63	Proof
2011 Proof	—	—	57,000

100000 DOLLARS

KM# 1209 10000.0000 g. 1.0000 Gold 321.49 oz. AGW   **Obv:** Bust right **Rev:** Bill Reid's sculpture: Spirit of Haida Gwaii **Note:** The sculpture is at the Canadian Embassy in Washington, D.C.

Date	Mintage	MS-63	Proof
2011 Proof	—	—	565,000

SILVER BULLION COINAGE

DOLLAR

KM# 617 1.5550 g. 0.9999 Silver 0.0500 oz. ASW 16 mm.   **Obv:** Crowned head right **Rev:** Holographic Maple leaf **Edge:** Reeded

Date	Mintage	MS-63	Proof
2003 Proof	—	—	4.50

KM# 621 1.5550 g. 0.9999 Silver 0.0500 oz. ASW 17 mm.   **Obv:** Crowned head right **Rev:** Maple leaf **Edge:** Reeded

Date	Mintage	MS-63	Proof
2004 Mint logo privy mark Proof	13,859	—	4.50

2 DOLLARS

KM# 618 3.1100 g. 0.9999 Silver 0.1000 oz. ASW 20.1 mm.   **Obv:** Crowned head right **Rev:** Holographic Maple leaf **Edge:** Reeded

Date	Mintage	MS-63	Proof
2003 Proof	—	—	7.50

KM# 622 3.1100 g. 0.9999 Silver 0.1000 oz. ASW 21 mm.   **Obv:** Crowned head right **Rev:** Maple leaf **Edge:** Reeded

Date	Mintage	MS-63	Proof
2004 Mint logo privy mark Proof	13,859	—	7.50

KM# 571 3.1100 g. 0.9999 Silver 0.1000 oz. ASW 21 mm.   **Obv:** Head right **Rev:** Lynx

Date	Mintage	MS-63	Proof
2005 Proof	—	—	7.50

3 DOLLARS

KM# 619 7.7760 g. 0.9999 Silver 0.2500 oz. ASW 26.9 mm.   **Obv:**
Crowned head right **Rev:** Holographic Maple leaf **Edge:** Reeded

Date	Mintage	MS-63	Proof
2003 Proof	—	—	15.00

KM# 623 7.7760 g. 0.9999 Silver 0.2500 oz. ASW 27 mm. **Obv:** Crowned head right **Rev:** Maple leaf **Edge:** Reeded

Date	Mintage	MS-63	Proof
2004 Mint logo privy mark Proof	13,859	—	12.50

KM# 572 7.7760 g. 0.9999 Silver 0.2500 oz. ASW 27 mm. **Obv:** Head right **Rev:** Lynx

Date	Mintage	MS-63	Proof
2005 Proof	—	—	12.50

4 DOLLARS

KM# 624 15.5500 g. 0.9999 Silver 0.4999 oz. ASW 34 mm. **Obv:** Crowned head right **Rev:** Maple leaf **Edge:** Reeded

Date	Mintage	MS-63	Proof
2004 Mint logo privy mark Proof	13,859	—	22.50

KM# 573 15.5500 g. 0.9999 Silver 0.4999 oz. ASW 34 mm. **Obv:** Head right **Rev:** Lynx

Date	Mintage	MS-63	Proof
2005 Proof	—	—	22.50

KM# 620 15.5500 g. 0.9999 Silver 0.4999 oz. ASW 33.9 mm. **Obv:** Crowned head right **Rev:** Holographic Maple leaf **Edge:** Reeded

Date	Mintage	MS-63	Proof
2003 Proof	—	—	25.00

5 DOLLARS

KM# 163 31.1000 g. 0.9999 Silver
0.9997 oz. ASW   **Obv:** Young bust
right, denomination and date below
Obv. Designer: Arnold Machin **Rev:**
Maple leaf flanked by 9999

Date	Mintage	MS-63	Proof
1988	1,155,931	35.00	—
1989 Proof	29,999	—	40.00
1989	3,332,200	35.00	—

KM# 187 31.1000 g. 0.9999 Silver
0.9997 oz. ASW   **Obv:** Crowned head

right, date and denomination below
Obv. Designer: Dora de Pedery-Hunt
Rev: Maple leaf flanked by 9999

Date	Mintage	MS-63	Proof
1990	1,708,800	35.00	—
1991	644,300	35.00	—
1992	343,800	35.00	—
1993	889,946	35.00	—
1994	1,133,900	35.00	—
1995	326,244	35.00	—
1996	250,445	42.50	—
1997	100,970	35.00	—
1998 Tiger privy mark	25,000	35.00	—
1998	591,359	35.00	—
1998 R.C.M.P. privy mark	25,000	35.00	—
1998 90th Anniversary R.C.M. privy mark	13,025	35.00	—
1998 Titanic privy mark	26,000	85.00	—
1999	1,229,442	35.00	—
1999 Rabbit privy mark	25,000	35.00	—
1999 "Y2K" privy mark	9,999	37.50	—
2000 Expo Hanover privy mark	—	45.00	—
2000 Dragon privy mark	25,000	35.00	—
2000	403,652	35.00	—
2001	398,563	35.00	—
2001 Reverse proof, Snake privy mark	25,000	—	45.00
2002	576,196	35.00	—
2002 Reverse proof, Horse privy mark	25,000	—	45.00
2003	—	35.00	—
2003 Reverse proof, sheep privy mark	25,000	—	45.00

KM# 363 31.1000 g. 0.9999 Silver 0.9997 oz. ASW   **Obv:** Crowned head right, date and denomination below **Rev:** Maple leaf flanked by 9999

Date	Mintage	MS-63	Proof
1999/2000 Fireworks privy mark	298,775	35.00	—

KM# 437 31.1035 g. 0.9999 Silver 0.9999 oz. ASW 38 mm.   **Obv:** Crowned head right, date and denomination below **Rev:** Radiant maple leaf hologram **Edge:** Reeded

Date	Mintage	MS-63	Proof
2001 Good fortune privy mark	29,906	75.00	—

KM# 436 31.1035 g. 0.9999 Silver 0.9999 oz. ASW 38 mm.   **Obv:** Crowned head right, date and

denomination below **Rev:** Three maple leaves in autumn colors, 9999 flanks **Rev. Designer:** Debbie Adams **Edge:** Reeded

Date	Mintage	MS-63	Proof
2001 Proof	49,709	—	40.00

KM# 505 31.1035 g. 0.9999 Silver 0.9999 oz. ASW 38 mm.   **Obv:** Crowned head right, date and denomination below **Rev:** Two maple leaves in spring color (green) **Edge:** Reeded

Date	Mintage	MS-63	Proof
2002	29,509	37.50	—

KM# 521 31.1035 g. 0.9999 Silver 0.9999 oz. ASW   **Obv:** Head right **Rev:** Maple leaf, summer colors **Rev. Designer:** Stan Witten

Date	Mintage	MS-63	Proof
2003	29,416	37.50	—

KM# 508 31.1035 g. 0.9999 Silver 0.9999 oz. ASW 38 mm.   **Obv:** Crowned head right, date and denomination below **Obv. Designer:** Dora de Pedery-Hunt **Rev:** Holographic Maple leaf flanked by 9999 **Edge:** Reeded

Date	Mintage	MS-63	Proof
2003 Proof	—	—	37.50

KM# 607 31.1200 g. 0.9999 Silver 1.0004 oz. ASW   **Obv:** Head right **Rev:** Maple leaf, winter colors

Date	Mintage	MS-63	Proof
2004	—	37.50	—

KM# 625 31.1035 g. 0.9999 Silver 0.9999 oz. ASW 38 mm.   **Obv:** Bust right **Obv. Designer:** Susanna Blunt **Rev:** Maple leaf **Edge:** Reeded

Date	Mintage	MS-63	Proof
2004 Mint logo privy mark Specimen	13,859	—	37.50
2004 Monkey privy mark Specimen	25,000	—	37.50
2004 D-Day privy mark Specimen	11,698	—	37.50
2004 Desjardins privy mark	15,000	37.50	—
2004 Capricorn privy Mark Reverse proof	5,000	—	37.50
2004 Aquarius privy mark Reverse proof	5,000	—	37.50
2004 Pisces privy mark Reverse proof	5,000	—	37.50
2004 Aries privy mark Reverse proof	5,000	—	37.50
2004 Taurus privy mark Reverse proof	5,000	—	37.50
2004 Gemini privy mark Reverse proof	5,000	—	37.50
2004 Cancer privy mark Reverse proof	5,000	—	37.50
2004 Leo privy mark Reverse proof	5,000	—	37.50
2004 Virgo privy mark Reverse proof	5,000	—	37.50
2004 Libra privy mark Reverse proof	5,000	—	37.50

Date	Mintage	MS-63	Proof
2004 Scorpio privy mark Reverse proof	5,000	—	37.50
2004 Sagittarius privy mark Reverse proof	5,000	—	37.50
2005	—	35.00	—
2005 Tulip privy mark Reverse proof	3,500	—	40.00
2005 Tank privy mark Reverse proof	7,000	—	60.00
2005 USS Missouri privy mark Reverse proof	7,000	—	60.00
2005 Rooster privy mark Reverse proof	15,000	—	50.00
2006	—	35.00	—
2006 Dog privy mark Reverse proof	—	—	50.00
2007	—	35.00	—
2007 F12 privy mark Reverse proof	—	—	130
2007 Pig privy mark Reverse proof	—	—	40.00
2008	—	35.00	—
2008 F12 privy mark Reverse proof	—	—	130
2008 Rat privy mark Reverse proof	—	—	40.00
2009	—	35.00	—
2009 Brandenberg Gate privy mark Reverse proof	—	—	50.00
2009 Tower Bridge privy mark Reverse proof	—	—	40.00
2009 Ox Privy mark Reverse proof	—	—	37.50
2010	—	35.00	—
2011	—	35.00	—
2012	—	35.00	—

KM# 522 31.1050 g. 0.9999 Silver 0.9999 oz. ASW   **Obv:** Head right **Rev:** Maple leaf, winter color **Rev. Designer:** Stan Witten

Date	Mintage	MS-63	Proof
2004	26,763	35.00	—

KM# 574 31.1035 g. 0.9999 Silver 0.9999 oz. ASW 38 mm.   **Obv:** Head right **Rev:** Lynx

Date	Mintage	MS-63	Proof
2005 Proof	—	—	37.50

KM# 660 31.1035 g. 0.9990 Silver 0.9990 oz. ASW   **Obv:** Bust right **Obv. Designer:** Susanna Blunt **Rev:** Silver maple, colorized **Rev. Designer:** Stan Witten

Date	Mintage	MS-63	Proof
2006	14,157	37.50	—

KM# 924 31.1050 g. 0.9999 Silver 0.9999 oz. ASW   **Rev:** Maple Leaf, laser engraved **Rev. Designer:** Joan Nguyen

Date	Mintage	MS-63	Proof
2005 Proof	25,000	—	60.00

KM# 550 31.1035 g. 0.9999 Silver 0.9999 oz. ASW   **Obv:** Head right **Rev:** Big Leaf Maple, colorized **Rev. Designer:** Stan Witten

Date	Mintage	MS-63	Proof
2005	21,233	35.00	—

KM# 625a 31.1050 g. 0.9999 Silver 0.9999 oz. ASW 38 mm.   **Rev:** Maple leaf, gilt

Date	Mintage	MS-63	Proof
2007	—	75.00	—
2008	—	75.00	—
2009	—	75.00	—
2009 Tower Bridge Privy Mark	—	75.00	—
2010	—	75.00	—

KM# 729 31.1050 g. 0.9990 Silver 0.9990 oz. ASW 38 mm.   **Obv:** Bust right **Rev:** Maple leaf orange multicolor

Date	Mintage	MS-63	Proof
2007 Proof	—	—	45.00

KM# 925 31.1050 g. 0.9990 Silver 0.9990 oz. ASW   **Obv:** Bust right **Obv. Designer:** Susanna Blunt **Rev:** Sugar maple, colorized **Rev. Designer:** Stan Witten

Date	Mintage	MS-63	Proof
2007	11,495	37.50	—

KM# 928 31.3900 g. 0.9990 Silver
1.0082 oz. ASW 38 mm.   **Rev:** Orange
sugar maple leaf **Rev. Designer:** Stan
Witten

Date	Mintage	MS-63	Proof
2007 Specimen	20,000	—	75.00

KM# 800 31.1050 g. 0.9990 Silver
0.9990 oz. ASW 38 mm.   **Subject:**
Vancouver Olympics **Obv:** Bust right
Obv. Designer: Susanna Blunt **Rev:**
Maple leaf, Olympic logo at left, turtle

Date	Mintage	MS-63	Proof
2008	—	37.50	—
2009	—	37.50	—
2010	—	37.50	—

KM# 798 31.1050 g. 0.9990 Silver
0.9990 oz. ASW 38 mm.   **Subject:**

Maple Leaf 20th Anniversary **Rev:**
Maple Leaf, selective gold plating

Date	Mintage	MS-63	Proof
2008 Proof	10,000	—	75.00

KM# 799 31.1050 g. 0.9990 Silver
0.9990 oz. ASW 38 mm.   **Subject:**
Breast Cancer Awareness **Rev:**
Multicolor, green maple leaf and pink
ribbon

Date	Mintage	MS-63	Proof
2008	11,048	85.00	—

KM# 800a 31.1050 g. 0.9999 Silver
0.9999 oz. ASW partially gilt 38 mm.
Rev: Maple leaf gilt, olympic logo at left

Date	Mintage	MS-63	Proof
2008	—	50.00	—

KM# 1056 31.1050 g. 0.9999 Silver
0.9999 oz. ASW 38 mm.   **Rev:** Maple

leaf in brown color, card diamond

Date	Mintage	MS-63	Proof
2008	—	50.00	—

KM# 1057 31.1050 g. 0.9999 Silver 0.9999 oz. ASW 38 mm. **Rev:** Maple Leaf in green color, card heart

Date	Mintage	MS-63	Proof
2008	—	50.00	—

KM# 1058 31.1050 g. 0.9999 Silver 0.9999 oz. ASW 38 mm. **Rev:** Maple leaf in green color, card club

Date	Mintage	MS-63	Proof
2008	—	50.00	—

KM# 1059 31.1050 g. 0.9999 Silver 0.9999 oz. ASW 38 mm. **Rev:** Maple Leaf in red color, card spade

Date	Mintage	MS-63	Proof
2008	—	50.00	—

KM# 863 31.1050 g. 0.9999 Silver 0.9999 oz. ASW 38 mm. **Subject:** Vancouver Olympics **Rev:** Thunderbird Totem **Rev. Designer:** Rick Harry

Date	Mintage	MS-63	Proof
2009	—	50.00	—

KM# 863a 31.1050 g. 0.9999 Silver 0.9999 oz. ASW partially gilt 38 mm. **Rev:** Thunderbird, gilt

Date	Mintage	MS-63	Proof
2009	—	60.00	—

KM# 1061 31.1050 g. 0.9999 Silver

0.9999 oz. ASW 38 mm.   **Rev:** Maple leaf in red color, support our troops yellow ribbon

Date	Mintage	MS-63	Proof
2009	—	70.00	—

KM# 998 31.1200 g. 0.9990 Silver 0.9995 oz. ASW 38 mm.   **Rev:** Olympic Hockey

Date	Mintage	MS-63	Proof
2010 Proof	—	—	42.50

KM# 998a 31.1050 g. 0.9999 Silver 0.9999 oz. ASW partially gilt 38 mm. **Rev:** Hockey player, gilt maple leaves flanking

Date	Mintage	MS-63	Proof
2010	—	50.00	—

KM# 1077 31.3900 g. 0.9990 Silver 1.0082 oz. ASW 34 mm.   **Rev:** Maple leaf on 45 degree angle left

Date	Mintage	MS-63	Proof
2010 Proof	9,000	—	80.00

KM# 1052 31.1050 g. 0.9999 Silver 0.9999 oz. ASW 38 mm.   **Rev:** Wolf standing with moonlight in background

Date	Mintage	MS-63	Proof
2011	1,000,000	40.00	—

KM# 1109 31.1050 g. 0.9990 Silver 0.9990 oz. ASW 38 mm.   **Rev:** Grizzly Bear walking right

Date	Mintage	MS-63	Proof
2011	—	40.00	—

KM# 1164 31.1050 g. 0.9990 Silver 0.9990 oz. ASW 38 mm. **Obv.** **Designer:** Susanna Blunt **Rev:** Cougar **Rev. Designer:** William Woodruff

Date	Mintage	MS-63	Proof
2012	1,000,000	40.00	—

10 DOLLARS

KM# 1158 31.1050 g. 0.9999 Silver 0.9999 oz. ASW 38 mm. **Obv:** Bust right **Rev:** Branch with three maple leaves

Date	Mintage	MS-63	Proof
2011 Proof	—	—	50.00

20 DOLLARS

KM# 1062 7.9600 g. 0.9999 Silver 0.2559 oz. ASW 27 mm. **Rev:** Five Maple leaves at left **Note:** Thick planchet

Date	Mintage	MS-63	Proof
2011	200,000	25.00	—

KM# 1176 7.9600 g. 0.9999 Silver 0.2559 oz. ASW 27 mm. **Obv:** Bust right **Rev:** Canoe and reflection **Rev. Designer:** Jason Bouwman **Edge:** Reeded **Note:** Thick planchet.

Date	Mintage	MS-63	Proof
2011	200,000	25.00	—

KM# 1226 7.9600 g. 0.9999 Silver 0.2559 oz. ASW 27 mm. **Obv:** Bust right **Rev:** Waterline view of polar bear swimming **Edge:** Reeded

Date	Mintage	MS-63	Proof
2012	250,000	25.00	—

50 DOLLARS

KM# 326 311.0350 g. 0.9999 Silver 9.9986 oz. ASW   **Subject:** 10th Anniversary Silver Maple Leaf **Obv:** Crowned head right **Rev:** Maple leaf flanked by 9999 **Edge:** 10th ANNIVERSARY 10e ANNIVERSAIRE

Date	Mintage	MS-63	Proof
1998 Proof	25,000	—	350

250 DOLLARS

KM# 676 1000.0000 g. 0.9999 Silver 32.146 oz. ASW   **Subject:** Kilo

Date	Mintage	MS-63	Proof
2006	—	1,350	—

KM# 1160 1000.0000 g. 0.9999 Silver 32.146 oz. ASW 101 mm.   **Rev:** Three maple leaves on branch

Date	Mintage	MS-63	Proof
2011	—	—	1,350

GOLD BULLION COINAGE

50 CENTS

KM# 888 1.2700 g. 0.9990 Gold 0.0408 oz. AGW 13.92 mm.   **Subject:** Red maple **Obv:** Bust right **Obv. Legend:** Elizabeth II 50 cents **Obv. Designer:** Susanna Blunt **Rev:** Two maple leaves **Rev. Legend:** Canada, Fine gold 1/25 oz or PUR 9999

Date	Mintage	MS-63	Proof
2009 Proof	150,000	—	90.00

KM# 1085 1.2700 g. 0.9990 Gold 0.0408 oz. AGW 13.92 mm.   **Rev:** Geese in flight left **Rev. Designer:** Emily Damstra

Date	Mintage	MS-63	Proof
2011 Proof	10,000	—	90.00

KM# 1214 1.2700 g. 1.0000 Gold 0.0408 oz. AGW 13.92 mm.   **Obv:** Bust right **Rev:** Three maple leaves, 2007-2012 above

Date	Mintage	MS-63	Proof
2012 Proof	—	—	90.00

KM# 1218 1.2700 g. 0.9999 Gold 0.0408 oz. AGW 13.92 mm.   **Obv:** Bust right **Rev:** Schooner sailing left

Date	Mintage	MS-63	Proof
2012 Proof	—	—	90.00

DOLLAR

KM# 238 1.5551 g. 0.9999 Gold 0.0500 oz. AGW   **Obv:** Crowned head right, denomination and date below **Rev:** Maple leaf flanked by 9999

Date	Mintage	MS-63	Proof
1993	37,080	BV+25%	—
1994	78,860	BV+25%	—
1995	85,920	BV+25%	—
1996	56,520	BV+25%	—
1997	59,720	BV+25%	—
1998	44,260	BV+25%	—
1999 oval "20 YEARS ANS" privy mark	—	BV+30%	—
2000 oval "2000" privy mark	—	BV+30%	—

KM# 365 1.5551 g. 0.9999 Gold 0.0500 oz. AGW   **Obv:** Crowned head right **Rev:** Maple leaf hologram

Date	Mintage	MS-63	Proof
1999	500	100.00	—

KM# 1138 1.5600 g. 0.9999 Gold 0.0501 oz. AGW 14 mm.   **Obv:** Bust right **Rev:** Maple leaf

Date	Mintage	MS-63	Proof
1911-2011	—	100.00	—

KM# 1213 1.5810 g. 1.0000 Gold 0.0508 oz. AGW 14.1 mm.   **Obv:** Bust right **Rev:** Three maple leaves, 2007-2012 above

Date	Mintage	MS-63	Proof
2012 Proof	—	—	110

2 DOLLARS

KM# 256 2.0735 g. 0.9999 Gold 0.0667 oz. AGW   **Obv:** Crowned head right, denomination and date below **Rev:** Maple leaf flanked by 9999

Date	Mintage	MS-63	Proof
1994	5,493	120	—

5 DOLLARS

KM# 135 3.1200 g. 0.9999 Gold 0.1003 oz. AGW   **Obv:** Young bust right, date and denomination below **Obv. Designer:** Arnold Machin **Rev:** Maple leaf flanked by 9999

Date	Mintage	MS-63	Proof
1982	246,000	BV+14%	—
1983	304,000	BV+14%	—
1984	262,000	BV+14%	—
1985	398,000	BV+14%	—
1986	529,516	BV+14%	—
1987	459,000	BV+14%	—
1988	506,500	BV+14%	—
1989	539,000	BV+14%	—
1989 Proof	16,992	—	185

KM# 188 3.1200 g. 0.9999 Gold 0.1003 oz. AGW   **Obv:** Elizabeth II effigy **Obv. Designer:** Dora dePedery-Hunt **Rev:** Maple leaf

Date	Mintage	MS-63	Proof
1990	476,000	BV+14%	—
1991	322,000	BV+14%	—
1992	384,000	BV+14%	—
1993	248,630	BV+14%	—
1994	313,150	BV+14%	—
1995	294,890	BV+14%	—
1996	179,220	BV+14%	—
1997	188,540	BV+14%	—
1998	301,940	BV+14%	—
1999 oval "20 Years ANS" privy mark	—	BV+19%	—
2000 oval "2000" privy mark	—	BV+19%	—

KM# 366 3.1200 g. 0.9999 Gold 0.1003 oz. AGW   **Rev:** Maple leaf hologram

Date	Mintage	MS-63	Proof
1999	500	200	—

KM# 439 3.1310 g. 0.9999 Gold 0.1006 oz. AGW 16 mm.   **Subject:** Holographic Maple Leaves **Obv:** Crowned head right **Rev:** Three maple leaves multicolor hologram **Edge:** Reeded

Date	Mintage	MS-63	Proof
2001	600	200	—

KM# 929 3.1300 g. 0.9990 Gold 0.1005 oz. AGW 16 mm.   **Obv. Designer:** Susan Blunt **Rev:** Maple leaf **Rev. Designer:** Walter Ott

Date	Mintage	MS-63	Proof
2007	—	—	200
2008	—	—	200
2009	—	—	200
2010	—	—	200
2011	—	—	200

KM# 1139 3.1300 g. 0.9990 Gold 0.1005 oz. AGW 16 mm. **Obv:** Bust right **Rev:** Maple leaf

Date	Mintage	MS-63	Proof
1911-2011	—	225	—

KM# 1212 3.1300 g. 1.0000 Gold 0.1006 oz. AGW 16 mm. **Obv:** Bust right **Rev:** Three maple leaves, 2007-2012 above

Date	Mintage	MS-63	Proof
2012 Proof	—	—	200

10 DOLLARS

KM# 136 7.7850 g. 0.9999 Gold 0.2503 oz. AGW **Obv:** Young bust right, date and denomination below **Obv. Designer:** Arnold Machin **Rev:** Maple leaf flanked by 9999

Date	Mintage	MS-63	Proof
1982	184,000	BV+10%	—
1983	308,800	BV+10%	—
1984	242,400	BV+10%	—
1985	620,000	BV+10%	—
1986	915,200	BV+10%	—
1987	376,000	BV+10%	—
1988	436,000	BV+10%	—
1989 Proof	6,998	—	500
1989	328,800	BV+10%	—

KM# 189 7.7850 g. 0.9999 Gold 0.2503 oz. AGW **Obv:** Crowned head right, date and denomination below **Obv. Designer:** Dora dePedery-Hunt **Rev:** Maple leaf flanked by 9999

Date	Mintage	MS-63
1990	253,600	BV+10%
1991	166,400	BV+10%
1992	179,600	BV+10%
1993	158,452	BV+10%
1994	148,792	BV+10%
1995	127,596	BV+10%
1996	89,148	BV+10%
1997	98,104	BV+10%
1998	85,472	BV+10%
1999 oval "20 Years ANS" privy mark	—	BV+15%
2000 oval "2000" privy mark	—	BV+15%

KM# 367 7.7850 g. 0.9999 Gold 0.2503 oz. AGW **Rev:** Maple leaf hologram

Date	Mintage	MS-63	Proof
1999	—	475	—

KM# 440 7.7970 g. 0.9999 Gold 0.2506 oz. AGW 20 mm. **Subject:** Holographic Maples Leaves **Obv:** Crowned head right **Rev:** Three maple leaves multicolor hologram **Edge:** Reeded

Date	Mintage	MS-63	Proof
2001	15,000	475	—

KM# 1140 7.7970 g. 0.9999 Gold 0.2506 oz. AGW 20 mm. **Obv:** Bust right **Rev:** Maple leaf

Date	Mintage	MS-63	Proof
1911-2011	—	475	—

KM# 1211 7.7970 g. 1.0000 Gold 0.2507 oz. AGW 20 mm. **Obv:** Bust right **Rev:** Three maple leaves, 2007-2012 above

Date	Mintage	MS-63	Proof
2012 Proof	—	—	475

20 DOLLARS

KM# 153 15.5515 g. 0.9999 Gold 0.4999 oz. AGW 32 mm. **Obv:** Young bust right, date and denomination below **Obv. Designer:** Arnold Machin **Rev:** Maple leaf flanked by 9999

Date	Mintage	MS-63	Proof
1986	529,200	BV+7%	—
1987	332,800	BV+7%	—
1988	538,400	BV+7%	—
1989	259,200	BV+7%	—
1989 Proof	6,998	—	925

KM# 190 15.5515 g. 0.9999 Gold 0.4999 oz. AGW **Obv:** Crowned head right, date and denomination below **Obv. Designer:** Dora dePedery-Hunt **Rev:** Maple leaf flanked by 9999

Date	Mintage	MS-63	Proof
1990	174,400	BV+7%	—
1991	96,200	BV+7%	—
1992	108,000	BV+7%	—
1993	99,492	BV+7%	—
1994	104,766	BV+7%	—
1995	103,162	BV+7%	—
1996	66,246	BV+7%	—
1997	63,354	BV+7%	—
1998	65,366	BV+7%	—
1999 oval "20 Years ANS" privy mark	—	BV+12%	—
2000 oval "2000" privy mark	—	BV+12%	—

KM# 368 15.5515 g. 0.9999 Gold 0.4999 oz. AGW **Rev:** Maple leaf hologram

Date	Mintage	MS-63	Proof
1999	500	925	—

KM# 441 15.5840 g. 0.9999 Gold 0.5010 oz. AGW 25 mm. **Subject:** Holographic Maples Leaves **Obv:** Crowned head right **Rev:** Three maple leaves multicolor hologram **Edge:** Reeded

Date	Mintage	MS-63	Proof
2001	600	925	—

50 DOLLARS

KM# 125.1 31.1030 g. 0.9990 Gold 0.9989 oz. AGW **Obv:** Young bust right, denomination and date below **Rev:** Maple leaf flanked by .999

Date	Mintage	MS-63	Proof
1979	1,000,000	BV+4%	—
1980	1,251,500	BV+4%	—
1981	863,000	BV+4%	—
1982	883,000	BV+4%	—

KM# 125.2 31.1030 g. 0.9999 Gold 0.9998 oz. AGW **Obv:** Young bust right, date and denomination below **Rev:** Maple leaf flanked by .9999

Date	Mintage	MS-63	Proof
1983	843,000	BV+4%	—
1984	1,067,500	BV+4%	—
1985	1,908,000	BV+4%	—
1986	779,115	BV+4%	—
1987	978,000	BV+4%	—
1988	826,500	BV+4%	—
1989 Proof	17,781	—	1,900
1989	856,000	BV+4%	—

KM# 191 31.1030 g. 0.9999 Gold
0.9998 oz. AGW **Obv:** Crowned head
right, date and denomination below
Obv. Designer: Dora dePedery-Hunt
Rev: Maple leaf flanked by .9999

Date	Mintage	MS-63	Proof
1990	815,000	BV+4%	—
1991	290,000	BV+4%	—
1992	368,900	BV+4%	—
1993	321,413	BV+4%	—
1994	180,357	BV+4%	—
1995	208,729	BV+4%	—
1996	143,682	BV+4%	—
1997	478,211	BV+4%	—
1998	593,704	BV+4%	—
1999 oval "20 Years ANS" privy mark	—	BV+7%	—
2000 oval "2000" privy mark	—	BV+7%	—
2000 oval fireworks privy mark	—	BV+7%	—

KM# 369 31.1030 g. 0.9999 Gold
0.9998 oz. AGW **Obv:** Crowned head
right, date and denomination below
Rev: Maple leaf hologram flanked by
9999, with fireworks privy mark

Date	Mintage	MS-63	Proof
2000	500	1,850	—

KM# 442 31.1500 g. 0.9999 Gold
1.0014 oz. AGW 30 mm. **Subject:**
Holographic Maples Leaves **Obv:**
Crowned head right **Rev:** Three maple
leaves multicolor hologram **Edge:**
Reeded

Date	Mintage	MS-63	Proof
2001	600	1,850	—

KM# 1042 31.1050 g. 0.9990 Gold
0.9990 oz. AGW 30 mm. **Rev:**
Vancouver logo and maple leaf **Edge:**
Reeded

Date	Mintage	MS-63	Proof
2008P	—	1,850	—

KM# 305 31.1030 g. 0.9999 Gold
0.9998 oz. AGW **Obv:** Crowned head
denomination below, within circle,
dates below **Rev:** Mountie at gallop
right, within circle **Rev. Designer:** Ago
Aarand **Shape:** 10-sided

Date	Mintage	MS-63	Proof
1997	12,913	1,850	—

KM# 1042a 31.1050 g. 0.9999 Gold
0.9999 oz. AGW partially enameled
30 mm.   **Rev:** Maple leaf in red
enamel, olympic logo at left

Date	Mintage	MS-63	Proof
2008	—	1,850	—

KM# 1037 31.1050 g. 0.9999 Gold
0.9999 oz. AGW 30 mm.   **Rev:**
Thunderbird **Edge:** Reeded

Date	Mintage	MS-63	Proof
2009	—	1,850	—

KM# 1037a 31.1050 g. 0.9999 Gold
0.9999 oz. AGW 30 mm.   **Rev:**
Thunderbird, stars in red enamel
highlights

Date	Mintage	MS-63	Proof
2009	—	1,850	—

KM# 1029 31.1050 g. 0.9999 Gold
0.9999 oz. AGW 30 mm.   **Rev:** Hockey
player flanked by maple leaves

Date	Mintage	MS-63	Proof
2010	—	1,850	—

KM# 1029a 31.1050 g. 0.9999 Gold
0.9999 oz. AGW 30 mm.   **Rev:** Hockey
player, red enameled maple leaves
flanking

Date	Mintage	MS-63	Proof
2010	—	1,850	—

KM# 1141 31.1050 g. 0.9999 Gold
0.9999 oz. AGW 30 mm.   **Obv:** Bust
right **Rev:** Maple leaf

Date	Mintage	MS-63	Proof
1911-2011	—	1,850	—

KM# 1210 31.1050 g. 1.0000 Gold
100000 oz. AGW   **Obv:** Bust right
Rev: Three maple leaves, 2007-2012
above

Date	Mintage	MS-63	Proof
2012 Proof	—	—	1,850

200 DOLLARS

KM# 750 31.1050 g. 1.0000 Gold 100000 oz. AGW 30 mm. **Rev:** Three maple leaves

Date	Mintage	MS-63	Proof
2007 Proof, T/E privy mark	500	—	1,850

KM# 786 31.1050 g. 1.0000 Gold 100000 oz. AGW 30 mm. **Obv:** Bust right on lathe-work background **Rev:** Two maple leaves on lathe-work background

Date	Mintage	MS-63	Proof
2008 Proof	—	—	1,850

KM# 1162 31.1050 g. 1.0000 Gold 100000 oz. AGW **Rev:** Maple leaf with lathe backgound

Date	Mintage	MS-63	Proof
2009 Proof	—	—	1,850

KM# 1163 31.1050 g. 0.9990 Gold 0.9990 oz. AGW **Subject:** Celebrating win **Rev:** Three athletics with hands raised

Date	Mintage	MS-63	Proof
2010 Proof	—	—	1,850

KM# 1165 31.1050 g. 1.0000 Gold 100000 oz. AGW 30 mm. **Obv. Designer:** Susanna Blunt **Rev:** Mountie on horseback, lathe backgound **Rev. Designer:** Ago Aarand

Date	Mintage	MS-63	P/L	Proof
2011	—	1,850	—	—

2500 DOLLARS

KM# 1161 1000.0000 g. 0.9999 Gold 32.146 oz. AGW 101 mm.   **Rev:** Three maple leaves on branch

Date	Mintage	MS-63	Proof
2011	—	—	56,000

1000000 DOLLARS

KM# 755 100000.0000 g. 0.9999 Gold 3214.6 oz. AGW   **Rev:** Maple leaf **Note:** Cast

Date	Mintage	MS-63	Proof
2007	10	5,630,000	—

PLATINUM BULLION COINAGE

DOLLAR

KM# 239 1.5552 g. 0.9995 Platinum
0.0500 oz. APW   **Obv:** Crowned head

right, date and denomination below
Rev: Maple leaf flanked by 9995

Date	Mintage	MS-63	Proof
1993	2,120	BV+30%	—
1994	4,260	BV+30%	—
1995	460	150	
1996	1,640	BV+30%	—
1997	1,340	BV+30%	—
1998	2,000	BV+30%	—
1999	2,000	BV+30%	—

2 DOLLARS

KM# 257 2.0735 g. 0.9995 Platinum
0.0666 oz. APW   **Obv:** Crowned head
right, date and denomination below
Rev: Maple leaf flanked by 9995

Date	Mintage	MS-63	Proof
1994	1,470	240	—

5 DOLLARS

KM# 192 3.1203 g. 0.9995 Platinum
0.1003 oz. APW   **Obv. Designer:**
dePedery-Hunt **Rev:** Maple leaf

Date	Mintage	MS-63	Proof
1990	9,000	BV+18%	—
1991	13,000	BV+18%	—
1992	16,000	BV+18%	—
1993	14,020	BV+18%	—
1994	19,190	BV+18%	—
1995	8,940	BV+18%	—
1996	8,820	BV+18%	—
1997	7,050	BV+18%	—
1998	5,710	BV+18%	—
1999	2,000	BV+18%	—

KM# 164 3.1203 g. 0.9995 Platinum
0.1003 oz. APW   **Obv:** Young bust
right, date and denomination below
Obv. Designer: Arnold Machin **Rev:**
Maple leaf flanked by 9995

Date	Mintage	MS-63	Proof
1988	74,000	BV+18%	—
1989 Proof	11,999	—	250
1989	18,000	BV+18%	—

10 DOLLARS

KM# 165 7.7857 g. 0.9995 Platinum
0.2502 oz. APW   **Obv:** Young bust
right, date and denomination below
Obv. Designer: Machin **Rev:** Maple
leaf flanked by 9995

Date	Mintage	MS-63	Proof
1988	93,600	BV+13%	—
1989	3,200	BV+13%	—
1989 Proof	1,999	—	550

KM# 193 7.7857 g. 0.9995 Platinum 0.2502 oz. APW   **Obv. Designer:** dePedery-Hunt **Rev:** Maple leaf

Date	Mintage	MS-63	Proof
1990	1,600	BV+13%	—
1991	7,200	BV+13%	—
1992	11,600	BV+13%	—
1993	8,048	BV+13%	—

Date	Mintage	MS-63	Proof
1994	9,456	BV+13%	—
1995	6,524	BV+13%	—
1996	6,160	BV+13%	—
1997	4,552	BV+13%	—
1998	3,816	BV+13%	—
1999	2,000	BV+13%	—

20 DOLLARS

KM# 166 15.5519 g. 0.9995 Platinum 0.4997 oz. APW   **Obv:** Young bust right, denomination and date below **Obv. Designer:** Machin **Rev:** Maple leaf flanked by 9995

Date	Mintage	MS-63	Proof
1988	23,600	BV+9%	—

Date	Mintage	MS-63	Proof
1989 Proof	1,999	—	1,000
1989	4,800	BV+9%	—

KM# 194 15.5519 g. 0.9995 Platinum 0.4997 oz. APW   **Obv. Designer:** dePedery-Hunt **Rev:** Maple leaf

Date	Mintage	MS-63	Proof
1990	2,600	BV+9%	—
1991	5,600	BV+9%	—
1992	12,800	BV+9%	—
1993	6,022	BV+9%	—
1994	6,710	BV+9%	—
1995	6,308	BV+9%	—
1996	5,490	BV+9%	—
1997	3,990	BV+9%	—
1998	5,486	BV+9%	—
1999	500	BV+15%	—

30 DOLLARS

KM# 174 3.1100 g. 0.9990 Platinum 0.0999 oz. APW   **Obv:** Crowned head right **Rev:** Polar bear swimming, denomination below **Rev. Designer:** Robert Bateman

Date	Mintage	MS-63	Proof
1990 Proof	2,629	—	210

KM# 198 3.1100 g. 0.9990 Platinum 0.0999 oz. APW   **Obv:** Crowned head right **Rev:** Snowy owl, denomination below **Rev. Designer:** Glen Loates

Date	Mintage	MS-63	Proof
1991 Proof	3,500	—	210

KM# 226 3.1100 g. 0.9990 Platinum 0.0999 oz. APW   **Obv:** Crowned head right **Rev:** Cougar head and shoulders, denomination below **Rev. Designer:** George McLean

Date	Mintage	MS-63	Proof
1992 Proof	3,500	—	210

KM# 240 3.1100 g. 0.9990 Platinum 0.0999 oz. APW **Obv:** Crowned head right **Rev:** Arctic fox, denomination below **Rev. Designer:** Claude D'Angelo

Date	Mintage	MS-63	Proof
1993 Proof	3,500	—	210

KM# 252 3.1100 g. 0.9990 Platinum 0.0999 oz. APW **Obv:** Crowned head right, date below **Rev:** Sea otter, denomination below **Rev. Designer:** Ron S. Parker

Date	Mintage	MS-63	Proof
1994 Proof	1,500	—	210

KM# 266 3.1100 g. 0.9990 Platinum 0.0999 oz. APW **Obv:** Crowned head right, date below **Rev:** Canadian lynx, denomination below **Rev. Designer:** Michael Dumas

Date	Mintage	MS-63	Proof
1995 Proof	620	—	210

KM# 278 3.1100 g. 0.9990 Platinum 0.0999 oz. APW **Obv:** Crowned head right, date below **Rev:** Falcon portrait, denomination below **Rev. Designer:** Dwayne Harty

Date	Mintage	MS-63	Proof
1996 Proof	489	—	210

KM# 300 3.1100 g. 0.9995 Platinum 0.0999 oz. APW **Obv:** Crowned head right, date below **Rev:** Bison head, denomination below **Rev. Designer:** Chris Bacon

Date	Mintage	MS-63	Proof
1997 Proof	5,000	—	210

KM# 322 3.1100 g. 0.9990 Platinum 0.0999 oz. APW **Obv:** Crowned head right, date below **Rev:** Grey wolf **Rev. Designer:** Kerr Burnett

Date	Mintage	MS-63	Proof
1998 Proof	2,000	—	210

KM# 359 3.1100 g. 0.9995 Platinum 0.0999 oz. APW **Obv:** Crowned head right, date below **Rev:** Musk ox **Rev. Designer:** Mark Hobson

Date	Mintage	MS-63	Proof
1999 Proof	1,500	—	210

KM# 405 3.1100 g. 0.9995 Platinum 0.0999 oz. APW 16 mm. **Obv:** Crowned head right, date below **Rev:** Pronghorn antelope head, denomination below **Rev. Designer:** Mark Hobson **Edge:** Reeded

Date	Mintage	MS-63	Proof
2000 Proof	600	—	210

KM# 429 3.1100 g. 0.9995 Platinum 0.0999 oz. APW 16 mm. **Obv:** Crowned head right **Rev:** Harlequin duck's head **Rev. Designer:** Cosme Saffioti and Susan Taylor **Edge:** Reeded

Date	Mintage	MS-63	Proof
2001 Proof	448	—	200

KM# 1097 3.1100 g. 0.9995 Platinum
0.0999 oz. APW 16 mm.   **Rev:** Great
Blue Heron

Date	Mintage	MS-63	Proof
2002 Proof	344	—	200

KM# 1101 3.1100 g. 0.9995 Platinum
0.0999 oz. APW 16 mm.   **Rev:** Atlantic
Walrus

Date	Mintage	MS-63	Proof
2003	365	—	250

KM# 1105 3.1100 g. 0.9995 Platinum
0.0999 oz. APW 16 mm.   **Rev:** Grizzly
Bear

Date	Mintage	MS-63	Proof
2004 Proof	380	—	250

50 DOLLARS

KM# 167 31.1030 g. 0.9995 Platinum
0.9994 oz. APW   **Obv:** Young bust

right, denomination and date below
Obv. Designer: Machin **Rev:** Maple leaf
flanked by 9995

Date	Mintage	MS-63	Proof
1988	37,500	BV+4%	—
1989 Proof	5,965	—	1,900
1989	10,000	BV+4%	—

KM# 195 31.1030 g. 0.9995 Platinum
0.9994 oz. APW   **Obv. Designer:**
dePedery-Hunt **Rev:** Maple leaf

Date	Mintage	MS-63	Proof
1990	15,100	BV+4%	—
1991	31,900	BV+4%	—
1992	40,500	BV+4%	—
1993	17,666	BV+4%	—
1994	36,245	BV+4%	—
1995	25,829	BV+4%	—
1996	62,273	BV+4%	—
1997	25,480	BV+4%	—
1998	10,403	BV+4%	—
1999	1,300	BV+10%	—

75 DOLLARS

KM# 175 7.7760 g. 0.9990 Platinum
0.2497 oz. APW   **Obv:** Crowned head
right **Rev:** Polar bear resting,
denomination below **Rev. Designer:**
Robert Bateman

Date	Mintage	MS-63	Proof
1990 Proof	2,629	—	520

KM# 199 7.7760 g. 0.9990 Platinum
0.2497 oz. APW   **Obv:** Crowned head
right **Rev:** Snowy owls perched on
branch, denomination below **Rev.
Designer:** Glen Loates

Date	Mintage	MS-63	Proof
1991 Proof	3,500	—	520

KM# 227 7.7760 g. 0.9990 Platinum 0.2497 oz. APW **Obv:** Crowned head right **Rev:** Cougar prowling, denomination below **Rev. Designer:** George McLean

Date	Mintage	MS-63	Proof
1992 Proof	3,500	—	520

KM# 241 7.7760 g. 0.9990 Platinum 0.2497 oz. APW **Obv:** Crowned head right **Rev:** Two Arctic foxes, denomination below **Rev. Designer:** Claude D'Angelo

Date	Mintage	MS-63	Proof
1993 Proof	3,500	—	520

KM# 253 7.7760 g. 0.9990 Platinum 0.2497 oz. APW **Obv:** Crowned head right, date below **Rev:** Sea otter eating urchin, denomination below **Rev. Designer:** Ron S. Parker

Date	Mintage	MS-63	Proof
1994 Proof	1,500	—	520

KM# 267 7.7760 g. 0.9990 Platinum 0.2497 oz. APW **Obv:** Crowned head right, date below **Rev:** Two lynx kittens,

denomination below **Rev. Designer:** Michael Dumas

Date	Mintage	MS-63	Proof
1995 Proof	1,500	—	520

KM# 279 7.7760 g. 0.9990 Platinum 0.2497 oz. APW **Obv:** Crowned head right, date below **Rev:** Peregrine falcon, denomination below **Rev. Designer:** Dwayne Harty

Date	Mintage	MS-63	Proof
1996 Proof	1,500	—	520

KM# 301 7.7760 g. 0.9990 Platinum 0.2497 oz. APW **Obv:** Crowned head right, date below **Rev:** Two bison calves, denomination below **Rev. Designer:** Chris Bacon

Date	Mintage	MS-63	Proof
1997 Proof	1,500	—	520

KM# 323 7.7760 g. 0.9990 Platinum 0.2497 oz. APW **Obv:** Crowned head right, date below **Rev:** Gray wolf **Rev. Designer:** Kerr Burnett

Date	Mintage	MS-63	Proof
1998 Proof	1,000	—	520

KM# 360 7.7760 g. 0.9990 Platinum 0.2497 oz. APW **Obv:** Crowned head right, date below **Rev:** Musk ox **Rev. Designer:** Mark Hobson

Date	Mintage	MS-63	Proof
1999 Proof	500	—	520

KM# 406 7.7760 g. 0.9990 Platinum 0.2497 oz. APW 20 mm. **Obv:**

Crowned head right **Rev:** Standing
pronghorn antelope, denomination
below **Rev. Designer:** Mark Hobson
Edge: Reeded

Date	Mintage	MS-63	Proof
2000 Proof	600	—	520

KM# 430 7.7760 g. 0.9995 Platinum
0.2499 oz. APW 20 mm.   **Obv:**
Crowned head right **Rev:** Harlequin
duck in flight **Rev. Designer:** Cosme
Saffioti and Susan Taylor **Edge:** Reeded

Date	Mintage	MS-63	Proof
2001 Proof	448	—	500

KM# 1098 7.7700 g. 0.9995 Platinum
0.2497 oz. APW 20 mm.   **Rev:** Great
Blue Heron

Date	Mintage	MS-63	Proof
2002 Proof	344	—	525

KM# 1102 7.7700 g. 0.9995 Platinum
0.2497 oz. APW 20 mm.   **Rev:** Atlantic
Walrus

Date	Mintage	MS-63	Proof
2003 Proof	365	—	550

KM# 1106 7.7700 g. 0.9995 Platinum
0.2497 oz. APW 20 mm.   **Rev:** Grizzly
Bear

Date	Mintage	MS-63	Proof
2004 Proof	380	—	550

150 DOLLARS

KM# 176 15.5520 g. 0.9990 Platinum
0.4995 oz. APW   **Obv:** Crowned head
right **Rev:** Polar bear walking,
denomination below **Rev. Designer:**
Robert Bateman

Date	Mintage	MS-63	Proof
1990 Proof	2,629	—	1,000

KM# 228 15.5520 g. 0.9990 Platinum
0.4995 oz. APW   **Obv:** Crowned head
right **Rev:** Cougar mother and cub,
denomination below **Rev. Designer:**
George McLean

Date	Mintage	MS-63	Proof
1992 Proof	3,500	—	1,000

KM# 200 15.5520 g. 0.9990 Platinum
0.4995 oz. APW   **Obv:** Crowned head
right **Rev:** Snowy owl flying,
denomination below **Rev. Designer:**
Glen Loates

Date	Mintage	MS-63	Proof
1991 Proof	3,500	—	1,000

KM# 242 15.5520 g. 0.9990 Platinum
0.4995 oz. APW   **Obv:** Crowned head
right **Rev:** Arctic fox by lake,
denomination below **Rev. Designer:**
Claude D'Angelo

Date	Mintage	MS-63	Proof
1993 Proof	3,500	—	1,000

KM# 254 15.5520 g. 0.9990 Platinum 0.4995 oz. APW **Obv:** Crowned head right, date below **Rev:** Sea otter mother carrying pup, denomination below **Rev. Designer:** Ron S. Parker

Date	Mintage	MS-63	Proof
1994 Proof	—	—	1,000

KM# 302 15.5520 g. 0.9990 Platinum 0.4995 oz. APW **Obv:** Crowned head right, date below **Rev:** Bison bull, denomination below **Rev. Designer:** Chris Bacon

Date	Mintage	MS-63	Proof
1997 Proof	4,000	—	1,000

KM# 268 15.5520 g. 0.9990 Platinum 0.4995 oz. APW **Obv:** Crowned head right, date below **Rev:** Prowling lynx, denomination below **Rev. Designer:** Michael Dumas

Date	Mintage	MS-63	Proof
1995 Proof	226	—	1,000

KM# 324 15.5520 g. 0.9990 Platinum 0.4995 oz. APW **Obv:** Crowned head right, date below **Rev:** Two gray wolf cubs, denomination below **Rev. Designer:** Kerr Burnett

Date	Mintage	MS-63	Proof
1998 Proof	2,000	—	1,000

KM# 280 15.5520 g. 0.9990 Platinum 0.4995 oz. APW **Obv:** Crowned head right, date below **Rev:** Peregrine falcon on branch, denomination below **Rev. Designer:** Dwayne Harty

Date	Mintage	MS-63	Proof
1996 Proof	100	—	1,000

KM# 361 15.5520 g. 0.9990 Platinum 0.4995 oz. APW **Obv:** Crowned head right **Rev:** Musk ox, denomination below **Rev. Designer:** Mark Hobson

Date	Mintage	MS-63	Proof
1999 Proof	500	—	1,000

KM# 407 15.5500 g. 0.9990 Platinum 0.4994 oz. APW 25 mm.   **Obv:** Crowned head right **Rev:** Two pronghorn antelope, denomination below **Rev. Designer:** Mark Hobson **Edge:** Reeded

Date	Mintage	MS-63	Proof
2000 Proof	600	—	1,000

KM# 431 15.5500 g. 0.9995 Platinum 0.4997 oz. APW 25 mm.   **Obv:** Crowned head right **Rev:** Two harlequin ducks **Rev. Designer:** Cosme Saffioti and Susan Taylor **Edge:** Reeded

Date	Mintage	MS-63	Proof
2001 Proof	448	—	1,000

KM# 1099 15.5500 g. 0.9995 Platinum 0.4997 oz. APW 25 mm.   **Rev:** Great Blue Heron

Date	Mintage	MS-63	Proof
2002 Proof	344	—	1,000

KM# 1103 15.5500 g. 0.9995 Platinum 0.4997 oz. APW 25 mm.   **Rev:** Atlantic Walrus

Date	Mintage	MS-63	Proof
2003 Proof	365	—	1,000

KM# 1107 15.5500 g. 0.9995 Platinum 0.4997 oz. APW 25 mm.   **Rev:** Grizzly Bear

Date	Mintage	MS-63	Proof
2004 Proof	380	—	1,000

300 DOLLARS

KM# 177 31.1035 g. 0.9990 Platinum 0.9990 oz. APW   **Obv:** Crowned head right **Rev:** Polar bear mother and cub, denomination below **Rev. Designer:** Robert Bateman

Date	Mintage	MS-63	Proof
1990 Proof	2,629	—	1,950

KM# 201 31.1035 g. 0.9990 Platinum 0.9990 oz. APW   **Obv:** Crowned head right **Rev:** Snowy owl with chicks, denomination below **Rev. Designer:** Glen Loates

Date	Mintage	MS-63	Proof
1991 Proof	3,500	—	1,950

KM# 229 31.1035 g. 0.9990 Platinum 0.9990 oz. APW **Obv:** Crowned head right **Rev:** Cougar resting in tree, denomination below **Rev. Designer:** George McLean

Date	Mintage	MS-63	Proof
1992 Proof	3,500	—	1,950

KM# 243 31.1035 g. 0.9990 Platinum 0.9990 oz. APW **Obv:** Crowned head right **Rev:** Mother fox and three kits, denomination below **Rev. Designer:** Claude D'Angelo

Date	Mintage	MS-63	Proof
1993 Proof	3,500	—	1,950

KM# 255 31.1035 g. 0.9990 Platinum 0.9990 oz. APW **Obv:** Crowned head right, date below **Rev:** Two otters swimming, denomination below **Rev. Designer:** Ron S. Parker

Date	Mintage	MS-63	Proof
1994 Proof	—	—	1,950

KM# 269 31.1035 g. 0.9990 Platinum 0.9990 oz. APW **Obv:** Crowned head right, date below **Rev:** Female lynx and three kittens, denomination below **Rev. Designer:** Michael Dumas

Date	Mintage	MS-63	Proof
1995 Proof	1,500	—	1,950

KM# 281 31.1035 g. 0.9990 Platinum 0.9990 oz. APW **Obv:** Crowned head right, date below **Rev:** Peregrine falcon feeding nestlings, denomination below **Rev. Designer:** Dwayne Harty

Date	Mintage	MS-63	Proof
1996 Proof	1,500	—	1,950

KM# 303 31.1035 g. 0.9990 Platinum 0.9990 oz. APW **Obv:** Crowned head right, date below **Rev:** Bison family, denomination below **Rev. Designer:** Chris Bacon

Date	Mintage	MS-63	Proof
1997 Proof	1,500	—	1,950

KM# 325 31.1035 g. 0.9990 Platinum 0.9990 oz. APW   **Obv:** Crowned head right, date below **Rev:** Gray wolf and two cubs, denomination below **Rev. Designer:** Kerr Burnett

Date	Mintage	MS-63	Proof
1998 Proof	—	—	1,950

KM# 362 31.1035 g. 0.9990 Platinum 0.9990 oz. APW   **Obv:** Crowned head right, date below **Rev:** Musk ox **Rev. Designer:** Mark Hobson

Date	Mintage	MS-63	Proof
1999 Proof	500	—	1,950

KM# 408 31.1035 g. 0.9990 Platinum 0.9990 oz. APW 30 mm.   **Obv:** Crowned head right, date below **Rev:** Four pronghorn antelope, denomination below **Rev. Designer:** Mark Hobson **Edge:** Reeded

Date	Mintage	MS-63	Proof
2000 Proof	600	—	1,950

KM# 432 31.1035 g. 0.9995 Platinum 0.9995 oz. APW 30 mm.   **Obv:** Crowned head right **Rev:** Two standing

harlequin ducks **Rev. Designer:** Cosme Saffioti and Susan Taylor **Edge:** Reeded

Date	Mintage	MS-63	Proof
2001 Proof	448	—	1,900

KM# 1100 31.1050 g. 0.9995 Platinum 0.9995 oz. APW 30 mm.   **Rev:** Great Blue Heron

Date	Mintage	MS-63	Proof
2002 Proof	344	—	1,950

KM# 1104 31.1050 g. 0.9995 Platinum 0.9995 oz. APW 30 mm.   **Rev:** Atlantic Walrus

Date	Mintage	MS-63	Proof
2003 Proof	365	—	1,950

KM# 1108 31.1050 g. 0.9995 Platinum 0.9995 oz. APW 30 mm.   **Rev:** Grizzly Bear

Date	Mintage	MS-63	Proof
2004 Proof	380	—	1,950

KM# 753 31.1050 g. 0.9999 Platinum 0.9999 oz. APW   **Rev:** Wooly mammoth

Date	Mintage	MS-63	Proof
2007 Proof	400	—	3,200

KM# 831 31.1050 g. 0.9990 Platinum 0.9990 oz. APW   **Rev:** Saber Tooth Scimitar cat

Date	Mintage	MS-63	Proof
2008 Proof	200	—	3,500

KM# 951 31.1600 g. 0.9990 Platinum 1.0008 oz. APW 30 mm.   **Rev:** Steppe Bison

Date	Mintage	MS-63	Proof
2009 Proof	200	—	3,500

KM# 1159 31.1050 g. 0.9990 Platinum 0.9990 oz. APW 30 mm.   **Rev:** Ground Sloth

Date	Mintage	MS-63	P/L	Proof
2010 Proof	—	—	—	1,900

KM# 1175 31.1050 g. 0.9995 Platinum 0.9995 oz. APW 30 mm.   **Obv:** Bust right **Rev:** Cougar head left

Date	Mintage	MS-63	Proof
2011 Proof	—	—	1,950

NEW BRUNSWICK

PROVINCE

STERLING COINAGE

HALFPENNY TOKEN

KM#1 Copper   **Obv:** Crowned head left **Obv. Legend:** VICTORIA DEI GRATIA REGINA **Rev:** Three masted ship **Rev. Legend:** NEW BRUNSWICK

Date	Mintage	VG-8	F-12	VF-20	XF-40	MS-60	MS-63	Proof
1843	480,000	4.00	7.50	15.00	45.00	300	400	—
1843 Proof	—	—	—	—	—	—	—	750

KM#3 Copper   **Obv:** Head left **Obv. Legend:** VICTORIA DEI GRATIA REGINA **Rev:** Three masted ship **Rev. Legend:** NEW BRUNSWICK

Date	Mintage	VG-8	F-12	VF-20	XF-40	MS-60	MS-63	Proof
1854	864,000	4.00	7.50	15.00	45.00	300	400	—

KM# 3a Bronze   **Obv:** Head left **Obv. Legend:** VICTORIA DEI GRATIA REGINA **Rev:** Three masted ship **Rev. Legend:** NEW BRUNSWICK

Date	Mintage	VG-8	F-12	VF-20	XF-40	MS-60	MS-63	Proof
1854 Proof	—	—	—	—	—	—	—	400

1 PENNY TOKEN

KM#2 Copper   **Obv:** Crowned head left **Obv. Legend:** VICTORIA DEI GRATIA
REGINA **Rev:** Three masted ship **Rev. Legend:** NEW BRUNSWICK

Date	Mintage	VG-8	F-12	VF-20	XF-40	MS-60	MS-63	Proof
1843	480,000	5.00	9.50	23.00	65.00	250	350	—
1843 Proof	—	—	—	—	—	—	—	800

KM#4 Copper   **Obv:** Head left **Obv. Legend:** VICTORIA DEI GRATIA REGINA
Rev: Three masted ship **Rev. Legend:** NEW BRUNSWICK

Date	Mintage	VG-8	F-12	VF-20	XF-40	MS-60	MS-63	Proof
1854	432,000	3.75	7.50	22.00	65.00	300	400	—

DECIMAL COINAGE

HALF CENT

KM# 5 Bronze   **Obv:** Laureate bust left **Obv. Legend:** VICTORIA D:G: BRITT:
REG: F:D: **Rev:** Crown and date within beaded circle, wreath surrounds

Date	Mintage	VG-8	F-12	VF-20	XF-40	MS-60	MS-63	Proof
1861	222,800	125	175	225	350	650	1,500	—
1861 Proof	—	—	—	—	—	—	—	2,200

CENT

KM# 6 Bronze   **Obv:** Laureate bust left **Obv. Legend:** VICTORIA D:G: BRITT:
REG: F:D: **Rev:** Crown and date within beaded circle, wreath surrounds **Rev.**
Legend: NEW BRUNSWICK

Date	Mintage	VG-8	F-12	VF-20	XF-40	MS-60	MS-63	Proof
1861	1,000,000	3.50	6.00	9.00	14.00	100.00	450	—
1861 Proof	—	—	—	—	—	—	—	450
1864 short 6	1,000,000	3.50	6.00	9.00	20.00	125	550	—
1864 long 6	Inc. above	4.00	6.50	13.00	24.00	175	650	—

5 CENTS

KM# 7 1.1620 g. 0.9250 Silver 0.0346 oz. ASW   **Obv:** Laureate head left **Obv.**
Legend: VICTORIA D: G: REG: / NEW BRUNSWICK **Rev:** Denomination and date
within wreath, crown above

Date	Mintage	VG-8	F-12	VF-20	XF-40	MS-60	MS-63	Proof
1862	100,000	65.00	100.00	225	500	1,700	3,200	—
1862 Proof	—	—	—	—	—	—	—	3,500
1864 small 6	100,000	65.00	100.00	225	1,000	2,200	4,900	—
1864 large 6	Inc. above	75.00	125	300	600	2,500	5,000	—

10 CENTS

KM# 8 2.3240 g. 0.9250 Silver 0.0691 oz. ASW   **Obv:** Laureate head left **Obv.**
Legend: VICTORIA D: G: REG: / NEW BRUNSWICK **Rev:** Denomination and date
within wreath, crown above

Date	Mintage	VG-8	F-12	VF-20	XF-40	MS-60	MS-63	Proof
1862	150,000	65.00	100.00	225	450	1,600	3,000	—
1862 recut 2	Inc. above	95.00	175	350	750	2,900	6,700	—
1862 Proof	—	—	—	—	—	—	—	2,850
1864	100,000	65.00	100.00	225	450	2,700	6,300	—

20 CENTS

KM# 9 4.6480 g. 0.9250 Silver 0.1382 oz. ASW   **Obv:** Laureate head left **Obv. Legend:** VICTORIA D: G: REG: / NEW BRUNSWICK **Rev:** Denomination and date within wreath, crown above

Date	Mintage	VG-8	F-12	VF-20	XF-40	MS-60	MS-63	Proof
1862	150,000	29.00	50.00	100.00	225	1,050	4,400	—
1862 Proof	—	—	—	—	—	—	—	2,850
1864	150,000	29.00	50.00	100.00	225	1,600	4,600	—

NEWFOUNDLAND
PROVINCE

CIRCULATION COINAGE

LARGE CENT

KM# 1 Bronze **Obv:** Laureate bust left **Obv. Legend:** VICTORIA D:G: BRITT: REG:F:D: **Rev:** Crown and date within circle, florals surround **Rev. Legend:** NEWFOUNDLAND

Date	Mintage	VG-8	F-12	VF-20	XF-40	MS-60	MS-63	Proof
1865	240,000	3.50	5.50	12.00	30.00	175	900	—
1872H	200,000	2.50	4.00	7.00	17.00	70.00	250	—
1872H Proof	—	—	—	—	—	—	—	800
1873	200,025	4.00	6.50	20.00	40.00	300	1,600	—
1873 Proof	—	—	—	—	—	—	—	3,000
1876H	200,000	3.50	7.00	15.00	60.00	300	1,600	—
1876H Proof, reported not confirmed	—	—	—	—	—	—	—	—
1880 round 0, even date	400,000	3.00	3.50	7.00	20.00	125	500	—
1880 round and low 0	Inc. above	4.50	12.00	20.00	50.00	400	2,600	—
1880 oval 0	Inc. above	200	300	500	950	2,000	6,000	—
1880 oval 0 Proof	—	—	—	—	—	—	—	2,500
1885	40,000	27.50	50.00	75.00	125	500	2,400	—
1885 Proof	—	—	—	—	—	—	—	2,500
1888	50,000	30.00	55.00	80.00	175	750	4,800	—
1890	200,000	3.00	6.00	15.00	45.00	300	1,200	—
1894	200,000	3.00	5.00	10.00	25.00	140	1,200	—
1894 Proof	—	—	—	—	—	—	—	1,500
1896	200,000	3.00	3.50	7.00	27.00	120	500	—
1896 Proof	—	—	—	—	—	—	—	1,500

KM# 9 Bronze **Obv:** Crowned bust right **Obv. Designer:** G.W. DeSaulles **Rev:** Crown and date within center circle, wreath surrounds, denomination above **Rev. Designer:** Horace Morehen

Date	Mintage	VG-8	F-12	VF-20	XF-40	MS-60	MS-63	Proof
1904H	100,000	10.00	18.00	30.00	75.00	400	1,300	—
1904H Proof	—	—	—	—	—	—	—	6,000
1907	200,000	3.00	5.00	11.00	35.00	250	1,000	—
1909	200,000	3.00	5.00	9.00	27.50	125	250	—
1909 Proof	—	—	—	—	—	—	—	600

KM# 16 Bronze   **Obv:** Crowned bust left **Obv. Designer:** E.B. MacKennal **Rev:** Crown and date within center circle, wreath surrounds, denomination above **Rev. Designer:** Horace Morehen

Date	Mintage	VG-8	F-12	VF-20	XF-40	MS-60	MS-63	Proof
1913	400,000	1.50	2.50	3.50	9.00	60.00	125	—
1917C	702,350	1.50	2.50	3.50	8.00	100.00	400	—
1917C Proof	—	—	—	—	—	—	—	950
1919C	300,000	1.50	2.50	4.00	14.00	225	750	—
1919C Proof	—	—	—	—	—	—	—	2,500
1920C	302,184	1.50	2.50	6.00	24.00	350	1,900	—
1929	300,000	1.50	2.50	3.50	7.00	85.00	175	—
1929C Proof	—	—	—	—	—	—	—	3,000
1936	300,000	1.50	2.00	2.50	5.00	40.00	100.00	—

SMALL CENT

KM#18 3.2000 g. Bronze 19 mm.   **Obv:** Crowned head left **Obv. Designer:** Percy Metcalfe **Rev:** Pitcher plant divides date, denomination below **Rev. Designer:** Walter J. Newman

Date	Mintage	VG-8	F-12	VF-20	XF-40	MS-60	MS-63	Proof
1938	500,000	0.45	0.95	1.25	3.50	24.00	70.00	—
1938 Proof	—	—	—	—	—	—	—	6,000
1940	300,000	1.25	2.25	4.50	14.00	95.00	600	—
1940 Re-engraved date	Inc. above	45.00	60.00	85.00	150	650	2,400	—
1940 Proof	—	—	—	—	—	—	—	2,500
1941C	827,662	0.45	0.70	0.95	2.50	29.00	200	—
1941C Re-engraved date	Inc. above	16.00	24.00	40.00	95.00	400	2,000	—
1942	1,996,889	0.45	0.70	0.95	2.50	40.00	250	—
1943C	1,239,732	0.45	0.70	0.95	2.50	22.50	100.00	—
1944C	1,328,776	1.50	2.50	9.00	35.00	300	2,000	—
1947C	313,772	0.95	1.25	4.00	19.00	100.00	350	—
1947C Proof	—	—	—	—	—	—	—	3,000

5 CENTS

KM# 2 1.1782 g. 0.9250 Silver 0.0350 oz. ASW   **Obv:** Laureate head left **Obv. Legend:** VICTORIA D: G: REG: / NEWFOUNDLAND **Rev:** Denomination and date within ornamental circle **Edge:** Reeded

Date	Mintage	VG-8	F-12	VF-20	XF-40	MS-60	MS-63	Proof
1865	80,000	35.00	50.00	150	300	1,200	3,000	—
1865 Proof	—	—	—	—	—	—	—	4,000
1870	40,000	65.00	125	225	500	1,900	3,000	—
1870 Proof	—	—	—	—	—	—	—	4,000
1872H	40,000	40.00	70.00	125	175	600	2,400	—
1873	44,260	125	200	450	1,100	4,600	—	—
1873H	Inc. above	950	1,400	2,000	3,700	12,500	22,000	—
1873 Proof	—	—	—	—	—	—	—	10,000
1876H	20,000	125	200	350	650	1,200	2,750	—
1880	40,000	45.00	65.00	150	300	1,600	2,400	—
1880 Proof	—	—	—	—	—	—	—	5,000
1881	40,000	45.00	65.00	150	300	1,900	2,500	—
1881 Proof	—	—	—	—	—	—	—	5,000
1882H	60,000	23.00	45.00	90.00	200	800	2,000	—
1882H Proof	—	—	—	—	—	—	—	2,000
1885	16,000	130	210	335	750	2,400	4,500	—
1885 Proof	—	—	—	—	—	—	—	7,500
1888	40,000	40.00	75.00	225	375	1,900	4,900	—
1888 Proof	—	—	—	—	—	—	—	7,500
1890	160,000	11.00	21.00	45.00	125	800	2,000	—
1890 Proof	—	—	—	—	—	—	—	5,000
1894	160,000	10.00	19.00	30.00	100.00	800	2,500	—
1894 Proof	—	—	—	—	—	—	—	5,000
1896	400,000	4.00	8.00	20.00	50.00	700	2,700	—
1896 Proof	—	—	—	—	—	—	—	5,000

KM# 7 1.1782 g. 0.9250 Silver 0.0350 oz. ASW   **Obv:** Crowned bust right **Rev:** Denomination and date within circle

Date	Mintage	VG-8	F-12	VF-20	XF-40	MS-60	MS-63	Proof
1903	100,000	5.00	11.00	29.00	70.00	450	1,700	—
1903 Proof	—	—	—	—	—	—	—	3,000
1904H	100,000	3.50	7.00	19.00	45.00	225	450	—
1904H Proof	—	—	—	—	—	—	—	1,800
1908	400,000	3.50	7.00	18.00	45.00	250	1,100	—

KM# 13 1.1782 g. 0.9250 Silver 0.0350 oz. ASW   **Obv:** Crowned bust left **Obv. Designer:** E.B. MacKennal **Rev:** Denomination and date within circle **Rev. Designer:** G.W. DeSaulles

Date	Mintage	VG-8	F-12	VF-20	XF-40	MS-60	MS-63	Proof
1912	300,000	1.75	2.50	6.00	24.00	125	250	—
1912 Proof	—	—	—	—	—	—	—	2,400
1917C	300,319	1.75	4.00	8.00	27.00	350	1,200	—

Date	Mintage	VG-8	F-12	VF-20	XF-40	MS-60	MS-63	Proof
1917C Proof	—	—	—	—	—	—	—	2,400
1919C	100,844	6.00	11.00	27.00	100.00	1,200	3,500	—
1919C Proof	—	—	—	—	—	—	—	2,400
1929	300,000	1.75	3.00	4.00	14.00	175	400	—

KM# 19 1.1782 g. 0.9250 Silver 0.0350 oz. ASW   **Obv:** Crowned head left **Obv. Designer:** Percy Metcalfe **Rev:** Denomination and date within circle **Rev. Designer:** G.W. DeSaulles

Date	Mintage	VG-8	F-12	VF-20	XF-40	MS-60	MS-63	Proof
1938	100,000	1.50	2.50	3.00	11.00	100.00	300	—
1938 Proof	—	—	—	—	—	—	—	1,600
1940C	200,000	1.50	2.50	3.00	11.00	100.00	350	—
1940C Proof	—	—	—	—	—	—	—	3,200
1941C	621,641	BV	1.75	2.50	4.00	22.00	35.00	—
1942C	298,348	BV	1.75	2.50	5.00	28.00	60.00	—
1943C	351,666	BV	1.50	2.50	5.00	22.00	45.00	—

KM# 19a 1.1664 g. 0.8000 Silver 0.0300 oz. ASW 15.67 mm.   **Obv:** Crowned head left **Obv. Designer:** Percy Metcalfe **Rev:** Denomination and date within circle **Rev. Designer:** G.W. DeSaulles **Edge:** Reeded

Date	Mintage	VG-8	F-12	VF-20	XF-40	MS-60	MS-63	Proof
1944C	286,504	1.50	1.75	2.50	9.00	70.00	150	—
1945C	203,828	1.50	1.75	2.50	4.00	22.50	35.00	—
1946C	2,041	550	600	700	900	2,100	3,000	3,000
1946C Prooflike	—	—	—	—	—	—	4,000	—
1947C	38,400	3.00	5.00	8.00	30.00	100.00	250	—
1947C Prooflike	—	—	—	—	—	—	2,100	—

10 CENTS

KM# 3 2.3564 g. 0.9250 Silver 0.0701 oz. ASW   **Obv:** Laureate head left **Obv. Legend:** VICTORIA D: G: REG: / NEWFOUNDLAND **Rev:** Denomination and date within ornamental circle

Date	Mintage	VG-8	F-12	VF-20	XF-40	MS-60	MS-63	Proof
1865	80,000	27.00	45.00	75.00	250	1,100	2,250	—

Date	Mintage	VG-8	F-12	VF-20	XF-40	MS-60	MS-63	Proof
1865 Proof, plain edge	—	—	—	—	—	—	—	5,500
1870	30,000	150	250	450	725	2,350	5,000	—
1870 Proof	—	—	—	—	—	—	—	10,000
1872H	40,000	22.00	35.00	80.00	200	800	1,700	—
1873 flat 3	23,614	55.00	70.00	250	650	4,000	5,000	—
1873 round 3	Inc. above	55.00	70.00	250	650	4,000	5,000	—
1873 Proof	—	—	—	—	—	—	—	12,000
1876H	10,000	55.00	70.00	225	350	1,400	2,500	—
1880/70	10,000	55.00	100.00	250	400	1,800	2,950	—
1880 Proof	—	—	—	—	—	—	—	7,500
1882H	20,000	30.00	55.00	150	475	2,200	6,700	—
1882H Proof	—	—	—	—	—	—	—	3,000
1885	8,000	70.00	130	300	800	2,200	4,250	—
1885 Proof	—	—	—	—	—	—	—	8,000
1888	30,000	35.00	70.00	200	700	4,000	5,000	—
1888 Proof	—	—	—	—	—	—	—	8,000
1890	100,000	9.00	19.00	35.00	150	1,100	3,200	—
1890 Proof	—	—	—	—	—	—	—	5,000
1894	100,000	8.50	12.00	25.00	125	1,200	3,000	—
1894 Proof	—	—	—	—	—	—	—	5,000
1896	230,000	5.00	10.00	25.00	90.00	1,200	3,200	—
1896 Proof	—	—	—	—	—	—	—	5,000

KM# 8 2.3564 g. 0.9250 Silver 0.0701 oz. ASW **Obv:** Crowned bust right **Rev:** Denomination and date within circle

Date	Mintage	VG-8	F-12	VF-20	XF-40	MS-60	MS-63	Proof
1903	100,000	11.00	30.00	90.00	250	2,400	5,500	—
1903 Proof	—	—	—	—	—	—	—	3,750
1904H	100,000	6.00	14.00	35.00	100.00	350	600	—
1904H Proof	—	—	—	—	—	—	—	2,250

KM# 14 2.3564 g. 0.9250 Silver 0.0701 oz. ASW **Obv:** Crowned bust left **Obv. Designer:** E.B. MacKennal **Rev. Designer:** G.W. DeSaulles

Date	Mintage	VG-8	F-12	VF-20	XF-40	MS-60	MS-63	Proof
1912	150,000	3.50	5.00	14.00	45.00	225	350	—
1917C	250,805	3.50	5.00	14.00	45.00	450	1,450	—
1919C	54,342	4.00	11.00	22.00	70.00	250	350	—

KM# 20 2.3564 g. 0.9250 Silver 0.0701 oz. ASW   **Obv:** Crowned head left **Obv. Designer:** Percy Metcalfe **Rev:** Denomination and date within circle **Rev. Designer:** G.W. DeSaulles

Date	Mintage	VG-8	F-12	VF-20	XF-40	MS-60	MS-63	Proof
1938	100,000	3.00	3.50	4.50	18.00	200	800	—
1938 Proof	—	—	—	—	—	—	—	3,200
1940	100,000	3.00	3.50	4.50	14.00	100.00	400	—
1940 Proof	—	—	—	—	—	—	—	4,000
1941C	483,630	BV	3.00	3.50	7.00	50.00	125	—
1942C	293,736	BV	3.00	3.50	7.00	70.00	200	—
1943C	104,706	BV	3.00	3.50	9.00	250	800	—
1944C	151,471	BV	3.50	11.00	27.00	350	1,300	—

KM# 20a 2.3328 g. 0.8000 Silver 0.0600 oz. ASW   **Obv:** Crowned head left **Obv. Designer:** Percy Metcalfe **Rev. Designer:** G.W. DeSaulles

Date	Mintage	VG-8	F-12	VF-20	XF-40	MS-60	MS-63	Proof
1945C	175,833	BV	2.50	3.00	7.00	100.00	400	—
1946C Proof	—	—	—	—	—	—	—	1,200
1946C	38,400	3.50	4.50	9.00	30.00	125	300	—
1947C	61,988	3.00	3.50	7.00	20.00	100.00	350	—

20 CENTS

KM# 4 4.7127 g. 0.9250 Silver 0.1401 oz. ASW 23.19 mm.   **Obv:** Laureate head left **Rev:** Denomination and date within ornamental circle

Date	Mintage	VG-8	F-12	VF-20	XF-40	MS-60	MS-63	Proof
1865	100,000	16.00	30.00	60.00	225	950	2,600	—
1865 Proof, plain edge	—	—	—	—	—	—	—	6,500
1865 Proof, reeded edge	—	—	—	—	—	—	—	10,000
1870	50,000	21.00	45.00	100.00	250	1,250	2,600	—
1870 Proof, plain edge	—	—	—	—	—	—	—	6,500
1870 Proof, reeded edge	—	—	—	—	—	—	—	6,500
1872H	90,000	12.00	25.00	60.00	140	750	1,800	—

Date	Mintage	VG-8	F-12	VF-20	XF-40	MS-60	MS-63	Proof
1873	45,797	21.00	65.00	175	550	5,400	8,000	—
1873 Proof	—	—	—	—	—	—	—	12,000
1876H	50,000	25.00	50.00	80.00	300	1,350	2,700	—
1880/70	30,000	27.00	55.00	100.00	350	2,000	3,000	—
1880 Proof	—	—	—	—	—	—	—	8,000
1881	60,000	12.00	25.00	80.00	300	1,200	2,900	—
1881 Proof	—	—	—	—	—	—	—	8,000
1882H	100,000	9.00	19.00	50.00	140	1,000	3,400	—
1882H Proof	—	—	—	—	—	—	—	3,500
1885	40,000	14.00	30.00	80.00	300	2,900	4,500	—
1885 Proof	—	—	—	—	—	—	—	10,000
1888	75,000	12.00	25.00	70.00	225	1,400	4,200	—
1888 Proof	—	—	—	—	—	—	—	10,000
1890	100,000	9.00	15.00	45.00	225	1,400	3,500	—
1890 Proof	—	—	—	—	—	—	—	6,500
1894	100,000	12.00	24.00	50.00	175	1,200	—	—
1894 Proof	—	—	—	—	—	—	—	6,500
1896 small 96	125,000	6.00	12.00	35.00	150	1,400	3,600	—
1896 large 96	Inc. above	7.00	15.00	50.00	200	1,700	4,500	—
1896 large 96, Proof	—	—	—	—	—	—	—	6,500
1899 hook 99	125,000	27.00	50.00	125	350	1,800	4,900	—
1899 large 99	Inc. above	5.00	12.00	30.00	125	1,400	3,600	—
1900	125,000	5.00	8.00	25.00	80.00	1,100	3,400	—
1900 Proof	—	—	—	—	—	—	—	6,500

KM# 10 4.7127 g. 0.9250 Silver 0.1401 oz. ASW **Obv:** Crowned bust right **Obv. Designer:** G.W. DeSaulles **Rev:** Denomination and date within circle **Rev. Designer:** W.H.J. Blakemore

Date	Mintage	VG-8	F-12	VF-20	XF-40	MS-60	MS-63	Proof
1904H	75,000	13.00	35.00	65.00	300	2,700	7,000	—
1904H Proof	—	—	—	—	—	—	—	2,400

KM# 15 4.7127 g. 0.9250 Silver 0.1401 oz. ASW **Obv:** Crowned bust left **Obv. Designer:** E.B. MacKennal **Rev:** Denomination and date within circle **Rev. Designer:** W.H.J. Blakemore

Date	Mintage	VG-8	F-12	VF-20	XF-40	MS-60	MS-63	Proof
1912	350,000	5.50	8.00	18.00	65.00	300	750	—
1912 Proof	—	—	—	—	—	—	—	2,500

25 CENTS

KM# 17 5.8319 g. 0.9250 Silver 0.1734 oz. ASW **Obv:** Crowned bust left **Obv. Designer:** E.B. MacKennal **Rev:** Denomination and date within circle **Rev. Designer:** W.H.J. Blakemore

Date	Mintage	VG-8	F-12	VF-20	XF-40	MS-60	MS-63	Proof
1917C	464,779	7.00	8.00	10.00	18.00	200	400	—
1917C Proof	—	—	—	—	—	—	—	3,000
1919C	163,939	7.00	8.00	15.00	35.00	450	2,000	—
1919C Proof	—	—	—	—	—	—	—	3,000

50 CENTS

KM# 6 11.7818 g. 0.9250 Silver 0.3504 oz. ASW 29.85 mm. **Obv:** Laureate head left **Obv. Legend:** VICTORIA DEI GRATIA REGINA NEWFOUNDLAND **Rev:** Denomination and date within ornamental circle

Date	Mintage	VG-8	F-12	VF-20	XF-40	MS-60	MS-63	Proof
1870	50,000	26.00	50.00	150	600	3,500	8,500	—
1870 Proof, plain edge	—	—	—	—	—	—	—	25,000
1870 Proof, reeded edge	—	—	—	—	—	—	—	25,000
1872H	48,000	18.00	35.00	90.00	400	1,600	3,600	—
1873	37,675	40.00	75.00	200	650	9,600	11,000	—
1873 Proof	—	—	—	—	—	—	—	40,000
1874	80,000	25.00	45.00	125	550	8,900	10,000	—
1874 Proof	—	—	—	—	—	—	—	40,000
1876H	28,000	35.00	85.00	150	450	2,250	5,250	—
1880	24,000	45.00	95.00	250	900	6,500	16,000	—
1880 Proof	—	—	—	—	—	—	—	40,000
1881	50,000	20.00	35.00	135	400	3,300	9,300	—
1881 Proof	—	—	—	—	—	—	—	40,000
1882H	100,000	12.00	30.00	95.00	350	1,600	5,400	—
1882H Proof	—	—	—	—	—	—	—	8,000
1885	40,000	30.00	60.00	175	650	2,800	7,100	—
1885 Proof	—	—	—	—	—	—	—	40,000

Date	Mintage	VG-8	F-12	VF-20	XF-40	MS-60	MS-63	Proof
1888	20,000	50.00	90.00	250	925	11,000	13,000	—
1888 Proof	—	—	—	—	—	—	—	40,000
1894	40,000	12.00	28.00	75.00	300	3,700	9,700	—
1896	60,000	8.50	16.00	65.00	300	3,000	8,100	—
1896 Proof	—	—	—	—	—	—	—	25,000
1898	76,607	8.50	13.00	60.00	200	3,100	8,100	—
1899 wide 9's	150,000	8.50	13.00	60.00	200	2,800	7,200	—
1899 narrow 9's	Inc. above	8.50	13.00	45.00	150	2,600	7,700	—
1900	150,000	8.50	13.00	45.00	175	2,600	7,200	—

KM# 11 11.7800 g. 0.9250 Silver 0.3503 oz. ASW 30 mm. **Obv:** Crowned bust right **Obv. Designer:** G.W. DeSaulles **Rev. Designer:** W.H.J. Blakemore

Date	Mintage	VG-8	F-12	VF-20	XF-40	MS-60	MS-63	Proof
1904H	140,000	13.00	14.00	20.00	60.00	350	1,000	—
1904H Proof	—	—	—	—	—	—	—	2,900
1907	100,000	13.00	14.00	25.00	75.00	400	1,200	—
1908	160,000	13.00	14.00	20.00	60.00	300	800	—
1909	200,000	13.00	14.00	22.00	60.00	350	1,000	—

KM# 12 11.7800 g. 0.9250 Silver 0.3503 oz. ASW 30 mm. **Obv:** Crowned bust left **Obv. Designer:** E.B. MacKennal **Rev:** Denomination and date within circle **Rev. Designer:** W.H.J. Blakemore

Date	Mintage	VG-8	F-12	VF-20	XF-40	MS-60	MS-63	Proof
1911	200,000	13.00	14.00	15.00	45.00	300	750	—
1917C	375,560	13.00	14.00	15.00	40.00	175	500	—
1917C Proof	—	—	—	—	—	—	—	3,250
1918C	294,824	13.00	14.00	15.00	40.00	175	500	—
1919C	306,267	13.00	14.00	15.00	40.00	300	1,200	—
1919C Proof	—	—	—	—	—	—	—	3,250

2 DOLLARS

KM# 5 3.3284 g. 0.9170 Gold 0.0981 oz. AGW   **Obv:** Laureate head left **Obv. Legend:** VICTORIA D: G: REG: / NEWFOUNDLAND **Rev:** Denomination and date within circle

Date	Mintage	F-12	VF-20	XF-40	AU-50	MS-60	MS-63
1865	10,000	150	225	300	375	1,100	8,500
1865 plain edge, Specimen-63, $15,000.	Est. 10	—	—	—	—	—	—
1870	10,000	150	225	300	450	1,500	7,500
1870 reeded edge, Specimen-63 $20,000.	Est. 5	—	—	—	—	—	—
1872	6,050	220	400	500	900	2,200	8,800
1872 Specimen-63 $12,500.	Est. 10	—	—	—	—	—	—
1880	2,500	800	1,000	1,200	2,300	4,650	14,250
1880/70	—	—	—	—	—	—	—

Note: Specimen. Bowers and Merena Norweb sale 11-96, specimen 64 realized $70,400.

Date	Mintage	F-12	VF-20	XF-40	AU-50	MS-60	MS-63
1881	10,000	150	200	250	325	1,600	2,500
1881 Specimen; Rare	—	—	—	—	—	—	—
1882H	25,000	150	200	250	300	700	2,200
1882H Specimen $4,250.	—	—	—	—	—	—	—
1885	10,000	150	200	250	300	850	2,750
1885 Specimen	—	—	—	—	—	—	—

Note: Bowers and Merena Norweb sale 11-96, specimen 66 realized $44,000

Date	Mintage	F-12	VF-20	XF-40	AU-50	MS-60	MS-63
1888	25,000	150	175	200	250	600	2,000
1888 Specimen; Rare	—	—	—	—	—	—	—

NOVA SCOTIA

PROVINCE

DECIMAL COINAGE

HALF CENT

KM# 7 Bronze **Obv:** Laureate bust left **Obv. Legend:** VICTORIA D:G: BRITT: REG:F:D: **Rev:** Crown and date within beaded circle, wreath of roses surrounds **Rev. Legend:** NOVA SCOTIA

Date	Mintage	VG-8	F-12	VF-20	XF-40	MS-60	MS-63	Proof
1861	400,000	5.00	7.00	8.00	13.00	60.00	300	—
1864	400,000	5.00	7.00	8.00	13.00	55.00	250	—
1864 Proof	—	—	—	—	—	—	—	300

CENT

KM# 8.2 Bronze **Obv:** Laureate bust left **Obv. Legend:** VICTORIA D:G: BRITT: REG:F:D: **Rev:** Crown and date within beaded circle, wreath of roses surrounds **Rev. Legend:** NOVA SCOTIA **Note:** Prev. KM#8. Small rosebud right of SCOTIA. The Royal Mint report records mintage of 1 million for 1862, which is considered incorrect.

Date	Mintage	VG-8	F-12	VF-20	XF-40	MS-60	MS-63	Proof
1861	800,000	3.00	4.50	5.00	11.00	125	400	—
1862	Est. 1,000,000	45.00	75.00	150	300	1,300	—	—
1864	800,000	3.00	4.50	5.00	16.00	150	450	—

STERLING COINAGE

HALFPENNY TOKEN

KM# 1 Copper   **Obv:** Laureate head left **Obv. Legend:** PROVINCE OF NOVA SCOTIA **Rev:** Thistle

Date	Mintage	VG-8	F-12	VF-20	XF-40	MS-60	MS-63	Proof
1823	400,000	3.00	6.00	13.00	60.00	275	—	—
1823 without hyphen	Inc. above	5.00	10.00	35.00	125	325	—	—
1824	118,636	6.00	12.00	27.00	65.00	450	—	—
1832	800,000	3.00	5.00	13.50	40.00	225	—	—

KM# 1a Copper   **Obv:** Laureate head left, draped collar **Obv. Legend:** PROVINCE OF NOVA SCOTIA **Rev:** Thistle

Date	Mintage	VG-8	F-12	VF-20	XF-40	MS-60	MS-63	Proof
1382 1382 (error)	—	500	700	1,650	—	—	—	—
1832/1382	—	10.00	15.00	50.00	150	—	—	—
1832 (imitation)	—	3.00	9.00	27.00	75.00	125	200	—

KM# 3 Copper   **Obv:** Head left **Obv. Legend:** PROVINCE OF NOVA SCOTIA **Rev:** Thistle

Date	Mintage	VG-8	F-12	VF-20	XF-40	MS-60	MS-63	Proof
1840 small 0	300,000	3.50	10.00	25.00	60.00	175	—	—
1840 medium 0	Inc. above	3.50	9.00	25.00	60.00	175	—	—
1840 large 0	Inc. above	4.00	10.00	40.00	125	225	—	—
1843	300,000	3.00	6.00	24.00	60.00	175	—	—

KM# 5 Copper

Date	Mintage	VG-8	F-12	VF-20	XF-40	MS-60	MS-63	Proof
1856 without LCW	720,000	3.00	4.00	7.50	23.00	175	—	—
1856 without LCW, Proof	—	—	—	—	—	—	—	600
1856 without LCW, inverted A for V in PROVINCE, Proof	—	—	—	—	—	—	—	600

KM# 5a   Bronze

Date	Mintage	VG-8	F-12	VF-20	XF-40	MS-60	MS-63	Proof
1856 with LCW, Proof	—	—	—	—	—	—	—	600

1 PENNY TOKEN

KM# 2   Copper   **Obv:** Laureate head left **Obv. Legend:** PROVINCE OF NOVA SCOTIA **Rev:** Thistle

Date	Mintage	VG-8	F-12	VF-20	XF-40	MS-60	MS-63	Proof
1824	217,776	4.00	10.00	26.00	85.00	400	—	—
1832	200,000	4.00	8.00	15.00	55.00	350	—	—

KM# 2a   Copper   **Obv:** Laureate head left **Obv. Legend:** PROVINCE OF NOVA SCOTIA **Rev:** Thistle

Date	Mintage	VG-8	F-12	VF-20	XF-40	MS-60	MS-63	Proof
1832 (imitation)	—	3.75	7.50	22.50	85.00	—	—	—

KM# 4   Copper 32 mm.   **Obv:** Head left **Obv. Legend:** PROVINCE OF NOVA SCOTIA **Rev:** Thistle

Date	Mintage	VG-8	F-12	VF-20	XF-40	MS-60	MS-63	Proof
1840	150,000	3.50	9.00	23.00	60.00	450	—	—
1843/0	150,000	45.00	75.00	250	—	—	—	—
1843	Inc. above	4.00	12.00	24.00	60.00	450	—	—

KM# 6   Copper   **Obv:** Crowned head left **Obv. Legend:** VICTORIA D: G:
BRITANNIA R: REG: F: D: **Rev:** Plant **Rev. Legend:** PROVINCE OF NOVA SCOTIA

Date	Mintage	VG-8	F-12	VF-20	XF-40	MS-60	MS-63	Proof
1856 without LCW	360,000	4.00	7.50	13.00	35.00	300	—	—
1856 with LCW	Inc. above	2.50	5.00	12.00	35.00	350	—	—

KM# 6a   Bronze   **Obv:** Crowned head left **Obv. Legend:** VICTORIA D: G:
BRITANNIA R: REG: F: D: **Rev:** Plant **Rev. Legend:** PROVINCE OF NOVA SCOTIA

Date	Mintage	VG-8	F-12	VF-20	XF-40	MS-60	MS-63	Proof
1856 Proof	—	—	—	—	—	—	—	400

PRINCE EDWARD ISLAND

PROVINCE

CUT & COUNTERMARKED COINAGE

CA. 1813

SHILLING

KM# 1 Silver   **Countermark:** Sunburst **Note:** Countermark on center plug of Spanish or Spanish Colonial 8 Reales.

Date	Mintage	VG-8	F-12	VF-20	XF-40	MS-60	MS-63	Proof
ND	1,000	2,000	3,000	5,000	—	—	—	—

5 SHILLING

KM# 3 Silver   **Countermark:** Sunburst **Note:** Countermark on holed Lima 8 Reales, KM#106.2.

Date	Mintage	VG-8	F-12	VF-20	XF-40	MS-60	MS-63	Proof
ND1809-11	1,000	2,000	3,000	5,000	—	—	—	—

KM# 2.1 Silver   **Countermark:** Sunburst **Note:** Countermark on holed Mexico City 8 Reales, KM#109.

Date	Mintage	VG-8	F-12	VF-20	XF-40	MS-60	MS-63	Proof
1791-1808	—	1,400	1,800	2,250	—	—	—	—

KM# 2.2 Silver   **Countermark:** Sunburst **Note:** Countermark on holed Mexico City 8 Reales, KM#110.

Date	Mintage	VG-8	F-12	VF-20	XF-40	MS-60	MS-63	Proof
ND1808-11	—	1,400	1,800	2,250	—	—	—	—

DECIMAL COINAGE

CENT

KM# 4 Bronze   **Obv:** Crowned head left within beaded circle **Obv. Legend:** VICTORIA QUEEN **Rev:** Trees within beaded circle **Rev. Legend:** PRINCE EDWARD ISLAND

Date	Mintage	VG-8	F-12	VF-20	XF-40	MS-60	MS-63	Proof
1871	2,000,000	2.50	4.00	6.50	20.00	100.00	185	—
1871 Proof	—	—	—	—	—	—	—	2,000

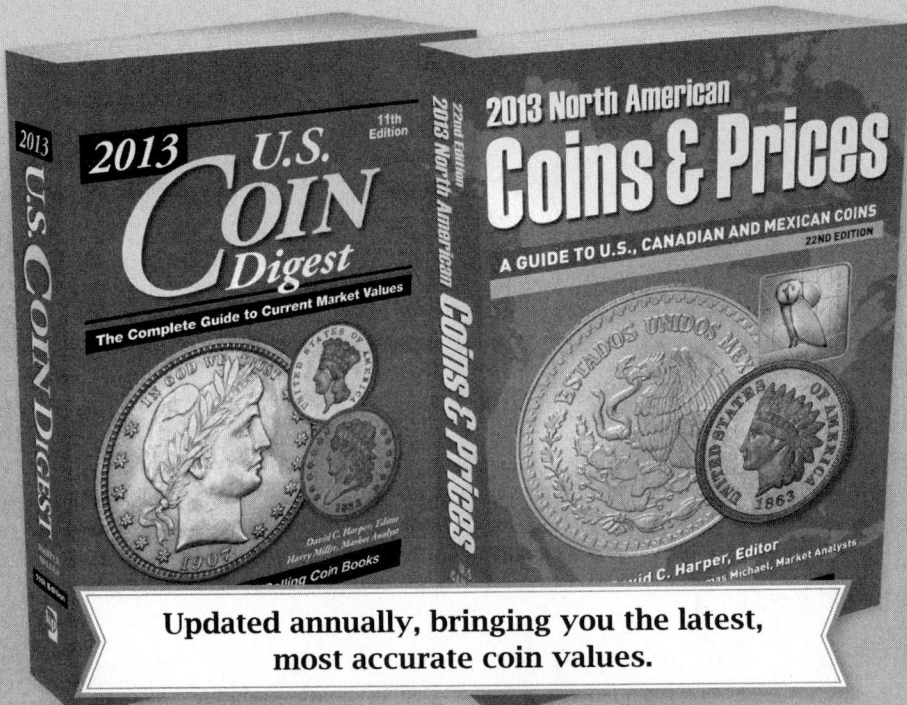

STANDARD CATALOGS
to bank on